Deep-Free

Marika Hanbury Tenison was █████████████ been interested in cooking and ███████████ long as she can remember. S█ ████████ domestic science training but learnt the hard way, by trial and error, and is still learning.

Married to the explorer and farmer Robin Hanbury Tenison, she now travels with him to little-known areas of the world. They have two children and live in a fourteenth-century farmhouse high up on Bodmin Moor. She finds her deep freeze invaluable as the family often entertains up to twenty people at weekends. She says, 'Without it, my food bills would soar and I would spend my entire time in the kitchen instead of being able to be with my family and friends.'

Her other cookery books include *Deep-Freeze Sense* and *Eat Well and Be Slim* (both available in Pan), *Soups and Hors d'Oeuvres* and *Left Over for Tomorrow*. She has also written two travel books and is now cookery editor for the *Sunday Telegraph*.

Other cookery books available in Pan

Ada Boni
The Talisman Italian Cook Book

Lousene Rousseau Brunner
New Casserole Treasury

Savitri Chowdhary
Indian Cookery

Theodora FitzGibbon
A Taste of Ireland
A Taste of London
A Taste of Scotland
A Taste of Wales
A Taste of the West Country

Dorothy Hall
The Book of Herbs

Robin Howe
Soups

Rosemary Hume and Muriel Downes
The Cordon Bleu Book of Jams, Preserves and Pickles

Kenneth Lo
Quick and Easy Chinese Cooking

Claire Loewenfeld and Philippa Back
Herbs for Health and Cookery

Marguerite Patten
Learning to Cook

Jennie Reekie
Traditional French Cooking

Constance Spry and Rosemary Hume
The Constance Spry Cookery Book

Marika Hanbury Tenison
Eat Well and Be Slim
Deep-Freeze Sense

Marika Hanbury Tenison

Deep-Freeze Cookery

Pan Books London and Sydney

First published 1970 by MacGibbon and Kee Ltd
This edition (slightly abridged) published 1972 by Pan Books Ltd,
Cavaye Place, London SW10 9PG
8th printing 1977
© Marika Hanbury Tenison 1970
ISBN 0 330 02953 3
Printed and bound in England by
Cox & Wyman Ltd, London, Reading and Fakenham

Contents

PART THREE: SEASONAL MENUS

Foreword

I once horrified a guest, at a dinner party I was giving, by telling her that the 'Lobster Newburg' she was enjoying so much had been made over two months previously. She seemed to find the idea most distasteful and I watched her merely picking at the 'Chicken in Lemon Sauce' and the 'Crêpes Suzette' which followed. That lady was one of many who still have an inbuilt mistrust of deep-freezing and any food that has been frozen.

In fact the food at that dinner party was the other half of a dinner I had given nine weeks before (to different guests). At that time I had made double quantities of all the dishes and put half in the freezer. If I had not mentioned it I am sure that my guests would never have guessed that I had not spent all day slaving over the kitchen stove.

Many people feel that a deep freeze is a luxury only for farmers' wives like myself, or for millionaires, and is of no use to anyone living in a town or city. I disagree wholeheartedly with this and honestly believe that no housewife (however small her family) who has not got all the time in the world to do the cooking and who cannot afford to employ a cook or to eat out at least three times a week, can *afford* to be without a deep freeze. To me it ranks far higher for housewives than a washing machine or spin drier, and is an economy that plays a major part in the never-ending battle of making both ends meet.

In Sweden and other countries where deep freezes are the rule rather than the exception, it is possible to hire a cook for one day a month. During that day the cook will prepare all the family meals for the rest of the month, packing them in the deep freeze ready for the time when they will be needed. I try to follow this plan myself, though being a person who finds it difficult to think too far ahead I do my family cooking once a fortnight, and so cut down my cooking time to a minimum for the remaining thirteen days.

Please do not get the wrong idea about me. I sound as if my one idea is to keep out of the kitchen but in fact I love cooking and trying out new recipes. To me it is much more than a job or chore that has to be done – it is a hobby and a delight. But I do like to be able to spend all the time I can with my husband and my family, also with my friends when they are staying with us or dining with us. To do this I try to use my deep freeze to its utmost potential and to do as much cooking as I can ahead of time. I also try to keep my deep freeze well stocked with items that can be cooked at a moment's notice so that when my husband suddenly tells me that he has asked six people to dinner, or when my daughter forgets to inform me that four of her school friends are turning up for Saturday lunch, I don't have to have a minor attack of hysterics and drive frantically to the nearest town which, in our case, is ten miles away.

This book is written not only for those who have a deep freeze and want to know more about its uses but also for anyone who is at all interested in food.

I have written it after eight years' experience of cooking for my family and friends and deep-freezing the majority of the dishes I cooked. During this time I have found no complete and comprehensive book that combines the basic rules for deep-freezing in its raw state with a wide variety of recipes that can be successfully frozen. All the recipes, or the ingredients they contain, that are contained in this book have been deep-frozen by me and I have made a point of passing on any problems or drawbacks that I have come across.

I have tried to include a very wide choice of recipes which I have collected from all over the world. Many of them you will recognize as being of international fame, some of them are my own invention and a large number have been begged, borrowed or stolen from friends in England and abroad. They range from the very economical and simple to the extravagant and flamboyant.

Unless otherwise stated, the quantities used in the recipes are for four generous portions.

I hope you will enjoy all that follows.

MARIKA

Written at Maidenwell with the ever-patient help and encouragement of Robin

1970

Weights and Measures

(*English cup measurements and level spoon measurements are used throughout the book*)

3 teaspoons	=	1 tablespoon
16 tablespoons	=	1 cup
1 cup	=	½ pint (10 fl ozs)
2 cups	=	1 pint
4 cups	=	1 quart
(American cup	=	8 fl ozs)

BUTTER   1 tablespoon equals ½ oz

CHOCOLATE   1 square   „   1 oz

FLOUR: bread flour 4 cups   „   1 lb
          cake flour 4½ cups   „   1 lb

RICE   2½ cups uncooked   „   1 lb
      1 cup raw   „   3–4 cups cooked

SUGAR: granulated 2 cups   „   1 lb
         caster 2 cups   „   1 lb
         brown 2 cups   „   1 lb
         icing 3½ cups   „   1 lb

GELATINE   1 envelope = 1 tablespoon = ½ oz: enough to thicken 2 cups or 1 pint of liquid.

LEMON:	Juice of 1 lemon = 2–3 tablespoons

YEAST:	1 cake compressed yeast = 1 oz

1 lb	=	454 grammes
8 oz	=	227 grammes
1 oz	=	28.4 grammes
2.21 lb	=	1 kilo
½ pint	=	2¼ decilitres
1 fluid oz	=	29.6 millilitres
1¾ pints	=	1 litre
1 cup cake flour	=	125 grammes
1 cup butter	=	225 grammes
1 cup sugar	=	190 grammes

PART ONE

The Deep Freezer

The Deep Freeze and its Uses

Although deep-freezing on a commercial basis was only started in America as recently as thirty-five years ago the method of preservation by ice has been practised in intensely cold parts of the world for centuries. As long ago as Elizabethan times meat was kept for months (as an alternative to salting) in underground chambers, reached by long tunnels. Ice packed round the walls kept these chambers at a very low temperature.

To demonstrate the effective results of freezing I must relate a story I heard whilst holidaying in Switzerland. A young couple were spending their honeymoon in the mountains above St Moritz. Sadly, the bridegroom fell into a crevasse of a glacier while they were out walking. His body was not found and his bride mourned for her young man for the next fifty years. Every year, on the date of their wedding anniversary, she returned to the mountains and threw a bunch of flowers into the foot of the glacier that had claimed her husband. Now, as you probably know, glaciers move slowly downwards year by year and on their fiftieth wedding anniversary the bridegroom appeared from the foot of the glacier, deep-frozen and in a complete state of preservation, as fresh and young-looking as the day he had slipped into the crevasse: fifty years younger than his faithful wife. The same thing has been known to happen with prehistoric mammoths which still appear from time to time in Siberia.

However, this book is concerned with a different kind of domestic freezing and although I am not going into the complicated chemistry of the freezing process I think it is important to know a bit about what happens inside your deep freeze once the lid is shut.

THE PROCESS OF FREEZING

Correctly frozen and stored food is the most successful form of preservation known today. It can be kept for long periods and on being defrosted will be virtually unchanged in flavour, texture, and nutritive values.

All foodstuffs are made up of minute cells which contain a combination of water, salts and minerals. On freezing, the water forms ice crystals inside the cells and the action of enzymes and bacteria in the food is arrested. The size of these crystals depends on the rate of freezing. Slow freezing causes large crystals which force their way through the fragile walls of the cells and cause damage to the texture and quality of the food. Small crystals leave the texture unharmed. To guarantee these small crystals, food should be rapidly frozen to 0°F or lower and stored at this temperature.

On defrosting, the crystals melt, leaving the texture of the food unchanged. The enzymes and the bacteria, having been dormant, start to function again and for this reason thawed food spoils quickly and should be used soon after defrosting.

FREEZING DOES NOT IMPROVE QUALITY, and the best result that can be achieved is that the food will retain the quality it had before it was frozen.

Some of the many advantages of deep freezes to the housewife

For the housewife living in the country the advantages of having a deep freeze are so numerous that it would be impossible to list them all. Freezing home products when they are at the height of their prime obviously rates high. Fruit and vegetables can be harvested at exactly the right moment, processed as soon as they have been picked, and stored through the year far more successfully and with far less preparation than by bottling or canning. Fresh fish and game can now be had in all seasons, baking can be done once a month and bulk buying can lead to a great saving of time and of the housekeeping account.

For housewives living in towns, in houses or flats, the advantages of owning a deep freeze are also enormous. Busy mothers with large families can cook for a month at a time, women with jobs can go to work knowing that the deep freeze is well stocked with ready-to-produce meals and people who entertain can pre-cook for their parties and achieve great banquets without ever appearing to have gone near the kitchen.

With careful planning and organization a deep freeze should easily pay for itself within two years of use.

4

At last it is possible to go to almost any refrigeration company and be shown a large selection of deep freezes and to choose one that will really suit your own requirements. Bear in mind that when buying a deep freeze one's eyes are *seldom* larger than one's stomach and it is a common fault to underestimate rather than overestimate the size required. Since I first had one seven years ago I have had to have two new ones of larger sizes and although my present model is 22 cubic feet, which stores 650 lb of frozen food, I could quite happily do with a larger one still.

Basically, deep freezes fall into three classifications – refrigerators with a deep-freezing compartment, upright-cupboard-type freezers, and the chest models with the lid opening from the top.

Types of deep freeze

1. A deep-freezing compartment combined with a refrigerator. The freezing compartment is usually at the top of the refrigerator and has a temperature control which can be lowered for the freezing of fresh and pre-cooked foods. Their capacity is not large, about a maximum of 50 lb of frozen food, and they can only quick freeze small amounts of fresh food at a time. Because of the relatively small space these combined refrigerator/freezers require, they are obviously most suited to housewives with small houses or flats who do not plan to freeze goods on a large scale.

2. The upright-cupboard type of deep freeze. These have the great advantage over the chest type of deep freezes of requiring far less floor space. Shelves or sliding baskets are provided by the manufacturers and frozen foods are easy to reach and easy to keep track of. Their disadvantage lies in the fact that when the door of the deep freeze is opened warm air rushes into the cabinet causing frosting on the walls and requiring an additional boost of power to keep the temperature regular. As a result these upright freezers are more expensive to run and require more frequent defrosting than the chest models.

3. The chest type of deep freeze. Because they have to negotiate the average doorway, these freezes are usually long and narrow and take up a lot of floor space with a certain amount of overhead space necessary to allow for the opening of the lid. Most manufacturers provide wire partitions for the bottom of the deep freeze and wire baskets for the top layer which slide sideways to enable the packages on the floor of the freeze to be reached.

Cost of running a deep freeze

Once you have bought your deep freeze you will find that the maintenance and repair costs are virtually nil and it is useful to note that the larger the freeze the relatively less expensive it is per cubic foot.

Deep freezes are thermostatically controlled. The amount of electricity they use depends to a large extent on the number of times they are opened, and the amount of work they have to do. On an average the operating costs work out at about the same as for the equivalent size of refrigerator (roughly that of a 200-watt electric bulb). Keeping your deep freeze in a cool place, keeping it as full as possible so that surplus air isn't circulating the whole time, and only opening the lid or door when necessary, helps to keep down the running costs.

Note

When looking at deep-freeze specifications you will see that the manufacturers refer to 'freezing capacity' and 'storage capacity'. The 'storage capacity' shows the amount of frozen food that the machine can actually store. The 'freezing capacity' shows the amount of fresh food that can be successfully quick-frozen within a twenty-four-hour period. The freezing capacity is about one-tenth of the storage capacity.

Where to put your deep freeze

The answer to this is wherever is most convenient, provided that it is in a reasonably cool situation with a gap between the back of the freeze and the wall. One of my friends keeps hers in her garage, side by side with her Mini, and because her garage is like an ice box itself most of the time, her running costs are very low indeed.

I found that I had such a lot of spare space, through using my deep freeze as a storage cupboard and being able to cut down on tinned and bottled products, that I was able to make room for it in the larder.

POWER FAILURE AND TECHNICAL FAULTS

Insist that the manufacturers provide your deep freeze with an alarm system. This is a loud buzzer operated by a battery, which goes off if the temperature inside the deep freeze begins to rise due to power failure or a technical fault.

Check the buzzer regularly to see that it is working and the batteries are not flat.

If the buzzer does go off *make sure that the lid of the deep freeze remains tightly shut.* Check that the power is working and that the plug of the deep freeze is not faulty. If the cause is neither of these things get on to your service engineer immediately.

Food can safely be left in the deep freeze for up to twenty-four hours after the current has gone off provided the lid is not opened. If repairs are going to take longer than this, most firms provide an emergency service of some kind to keep the food frozen.

It is possible to take out an insurance policy at a very small premium to guard against any damage to food contained inside the deep freeze. Luckily disasters are very rare.

CARE OF THE DEEP FREEZE

Have your machine serviced once a year.

Defrost when necessary. Normally this only needs to be done about once every six months. Frost will always form on the wall of the deep freeze but this should not be allowed to reach a depth of more than $\frac{1}{4}$ inch. Heavy frosting increases running costs and decreases the efficiency of the machine.

When taking a deep freeze as a trade-in for another machine the manufacturers will take into account the condition of the top surface. If you use this as extra counter space it is as well to protect it with a layer of contact paper to prevent scratching. A light polish with a silicone cloth will keep the rest of the paintwork in good condition.

DEFROSTING

Work fast.

Remove all the packages and keep them in the coldest place possible. Wrapping them in layers of newspaper will help to prevent any thawing. Turn freezer to 'defrost', or unplug it. (Follow manufacturer's instructions.)

Scrape the ice off the walls with a stiff brush or a wooden scraper. Do not use a knife as this will scratch the walls of the freeze. Remove as much of the ice as possible. Place bowls of boiling water on the floor of the freezer, replacing the water as it cools until all the ice has melted. Remove all the water with a cloth.

Finally, wipe over the inside of the cabinet with a solution of 1 cup of vinegar and 2 teaspoons of bicarbonate of soda to 1 gallon of water, to remove any smells. Thoroughly dry out the inside with a soft cloth.

Switch on and leave to get cold for 1 hour. Replace packages, checking them as you do so.

WEAR GLOVES AS IT'S COLD INSIDE.

How to Use your Deep Freeze

WHAT TO PUT IN THE DEEP FREEZE

Freeze only produce that is fresh, young, tender and of the highest quality. Remember that freezing does not improve the quality of food.

Freeze:

1. Fresh vegetables, fruit, meat, fish, shellfish.
2. Pre-cooked soups, first courses, main courses, puddings, sauces and savouries.
3. Cakes, breads and pastries.
4. Some dairy produce.

Because of the action of ice crystals formed by freezing, the following foods do not react well to freezing.

Do not freeze:

1. Eggs in their shells: the liquid of the eggs expands, breaking the shells.
2. Hard-boiled eggs: the yolk of the egg hardens and goes leathery.
3. Whites and yolks of eggs together: the yolk hardens.
4. Garlic flavouring: kept for longer than a week the garlic tends to develop an off-flavour.
5. Salad greens: freezing discolours lettuces, etc, and leaves them soft and mushy.

6. Cream below 40 per cent butter fat: separates.

7. Cream cheese below 40 per cent butter fat: separates.

8. Boiled potatoes in pre-cooked dishes: the potato hardens and goes leathery, unless mashed.

DO NOT RE-FREEZE ANYTHING THAT HAS ALREADY BEEN FROZEN AND DEFROSTED UNLESS YOU COOK IT IN BETWEEN.

PLANNING: THE SECRET OF SUCCESSFUL FREEZING

Careful planning is one of the most important factors enabling you to get the utmost value from your deep freeze. PLAN your meals well in advance so that you can cook two or three of the same dishes at once. Eat one and store the others. PLAN your garden so that you have plenty of fresh produce to freeze and store. PLAN to cook emergency meals that can be frozen and stored for the unexpected guests and last-minute parties. PLAN to buy in bulk when things are cheaper and in season. PLAN so that you do not overstock your deep freeze with any one item.

Economizing with your deep freeze

I live ten miles from the nearest town and before I had a deep freeze I used to spend a small fortune on petrol, driving to town almost every other day to do the shopping. Now I do my shopping once a fortnight buying bread, butter, lard, etc, in large quantities and storing them in the freezer.

If you look around it is possible to buy almost anything in bulk and at a great saving. Any good butcher will give you a sizeable reduction (your local slaughter house will give you an even larger one) if you buy in bulk. He will supply you with a whole or half-lamb cut into convenient joints at a saving of about 20 per cent. The same thing applies to pork and veal and to beef which can be bought by the fore- or hind-quarter. As a fore-quarter is mostly stewing meat it is cheaper than a hind-quarter which is composed mainly of roasting meat.

Wholesalers of bacon, sausages and lard are prepared to sell reasonably small quantities, and I find that I save an average of about 20 per cent on 10-lb quantities of these items. Ten pounds of sausages sounds a lot but if you have the room in your deep freeze it adds up to a considerable saving and you will find they are soon used up.

If you use commercial frozen products you will find you can economize by buying these in bulk from your nearest deep-freeze wholesaler. If you are lucky they will sometimes deliver to your home. It is important to see that pre-frozen food has no chance to thaw before being put into your own deep freeze. Make sure that the food you buy is taken out of the cold room when you are ready to leave the shop and not left standing in a thawing draught whilst you pay the bill. Wrap it in plenty of newspaper and pack in cardboard boxes. Transfer the goods to your own deep freeze as soon as possible.

Buy fruit and vegetables, meat, game and fish when it is plentiful and in season. The price of fish, particularly, varies considerably at different times of the year.

Greengrocers often find themselves overstocked with vegetables and fruit and will be happy to sell you a box or tray of some produce at a greatly reduced price.

Keep your eyes open for bargains and you will be surprised how soon you will have paid for your deep freeze with the amount you have saved by planned buying.

Dog food. Dog food can be expensive if you have more than one dog; buying their food in tins is uneconomical and not entirely satisfactory. Use your deep freeze to cut down on costs. Buy cheap offal from your butcher or slaughter house. Package it in suitable-sized polythene bags for one meal. Meat unsuitable for human consumption can often be bought from a slaughter house for very little, but beware of any meat that is off or in the least smelly.

If you don't like dealing with uncooked dog meat, it is now possible to make a contract with a wholesale frozen-dog-food merchant who will deliver the frozen processed meat to your door. Buy as much as you can store at one time. The greater the quantity you buy the greater the saving.

Use your deep freeze as a store cupboard

One of the compartments in my deep freeze I try to keep entirely as a kind of store cupboard stocked with items packed in small quantities which can be quickly thawed and used as a time-saver when I am cooking, and in emergencies. Below is a sample list:

Eggs. Separated, packed and stored in twos in ice-cube moulds or small tubs. I do this especially with yolks or whites of eggs left over from cooking. No more problems of wondering what to do with the egg whites when you have been making a custard or mayonnaise, just store them in the deep freeze until you feel like making meringues.

Stock. Whenever you have meat bones or trimmings available make a stock, cool well, and remove all the fat and store in ½-pint cartons. (Or reduce by boiling and store the concentrated stock in ice-cube moulds.)

Mixed vegetables. Cut into small cubes. Pack into small polythene bags and use in soups and stews. (See vegetable charts for the preparation of vegetables for freezing.)

Sauces. eg, mushroom, tomato, meat, barbecue, Hollandaise, apple (sweet and savoury), chocolate. Store in quantities for four people in waxed containers.

Herbs. Fresh herbs (so much more flavourful than dried ones) packed in polythene bags, eg, parsley, chives, fennel, mint, basil, thyme. When required, thaw for whole leaves or crumble the frozen leaves to save chopping.

Pastry. Short, savoury and sweet, puff, rough-puff and so on.

Flan cases. Pre-baked and uncooked.

Doughs. For scones, breads and biscuits.

Flavoured butters. Parsley, horseradish, chive and brandy butter.

Mushrooms. Sautéed in butter if they are large; just as they are if very small and fresh.

Green Peppers. Chopped and blanched.

Fruit juices. Lemon and orange juice, raspberry, blackcurrant purée, etc.

Concentrated fruit juices. For making fruit juices and lemonade. Frozen in ice-cube trays.

Concentrated strong coffee, tea and mint tea. Frozen in ice cubes to use for instant iced coffee and tea.

TWELVE GOLDEN RULES FOR SUCCESSFUL DEEP-FREEZING

1. Freeze food of top quality. Freezing will preserve the original quality, texture, flavour, colour and nutritive value of the food.

2. Ensure that all your utensils, etc, are clean. Freezing does not kill bacteria and germs in food.

3. Prepare individual items as directed.

4. Cool quickly if the produce has been cooked or blanched.

5. Package carefully in waterproof containers or paper. Seal

well to exclude all excess air. Moisture and exposure to air damage frozen goods.

6. Label each packet carefully.

7. Freeze quickly in the coldest part of your deep freeze, on the floor or next to the walls.

8. Store frozen food at 0°F or lower.

9. Do not keep frozen food for longer than the recommended time.

10. Keep a close check on the contents of your deep freeze so that packages do not get overlooked.

11. Thaw according to directions.

12. Never re-freeze anything once it has thawed.

Packaging

All food must be cooled before packaging and freezing. Everything for the deep freeze must be packaged in waterproof and vapour-proof airtight containers. If this is not done the food will deteriorate and dehydrate, and strong odours will contaminate other foodstuffs.

It is now possible to buy containers and special polythene bags at most large stationers and general stores. Some deep-freeze manufacturers supply their own range of packaging materials.

Glass containers are used extensively for storing liquids but extra care has to be taken with these to ensure that the liquid has plenty of room for expansion. If they are filled too full they will break. I seldom use glass containers myself having had a very nasty experience with a bottle of champagne. We had a young man staying with us whose wife suddenly produced a baby three weeks early. Feeling that we ought to celebrate that evening I put a bottle of champagne in the deep freeze to cool quickly. I left the bottle there too long and the next thing I knew was that there was a loud explosion. Rushing to the deep freeze I found that the bottle had burst and the freeze was covered in a terrible mixture of broken glass and frozen champagne.

If you have any trouble getting packaging materials, get in touch with your deep-freeze manufacturers and they will give you the name of a supplier.

Cooling

Any foods that have been cooked or blanched should be cooled as quickly as possible before being packaged. The quickest way of cooling is to set the food either directly in iced water, or in the case of pre-cooked food to put the container it has been prepared in into iced water, adding more ice as the water warms up.

THE MOST USUAL TYPES OF CONTAINERS AND PACKAGING MATERIALS

1. *Glass jars (specially toughened) with screw lids.* Used for storing liquids, soups, etc.

2. *Waxed cardboard tubs with snap-on lids in various sizes.* Used for storing berries, liquids and sauces.

3. *Waxed cardboard cartons in various sizes, supplied with moisture- and vapour-proof liners.* Used for storing vegetables, fruit and minced meats.

4. *Waxed cardboard boxes in various sizes.* Used for storing sliced meat, patties, vegetables and fruit.

5. *Polythene and plastic containers in various sizes with snap-on lids.* Used for storing ice-cream, vegetables, fruit, and meat and poultry in sauces.

6. *Polythene bags in various sizes.* Used for storing meat, poultry, game, and small joints, vegetables and fruit.

7. *Aluminium boxes and pie plates in various sizes.* Used for cooking and storing pies and flans.

8. *Aluminium foil.* Used as protective covering for joints, poultry, and fish.

9. *Tins with close-fitting lids (in rustless aluminium).* Used for storing cream, ice-cream, and fruit in syrup.

10. *Thin moisture- and vapour-proof plastic wrapping in sheets.* Used for separating individual joints, steaks and patties before they are wrapped in tin foil or plastic bags.

11. *Waxed paper wrapping, specially toughened for freezing.* Used for short-term wrapping of meat and fish.

12. *Cotton stockinette.* Used as an inside wrapping for meat and poultry to provide protection from freezer burn for long-term freezing.

13. *Labels specially treated for deep-freezing.*

14. *Metal tags for sealing polythene bags.*

15. *Specially prepared waterproof sealing tape.*

Note: It is now possible to buy casseroles and dishes in attractive designs guaranteed to go safely from the freezer to the oven.

Notes on filling containers for freezing

Remember that liquids expand when frozen, and allow plenty of room when filling a container. For instance, leave half an inch of head space at the top of a pint carton of soup to allow for expansion, otherwise you will find the liquid forcing up the lid of your container as it freezes.

Close packing eliminates excess air so pack vegetables and fruit as closely as you can in boxes without bruising the product.

Always press polythene bags gently to get rid of excess air before sealing. If it is necessary to leave quite a large air space in boxes or cartons, fill up this space with crumpled moisture-proof freezer paper.

Individual poultry joints, hamburgers, steaks, patties, fish fillets, etc, will stick together when frozen so separate each item with a layer of thin polythene before packing.

When filling polythene bags (the most versatile of the packaging materials) with soups, purées and other liquids, place the bag inside a waxed carton or other container. Smooth the bag over the inside of the container and turn the top of the bag down over the outside of the container. Pour in the liquid. Seal the bag and freeze in the container. When frozen solid, the bag can be removed from the container and will then be in a suitable shape to stack for storage.

Polythene bags can be used over and over again. To wash the bag, turn inside out, wash in warm soapy water, rinse, and dry carefully.

Never fill waxed tubs or cartons with hot liquid. The wax melts and the box becomes porous.

When freezing pre-cooked dishes in the casseroles or utensils they have been cooked in, make sure that the containers are unbreakable, odourless and rustproof.

When packing meat, poultry and fish in aluminium foil or in freezer paper, make sure that the food is completely and adequately covered. Make up a neat parcel with as few open ends that need sealing as possible.

Certain foods that are fragile or easily damaged such as croquettes, stuffed tomatoes and individual patties should be placed separately on a tray and frozen before being packed. When solid they should be carefully packed in a rigid container and separated

14

by a layer of moisture- and vapour-proof wrapping. The wrapping will help to make them easy to separate for cooking whilst still frozen.

A ROUGH GUIDE TO PACKAGING VARIOUS FOODS

Bread	Polythene bags.
Cakes	Polythene bags, waxed boxes.
Eggs	Waxed tubs or cartons.
Fruit (berries)	Waxed tubs or cartons.
Fruit (general)	Polythene bags, cartons, tins.
Fruit purée	Waxed cartons, or tins. (Fruit purée tends to leak so make sure it is packed in a waterproof container.)
Fish	Tin foil covered with a polythene bag.
Ice-cream	Waxed containers, tins or polythene containers.
Meat	Stockinette covered by a polythene bag, for long storage, or in freezer paper.
Game	Stockinette covered by polythene bags.
Pies	Aluminium-foil dishes or unbreakable pie dishes in polythene bags.
Pre-cooked dishes	Waxed boxes, aluminium dishes, or the dishes they are to be served in, covered by polythene bags.
Poultry	Stockinette covered by a polythene bag.
Vegetables	Small vegetables in waxed tubs or containers.
Sauces, soups and stocks	Waxed containers, jars or tins.

SEALING

Having carefully prepared your food for the deep freeze and packaged it in a suitable container, *make sure that it is completely sealed with as much air as possible excluded from the package.*

Correct sealing ensures that air and odours do not reach the frozen food. Incorrect and careless sealing will lead to disappointment when the food is defrosted.

Each individual package in the deep freeze must be well packaged and carefully sealed for really good results.

METHODS FOR SEALING DIFFERENT TYPES
OF CONTAINERS

1. POLYTHENE BAGS

(a) Heat-sealing

This sounds very professional but is in fact very easy. Fill the bag
and place the open end on a flat surface. Gently press the bag to
exclude as much air as possible. Place a thin strip of brown paper
over the open end of the bag and run a warm iron over the paper.
You will find this forms an airtight seam.
Note: It is now possible to buy a special sealing iron and specially
treated paper with a built-in strip for quick, easy heat-sealing.

(b) Sealing with wire tags

This is a simple method and perfectly adequate for short-term
freezing but I have found that the tags sometimes work loose after
a time. Press the bag gently to exclude all possible air and secure
the opening of the bag with three twists of the wire tag. This
method of sealing is especially good for vegetables and you end
up with a neat uniform parcel instead of a rather oddly shaped
bag.
Note: A number of paper-covered wire tags are usually supplied
with each packet of polythene bags but it is now possible to buy
coloured plastic-covered tags that can be used again and again
and are useful for giving a rough guide to the contents of a package.

2. TUBS, CARTONS, BOXES, AND TINS

Seal all round the lids with specially prepared waterproof sealing
tape or place the container in a polythene bag and seal with a
metal tag.

3. PACKAGES WRAPPED IN ALUMINIUM FOIL
OR FREEZER PAPER

Seal all the joins and overlaps in the paper with specially prepared
waterproof sealing tape.

LABELLING

Correct labelling is very important

When a package freezes it clouds over and is covered by a thin film of ice. What was clearly a leg of lamb wrapped in a polythene bag when you put it in the deep freeze, could easily be taken for a sheep's head the next day.

Write on your tubs and cartons with a waterproof felt pen or a chinagraph pencil (obtainable from any stationers), stating clearly the date of packaging, the contents, and the quantity. Stick waterproof labels to foil and paper packages, and tie clearly-marked labels on all your polythene bags. Make sure that stick-on labels are suitable for deep-freezing and will not come off when in contact with ice.

Example of labelling

9.9.70	BROAD BEANS	1 lb
3.10.70	FISH PIE	For 6 servings

Freezing

The quicker you freeze your produce the better it will be preserved. When freezing, turn the control on your deep freeze down to its lowest.

Since the bottom and the sides of the deep freeze are the coldest (warm air rises, therefore the top of the deep freeze is the least cold), always try to leave a clear area where packages can be placed close to the walls of the freezer to freeze quickly.

The smaller the package the faster it will freeze so do not freeze produce in too great a quantity. For instance, freeze a 2-lb quantity of peas in two 1-lb containers.

Do not allow food to come into contact with packages already frozen as this tends to cause uneven freezing and to damage frozen products.

17

STORAGE

Make life easier for yourself by dividing your deep freeze into compartments by means of the wire baskets and partitions provided, and by storing the same classification of produce in one compartment. In this way you will save time when looking for a particular package, knowing that it will be in a certain part of the deep freeze.

I have mine divided into six compartments:

Vegetables	Fruit	Store Cupboard
Meat	Fish	Pre-cooked Foods

STORAGE TIME OF FROZEN FOODS

Have you ever wondered how it is that restaurants can serve grouse for lunch on August 12th, the very day that opens the grouse season? The answer, of course, is that they have been sitting in the deep freeze since the previous season. Game and most meat will keep satisfactorily for a least a year at the right temperature. Pre-cooked foods should not be kept for longer than 3 months. I have included a general list to be used as a rough guide to storage time of most foods.

A GENERAL GUIDE TO THE LENGTH OF TIME TO KEEP VARIOUS FOODS IN THE DEEP FREEZE

Beef in joints	12 months
Beef, minced or chopped	4 ,,
Bread	3 ,,
Butter, salted	3 ,,
Butter, unsalted	6 ,,
Cakes	3 ,,
Cheese	6 ,,
Cream	3 ,,
Eggs	6 ,,

18

Fish, lean	6	„
Fish, fat	4	„
Fruit with sugar and juices	9	„
Fruit without sugar	3	„
Game	12	„
Ice-cream	3	„
Lamb	9	„
Mutton	9	„
Pork, salted	3	„
Pork, unsalted	9	„
Poultry	12	„
Pre-cooked dishes	3	„ on an average. See recipes
Sausages, salted	2–4	„
Sausages, unsalted	9	„
Shellfish	3	„
*Vegetables	9	„
Veal	12	„

From this list you will see that salted foods should be kept for a shorter time than unsalted ones. This is because salt acts on fat after a certain length of time and causes it to have rather a rancid taste. Also note that fat foods keep for a shorter time than lean foods.

SOME PROBLEMS OF DEEP-FREEZING AND HOW TO AVOID THEM

Packages being overlooked

Nothing is more aggravating than finding, at the bottom of your deep freeze, an exotic and delicious dish that you once took great care to produce and freeze that has been sitting there for well over the allotted time, and which consequently you have to throw away. Avoid this by labelling everything with care and keeping a running chart on the contents of your deep freeze.

Freezer burn

This is a condition affecting meat and poultry, which becomes white and blotchy on the skin, and when cooked is dry and tasteless. Freezer burn is caused by insufficient packing and bad sealing. Air gets to the surface of the meat and makes it dehydrate.

* This is a rough guide. Carrots and cauliflower are best used within 6 months. Beans and Brussels sprouts will keep for 1 year.

19

Tainted foods

Again the cause of this is bad packing. Some foods: asparagus, sweetcorn, smoked fish and smoked meat, for example, have particularly strong and penetrating odours which are absorbed by the ice on the inside of the cabinet and also by other carelessly packed goods, especially dairy produce.

Avoid any smells by careful packaging and sealing.

If your deep freeze should start to smell a bit stale, wipe the inside of the cabinet with a cloth soaked in a solution of vinegar and water.

Bad quality foods

If food from the deep freeze is not of the best quality it is due to one of three things: being kept too long; being badly packed; or, most likely, to the food having been of poor quality in the first place. *Deep-freezing does not improve the quality or the taste of food.*

THAWING FROZEN FOOD

There are six methods of thawing food taken from the deep freeze:

1. Thawing in the refrigerator.
2. Thawing at room temperature.
3. Thawing in front of an electric fan.
4. Thawing in cold or warm water.
5. Thawing in a slow oven.
6. Thawing by cooking food from the frozen state.

For the best results different foods require different thawing processes. As a rough guide:

Vegetables should be cooked while still frozen, in a small quantity of boiling water.

Fruit that is to be eaten without being cooked or prepared should be thawed as slowly as possible in a refrigerator.

Whole fish, meat, poultry and game that is to be baked, roasted or fried should be thawed slowly in a refrigerator.

Small cuts of meat less than 1 inch thick such as chops, steaks or hamburgers, can be cooked without thawing.

Breads and rolls can be thawed by placing them in a warm oven.

Pre-cooked dishes that require further cooking or which are to be eaten hot can be cooked or heated from the frozen state.

Pre-cooked dishes that are to be eaten cold should be thawed as slowly as possible in a refrigerator.

Thawing in the refrigerator

Food should be left in its original wrapping to thaw. If meat is unwrapped before thawing it tends to bleed and lose some quality and colour. Fruit loses some of its juice and tends to become mushy. Although thawing in this way is by far the most satisfactory method for large joints of meat, poultry, game, fish, fruit, and pre-cooked dishes that are to be eaten cold (since there is less danger of toughening and of the food being unevenly cooked) it has the disadvantage of taking quite a considerable time. For instance a 5-lb roast will need about 20 hours to thaw completely.

Thawing at room temperature

Faster; a 5-lb roast will thaw in about 4 hours.

Thawing in cold or warm water

This can be done either by placing the food, still wrapped, in water or by holding it under a running tap. This is a quick method of thawing and useful in emergencies but is not absolutely reliable as it is difficult to know when the food has thawed completely and there is always a danger of the food coming into contact with the water.

Thawing in a slow oven

This is a successful method for breads and rolls but dangerous with meat and poultry as these tend to cook on the outside before the inside has thawed.

Thawing by cooking food from the frozen state

Not at all reliable with large joints of meat or poultry, which tend to become fully cooked on the outside while still raw in the middle. Also it causes toughness in the meat. Fish and small cuts of meat react better to being cooked whilst still frozen, especially if they are to be fried. Stews, pre-cooked pies and casseroles are completely successful when cooked in this way but remember to test well to ensure that the dish is cooked right through. Vegetables should always be cooked whilst still frozen and since they will have been blanched before freezing remember that they will require less time to cook than fresh vegetables.

THAWING TIMES

It is almost impossible to lay down hard and fast rules for the time required to thaw different types of food. So much depends on temperature and the size, weight and bulk of the food to be thawed.

You will find that by experience you will soon be able to judge the time needed to thaw frozen food.

As a rough guide:

1 pint fruit in syrup	1 lb meat	1 lb fish
Refrigerator – 4 hours	$3\frac{1}{2}$ hours	3–4 hours
Room temperature – $2\frac{1}{2}$ hours	1 hour	1 hour

Note: Fruit packed in dry sugar takes an hour less to thaw than fruit in syrup.

As a general rule thaw all foods in their wrapping, as this prevents drying and loss of texture.

Vegetables

GROWING VEGETABLES FOR THE DEEP FREEZE

Most seed catalogues now specially recommend varieties of seed for growing vegetables for deep-freezing, and I have had very good results from following this advice.

The most important thing is to select a variety of seed that does well in your garden and above all to pick the vegetables when they are young and at their prime. Never later. It is also important not to pick too large a quantity at one time as the quicker you can get your vegetables from the garden to the deep freeze the better the result will be. They will stay far fresher on the stalk than they will sitting around your kitchen.

Bear in mind your family's taste in vegetables. It is far more valuable to grow and freeze vegetables that they enjoy than to stock up with large quantities of something they will only eat with reluctance.

VARIETIES RECOMMENDED FOR GROWING AND FREEZING

Broad beans	Carter's Green Leviathan: Green Longpod.
Dwarf french beans	Masterpiece: Carter's Blue Lake.
Runner beans	Carter's Streamline: Carter's White Monarch.
Peas: first crop	Kelvedon Wonder: Progress.
Peas: second crop	Early Onward: Onward: Carter's Raynes Park.
Sprouting broccoli	Green Sprouting Broccoli.
Brussels sprouts	Cambridge Special.
Carrots	Carter's Improved Early Horn: Carter's Early Gem: Early Market.
Cauliflower	Carter's Forerunner.
Spinach	Carter's Goliath.

PREPARING VEGETABLES FOR THE DEEP FREEZE

On the whole, vegetables in their natural state are well suited to deep-freezing. The only exceptions are potatoes, tomatoes and salad stuffs.

The preparation of vegetables is of great importance. To ensure that they keep their original taste, tenderness and colour they must be frozen as soon as possible after picking, blanched in boiling water, cooled quickly, and packed carefully in the right containers.

Equipment

1. A large saucepan of boiling water.
2. A wire-mesh basket to fit in the saucepan. I have never managed to find a basket with a small enough mesh to hold peas, so I solved this problem by making a butter-muslin bag with a draw-string at the neck which I find very useful.
3. A quantity of iced water or very cold running water.
4. Packaging materials.
5. Ascorbic acid (Vitamin C), obtainable from chemists.
6. An accurate weighing machine.

Preparation

1. Choose only vegetables that are fresh and in perfect condition. If anything they should be a little on the young side and never overgrown.
2. Prepare the vegetables in the normal way, first making sure that they are absolutely clean, ie, shell peas or broad beans, string and cut runner beans, cut asparagus to uniform lengths.
3. Weigh the vegetables.
4. Bring a saucepan of water to the boil. Use 1 gallon of water to 1 lb of vegetables.
5. Working with small quantities, 1 lb at a time, plunge them into the boiling water in the wire basket or bag. Bring the water back to the boil. Time the blanching process carefully, following the chart below. Agitate the basket or bag to make sure that the vegetables are all equally well heated.
6. Plunge the vegetables immediately into iced or cold running water. Agitate until they are cooled through.
7. Drain, package, seal, label, and freeze at once.

Notes

Vegetables that are apt to lose their colour in cooking should have 2 teaspoons of ascorbic acid added to each gallon of blanching water. See chart. Lemon juice will also prevent discoloration. Some vegetables have to be fully cooked before freezing. See chart.

Defrosting and cooking of frozen vegetables

Because of the blanching process, vegetables that have been deep-frozen usually cook in a third to a half of the time taken for fresh vegetables. They are usually best cooked straight from the deep freeze without defrosting.

Put frozen vegetables into a small quantity of fast-boiling water, about $\frac{1}{4}$ pint to each 1 lb of vegetables, bring the water back to the boil and break the vegetables gently apart with a fork. Boil until tender.

I also find it very successful to cook frozen vegetables in the French manner with no water but, instead, about 2 tablespoons of butter to every 1 lb of vegetables.

If you defrost vegetables before cooking make sure to cook them immediately they have thawed, otherwise they will lose some of their flavour and texture.

If cooking vegetables in a pressure cooker, thaw them enough to be able to break them apart with a fork. Use $\frac{1}{8}$ pint water to each 1 lb of vegetables and check cooking time carefully.

Vegetable	Preparation
ARTICHOKE, GLOBE	Wash and trim stem.
ASPARAGUS	Clean. Cut into uniform sizes. Tie in bundles.
BEANS, BROAD	Select plump young pods. Shell.
BEANS, LIMA	Shell.
BEANS, FRENCH OR RUNNER	Select young pods. Top and tail. Cut into uniform pieces or leave whole.
BEETROOT	Freeze small round beetroot not over 2″ in diameter. Freeze whole or sliced.
BROCCOLI	Select tender stalks. Cut into uniform lengths. Wash in salt water.
BRUSSELS SPROUTS	Select small, firm heads. Wash well. Trim stalks.
CABBAGE	Select tender, firm heads. Shred or cut into wedges. Wash well in salt water.
CARROTS	Select tender carrots. Leave small carrots whole. Cube large carrots or cut into thin strips. Remove tops. Wash. Peel if necessary.

Blanching time in 1 gallon of boiling water	Packing
7 minutes.	Pack in individual polythene bags.
2–4 minutes.	Pack carefully in waxed or polythene boxes.
2 minutes.	Pack in polythene bags or containers, leaving $\frac{1}{2}''$ for head space.
2–4 minutes, depending on size.	Pack in suitable waterproof containers, leaving $\frac{1}{2}''$ for head space.
2 minutes.	Pack in suitable waterproof containers, leaving $\frac{1}{2}''$ for head space.
Cook until tender.	Pack in waterproof containers to avoid leakage, leaving $\frac{1}{2}''$ head space.
3 minutes.	Pack in waxed or polythene boxes.
3 minutes.	Pack in suitable containers.
Cook until tender.	Pack in suitable containers, leaving $\frac{1}{2}''$ head space.
Whole carrots 3 mins. Thin strips 2 mins.	Pack in suitable containers, leaving $\frac{1}{2}''$ head space.

Vegetable	Preparation
CAULIFLOWER	Clean. Leave small heads whole. Separate large heads into uniform branches.
CELERY	Select crisp tender stalks. Remove any tough fibres. Clean. Cut into uniform pieces.
CHICORY	Select compact heads. Trim stalks and remove any bruised outside leaves.
CORN; SWEET, ON-THE-COB	Select ears with plump, tender kernels. Husk and remove silk. Wash.
CORN; SWEET, WHOLE-KERNEL AND CREAM-STYLE	Select ears with plump tender kernels. Husk and remove silk. Wash. Cut kernels from ears after blanching.
COURGETTES	Select young vegetables. Cut into 1″ lengths. Peel if necessary.
EGGPLANT OR AUBERGINE	Cut into halves or slices.
GREENS, BEETROOT, CHARD, COLLARDS, KALE, MUSTARD, OR TURNIP	Select young tender leaves. Remove tough stems. Shred if desired. Wash well.

TIME OF VEGETABLES FOR FREEZING

Blanching time in 1 gallon of boiling water	Packing
Small heads 4 mins. Branches 3 mins.	Pack whole heads in polythene bags. Branches in waxed boxes or containers.
3 minutes.	Pack in suitable containers, leaving $\frac{1}{2}''$ head space.
2 minutes. (Add 2 tablespoons lemon juice to prevent browning.) *Note:* Chicory absorbs a lot of water in cooking. Be careful to drain well.	Pack in waxed boxes or polythene containers.
Small 7 minutes. Medium 9 minutes. Large 11 minutes.	Pack in suitable containers or wrap in moisture- and vapour-proof freezer paper.
4 minutes.	Pack into containers, leaving $\frac{1}{2}''$ head space.
3 minutes.	Pack in suitable containers leaving $\frac{1}{2}''$ head space.
4 minutes. (Add 2 teaspoons of ascorbic acid to prevent browning.)	Pack in suitable containers.
2–3 minutes.	Pack in suitable containers leaving $\frac{1}{2}''$ head space.

Vegetable	Preparation
KOHLRABI	Select young tender roots. Cut off tops and roots. Wash and peel. Leave whole or dice into cubes.
MARROW	Select young vegetables. Cut into 1″ lengths. Peel if necessary.
MUSHROOMS	Small, fresh mushrooms may be washed and frozen raw. These should not be kept in the deep freeze for more than 1 month. Wash, peel and slice large mushrooms in a solution of 1½ teaspoons ascorbic acid to 1 pint water to avoid discoloration.
OKRA	Select young, tender, green pods. Cut off stems and wash well.
PARSNIPS	Scrub small parsnips. Peel and dice large ones.
PEAS	Select tender, full pods. Shell, discarding any tough peas.
PEAS, MANGE-TOUT	Select flat, young pods. Top and tail.
PEPPERS, GREEN	Freeze uncooked for use in uncooked dishes. Blanch for use in cooked dishes. Select firm crisp peppers. Wash, cut out stems, halve and remove seeds. Cut into strips or rings if desired.

Blanching time in 1 gallon of boiling water	Packing
Whole 3 minutes. Cubed 1 minute.	Pack in suitable containers or wrap whole roots in moisture- and vapour-proof freezer paper.
3 minutes.	Pack in suitable containers leaving $\frac{1}{2}''$ head space.
Steam for 3 minutes, or fry lightly in butter.	Pack in suitable containers, leaving $\frac{1}{2}''$ head space.
Small pods 3 minutes. Large pods 4 minutes.	Pack in suitable containers leaving $\frac{1}{2}''$ head space.
3–4 minutes.	Pack in suitable containers leaving $\frac{1}{2}''$ head space.
2 minutes.	Pack in suitable containers leaving $\frac{1}{2}''$ head space.
3 minutes.	Pack in suitable containers leaving $\frac{1}{2}''$ head space.
Slices 2 minutes. Halves 3 minutes.	Pack in suitable containers leaving no head space for raw peppers, $\frac{1}{2}''$ head space for blanched peppers.

Vegetable	Preparation
PIMENTOS	Select firm, crisp, well-coloured pimentos. Roast in a hot oven for 4 mins and remove skins.
POTATOES (NEW)	Scrub well.
PUMPKIN	Select well-coloured, mature pumpkins. Wash. Cut into slices or cubes. Remove seeds.
SALSIFY or Oyster Plant	Select tender roots. Scrape the roots and cut into $2\frac{1}{3}$–3″ chunks.
SEA KALE	Select pale leaf stalks. Trim and wash. Cut into uniform lengths. Tie into bundles of 6–8 stalks.
SPINACH	Select tender leaves. Pick over and wash well.
SQUASH, SUMMER	Select young tender squash. Wash and cut into slices.
SQUASH, WINTER	Select firm, mature squash. Wash, cut into pieces, remove seeds.
SWEET POTATOES	Choose mature sweet potatoes that have been cured.

Blanching time in 1 gallon of boiling water	Packing
4 minutes.	Pack in suitable containers leaving $\frac{1}{2}''$ head space.
Blanch 2–4 minutes.	Seal in polythene bags. Will keep up to 1 year.
Cook until tender. Remove skin and mash.	Pack in cartons or boxes leaving $\frac{1}{2}''$ head space.
3–4 minutes. Add 2 tablespoons lemon juice to prevent browning.	Pack in polythene bags or suitable containers leaving $\frac{1}{2}''$ head space.
2–4 minutes.	Pack carefully in waxed boxes or polythene containers.
$2\frac{1}{2}$ minutes.	Pack in suitable containers leaving $\frac{1}{2}''$ head space.
3 minutes.	Pack in suitable containers leaving $\frac{1}{2}''$ head space.
Cook until tender. Remove rind and mash.	Pack in suitable containers leaving $\frac{1}{2}''$ head space.
Cook until almost tender. Peel, slice in half or mash. Cooked potato slices can be rolled in sugar before freezing.	Pack in suitable containers leaving $\frac{1}{2}''$ head space.

Vegetable	Preparation
TOMATOES (*Note:* Whole tomatoes do not freeze well)	*Juice*. Choose firm ripe tomatoes. Cut into quarters.
	Stewed. Choose firm ripe tomatoes. Peel and quarter.
TURNIPS	Select small, firm turnips. Peel and slice or dice.
ZUCCHINIS	Select young vegetables. Cut into 1″ lengths. Peel if necessary.

TIME OF VEGETABLES FOR FREEZING

Blanching time in 1 gallon of boiling water	Packing
Simmer 5–10 minutes. Press through a sieve.	Pack in cartons or tubs leaving head space for liquid expansion.
Cook until tender. 10–20 minutes.	Pack in suitable containers leaving head space for liquid expansion.
2 minutes.	Pack in suitable containers leaving ½" head space.
3 minutes.	Pack in suitable containers leaving ½" head space.

COOKING IN BOILING WATER

Cooking time after water boils

VEGETABLE	Minutes
Asparagus	5–10
Beans, lima:	
large	6–10
small runner	15–20
Beans, snap, green or wax:	
1-inch pieces	12–18
Beans, green, French	10–20
Beet greens	6–12
Broccoli	5–8
Brussels sprouts	4–9
Carrots	5–10
Cauliflower	5–8

VEGETABLE	Minutes
Corn:	
whole-kernel	3–5
on-the-cob	3–4
Kale greens	8–12
Mustard greens	8–15
Peas	5–10
Spinach	4–6
Squash, runner	10–12
Turnip greens	15–20
Turnips	8–12

COOKING IN A PRESSURE COOKER

Cooking time after correct pressure has been reached

VEGETABLE	Minutes
Asparagus	$\frac{1}{2}$
Beans, lima	2
Beans, runner, snap, green or wax:	
(1-inch pieces)	$\frac{1}{2}$
Beet greens	$\frac{3}{4}$
Broccoli	$\frac{3}{4}$
Brussels sprouts	1

VEGETABLE	Minutes
Cauliflower	$\frac{1}{2}$
Corn:	
whole-kernel	$\frac{1}{2}$
on-the-cob	$2\frac{1}{2}$–3
Peas	$\frac{1}{4}$
Spinach	$\frac{3}{4}$

Fruit

GROWING FRUIT FOR THE DEEP FREEZE

Eating summer fruit throughout the winter is one of the greatest luxuries to be gained from owning a deep freeze. Most fruits deep-freeze very successfully. Raspberries in particular, if treated correctly, are almost impossible to tell from fresh ones. If you are lucky enough to have your own garden, I would suggest that you grow and freeze as much fruit as you can comfortably cope with.

Harvest the fruit when it is fully ripe and well coloured. Never freeze fruit that has over-ripened and gone mushy, fruit that has been damaged or blemished, fruit that has been picked when wet. *Note:* If you use spray insecticides on your fruit make sure that it is carefully washed before being frozen.

PREPARING FRUIT FOR THE DEEP FREEZE

Except for berries most fruits freeze more successfully if mixed with sugar or syrup if they are puréed. Fruit frozen raw without sugar (with the exception of raspberries and currants) should not be kept for longer than 3 months.

The less fruit is handled the less likely it is to be bruised. In the case of raspberries and currants I find the most satisfactory method is to pick the berries carefully, watching for any imperfections, and put them straight into the containers they are to be frozen in. Fruit from one's garden seldom needs to be washed and in this way there is only one step between picking the fruit and freezing it.

Pick the fruit as it reaches its prime and not after. Pick and process as you go along. It is far better to deal with small quantities of fruit at one time than to pick the fruit and let it stand around until you have time to freeze it.

Only freeze perfect fruit raw. Bruised imperfect fruit can be stewed or puréed and then frozen.

One of the problems that may occur when freezing fruit is that some fruit turns brown and discolours when peeled. This can be avoided by adding lemon juice or ascorbic acid (Vitamin C) to the fruit before freezing. Ascorbic acid can be obtained in crystal form and can either be added to sugar or to sugar-syrup.

Fruit that needs to be washed should be washed in cold or iced water and dried carefully. Do not remove stalks or flower heads before washing.

1. *Raw, without sugar or syrup.* Make sure that the fruit is clean, if necessary rinse it gently in iced water. Place the fruit in a single layer on a shallow tray in the freezer. When it is frozen through, package the frozen berries in waxed tubs.

2. *Raw, with sugar.* Make sure the fruit is clean. Place it in a shallow tray and sprinkle the sugar over it. Shake the tray until the fruit is evenly coated with sugar. Package in polythene bags or waxed tubs.

3. *Raw, covered with syrup.* Make a light syrup by heating together sugar and water until the sugar has dissolved. Allow it to cool and pour it over the fruit. Package in waxed tubs or cartons.

4. *Stewed with sugar.* Stew the fruit in the normal way, with sugar to sweeten.

5. *Puréed.* Pass ripe fruit through a fine sieve and sweeten to taste. Pack in tubs or cartons.

6. *Fruit juice.* Extract juices and freeze with the addition of sugar.

Note: Fruit and fruit juices for making jam can be kept in quantity in the deep freeze. Jam made from frozen fruit has a much fresher flavour than jam kept on a larder shelf for 6 months.

Syrups

Sugar-syrups can be made a few days in advance and kept in a cool place until needed. See chart for the strength of syrup needed for individual types of fruit.

A quarter of the quantity of the sugar in the syrup may be replaced by corn syrup or honey to provide a change of flavour.

To make the syrup, heat the water and sugar together (do not boil) until the sugar has melted, or add the sugar to cold water and stir until the sugar has completely dissolved. The syrup should always completely cover the fruit when it is packed.

Adding lemon juice or ascorbic acid to fruit before freezing

(See chart for the amount of ascorbic acid to use for individual fruits.) Mix ascorbic acid crystals in water before adding them to the syrup. Add lemon juice to the syrup.

Packing

Pack whole fruit in rigid containers to avoid damage while in the deep freeze.

Pack fruit slices, purées, etc, in polythene bags or other suitable containers.

Always allow head room for expansion in cartons, boxes or tubs.

When packing whole fruit in syrup, pack the head space with some crumpled freezer paper, to keep the fruit well covered by the syrup.

Thawing

If the fruit is to be served raw, thaw it in its container in the refrigerator. Serve it very slightly frozen if possible.

A 1-lb pack will require about 6 hours' defrosting in a refrigerator.

If the fruit is to be cooked, thaw enough to be able to separate the fruit and cook it as usual.

Note: When preparing, cooking or freezing fruit do not allow it to come into contact with any copper, iron, tin or galvanized tin utensils or containers, as these will affect the taste and colour of the fruit.

APPLES

Choose ripe apples with a strong flavour. Discard any that are bruised or badly blemished.

1. Peel, core and remove blemishes. Slice or chop.

1 QUART = 32 Fl oz
OR = 900 ML

APRICOTS

Choose ripe, golden fruit with firm skins.

1. Wash in iced water. Dry well on kitchen paper. Leave whole.

2. Skin fruit by covering for 30 seconds with boiling water. Rub off skins. Stone, halve or quarter.
3. Clean fruit.

AVOCADOS

Choose soft, ripe fruit with unblemished skins.

1. Whole, wipe skin. . . . .
2. Wash and peel fruit and remove stone. Purée.

40

Method	Freezing
1. Blanch for 1½ minutes in 1 quart of water with 3 tablespoons lemon juice. Cool quickly in cold running water. Dry gently on kitchen paper.	1. Pack without sugar in polythene bags or waxed containers. Leave ½″ head space for expansion.
2. Blanch in a light syrup, 14 oz sugar to 1 pint water, 1 tablespoon lemon juice.	2. Pack in waxed containers. Cover with syrup. Leave ½″ head space for expansion.
3. Cook with or without sugar until tender. Purée.	3. Pack in cartons. Leave 1″ head space for expansion.
1. Drop the fruit into a mixture of 3 tablespoons of lemon juice to 1 quart of water. Dry well.	1. Pack in rigid containers. Leave ½″ head space for expansion.
2. Cover fruit with prepared syrup of 1 lb of sugar to 1 pint of water.	2. Pack in polythene bags or containers. Leave ½″ head space for expansion.
3. Cook until tender in a little water. Stone and purée. Sweeten to taste.	3. Pack purée in jars or cartons. Leave 1″ head space for expansion.
....	1. Pack in polythene bags.
2. Add ¼ teaspoon ascorbic acid or 3 tablespoons lemon juice to 1 quart of purée.	2. Pack in jars or cartons. Leave 1″ head space for expansion.
3. Add ½ lb sugar to 1 quart of purée.	3. As for 2.

Preparation

BANANAS   *FREEZING IS NOT*

BLACKBERRIES
Choose firm, ripe fruit.

1. Wash in iced water. Dry well. Remove stalks.

BLUEBERRIES
Choose firm, ripe fruit.

1. Wash berries in iced water. Dry well on kitchen paper.

Method	*Freezing*

RECOMMENDED

1. Freeze berries without sugar.	1. Pack in rigid containers. Leave ½″ head space for expansion.
2. Place berries in a shallow tray, cover with 1 lb sugar to 4 lb fruit and shake well until the fruit is evenly coated.	2. Pack in rigid containers. Leave ½″ head space for expansion.
3. Cook berries in a small amount of water until tender. Sweeten to taste.	3. Pack in jars or tubs. Leave 1″ head space for expansion.
4. Drop berries into a prepared syrup of 2 lb of sugar to 1 pint of water.	4. Cover with syrup and pack in jars or tubs. Leave 1″ head space for expansion.

1. Steam-blanch berries in a colander or wire basket, suspended over boiling water, for 1 minute. This stops the skins from toughening. Cool.	1. Pack in rigid containers. Leave ½″ head space for expansion.
2. Place berries in a shallow tray. Sift 1 lb sugar to 4 lb berries over the fruit. Shake berries until they are evenly coated with sugar.	2. Pack in rigid containers. Leave ½″ head space for expansion.
3. Drop berries into a prepared syrup of ¾ lb sugar to 1 pint water.	3. Pack in polythene bags or suitable containers. Leave 1″ head space for expansion.

CHERRIES, SOUR

Choose fruit that is uniform in size, well coloured and with a sharp acid flavour.

1. Wash fruit in iced water. Dry well. Remove stalks, and stones if preferred.

CHERRIES, SWEET

Choose large, ripe uniform fruit with tender skins and a strong flavour.

1. Wash in iced water. Dry well and remove stalks, and stones if preferred.

COCONUT, FRESH

Only freeze fully ripe coconuts which still contain water.

1. Husk coconut. Break into halves and grind or grate the meat.

CRANBERRIES

Choose bright red berries that are fully ripe. Discard green or blemished fruit.

1. Wash and stem. Dry well.

Method	Freezing
1. Cover fruit with a prepared syrup of 1¾ lb of sugar to 1 pint of water.	1. Pack in suitable containers. Leave 1″ head space for expansion.
2. Mix cherries with sugar, 6 oz sugar to 1 lb cherries.	2. Pack in suitable containers. Allow ½″ head space for expansion.
1. Freeze whole cherries on a shallow tray before packing.	1. Pack in rigid containers. Leave ½″ head space for expansion.
2. Cover fruit with a prepared syrup of 1 lb sugar to 1 pint of water.	2. Pack in suitable containers and leave 1″ head space for expansion.
3. Mix cherries with ¾ lb of sugar to 1 lb cherries.	3. Pack in rigid containers and allow ½″ head space for expansion.
1. Freeze raw without sugar.	1. Pack in waxed tubs, pressing coconut down firmly.
2. Mix ¼ lb sugar with 2 lb grated coconut.	2. Pack in waxed tubs, pressing coconut down firmly.
1. Pack without sugar.	1. Pack in rigid containers. Leave ½″ head space for expansion.
2. Mix ¼ lb sugar with 1 lb fruit. Shake the fruit gently with the sugar until the berries are evenly coated.	2. Pack in rigid containers. Leave ½″ head space for expansion.

Preparation

CURRANTS, RED, WHITE, AND BLACK
Choose firm, fully ripened fruit. Discard soft or blemished berries.

1. Wash, stem, and dry well.

DATES
Choose fruit that is tender and well flavoured.

1. Wash and dry well. Stone if preferred.

FIGS
Choose fruit that is soft and ripe with a rich flavour.

1. Wash in iced water. Stem and peel, as the skin tends to toughen when frozen. Leave whole, halve or slice.

GOOSEBERRIES
Choose firm, ripe fruit.

1. Wash. Top and tail.

Method	*Freezing*

1. Freeze raw fruit without sugar.

2. Crush slightly with a fork. Cover with 1 lb sugar to 3 lb fruit.

3. Cover with a light syrup of 14 oz sugar to one pint water.

4. Purée adding $\frac{1}{2}$ lb sugar to 2 lb fruit.

1. Pack in suitable containers leaving $\frac{1}{2}''$ head space for expansion.

2.
3. } As above.
4.

---

1. Pack without sugar.

1. Pack in suitable containers leaving $\frac{1}{2}''$ head space for expansion.

---

1. Freeze whole fruit on a shallow tray before packing. (Do not keep longer than 3 months.)

2. Cover with a prepared syrup of $\frac{1}{2}$ lb sugar to 1 pint water and $\frac{3}{4}$ teaspoon ascorbic acid or 4 tablespoons lemon juice.

1. Wrap each fig in a layer of freezer paper, before packing in a rigid container.

2. Pack in a suitable container. Fill head space with crumpled freezer paper.

---

1. Crush slightly with a fork and add 1 lb sugar to 3 lb fruit.

1. Pack in suitable containers leaving 1'' head space for expansion.

Preparation

GRAPEFRUIT
Choose fruit that has ripened on the tree and is juicy and well flavoured.

1. Wash. Peel and remove membrane. Break into segments and remove skin and pips.

GRAPES
Choose firm ripe fruit with tender skins.
(*Note:* Frozen grapes are only suitable for pies, fruit cocktails and jellies.)

1. Wash. Remove stems. Skin and remove pips.

GUAVA
Choose fruit that is ripe and tender.

1. Wash. Peel and cut in half.

LOGANBERRIES
Choose ripe fruit, well coloured and strongly flavoured. Discard unripe or blemished fruit.

1. Wash fruit in iced water. Dry gently on kitchen paper.

Method	Freezing
1. Cover fruit with a prepared syrup of 14 oz sugar to 1 pint of water.	1. Pack in suitable containers. Leave 1″ head space for expansion.
1. Cover fruit with a prepared syrup of 14 oz sugar to 1 pint of water.	1. Pack in suitable containers. Leave 1″ head space for expansion.
1. Cook until tender in a prepared syrup of $\frac{1}{2}$ lb sugar to 1 pint water.	1. Pack in rigid containers. Leave 1″ head space for expansion.
1. Freeze berries unwrapped in a single layer on a shallow tray.	1. Pack in rigid containers. Leave $\frac{1}{2}$″ head space for expansion.
2. Place berries on a shallow tray. Cover with 1 lb sugar to 4 lb berries. Shake the tray gently until the fruit is evenly coated with sugar.	2. Pack in suitable containers. Leave 1″ head space for expansion.
3. Cover berries with a prepared syrup of 1 lb sugar to 1 pint water.	3. Pack in suitable containers. Leave 1″ head space for expansion.
4. Rub ripe loganberries through a fine sieve. Mix in $\frac{1}{2}$ lb sugar to 2 lb fruit.	4. Pack in tubs or cartons. Leave 1″ head space for expansion.

Preparation

MANGOES
Choose firm but ripe fruit.

1. Wash and peel. Cut off a slice from stem end and around the seed.

MELONS
Choose fruit that is fully ripe but has not softened. (*Note:* Melon is best used while still slightly frosty as it tends to turn mushy when defrosted.)

1. Wash. Peel. Cut in half and remove seeds. Slice, cube or cut into balls.

NECTARINES
Choose soft, ripe but not mushy fruit, with a smooth texture.

1. Wash. Peel and stone. Cut into halves or slices.

ORANGES
Choose fruit that has ripened naturally, if possible.

1. Peel. Remove pith and leave whole.
2. Peel, divide into segments, or cut into slices, remove membrane and pips.

PEACHES
Choose firm, fully ripe fruit with rich yellow or orange-coloured flesh.

1. Wash gently. Peel with a knife or rub off skins after covering with boiling water for 1 minute. Stone and cut into halves or slices.

Method	*Freezing*
1. Slice fruit directly into a prepared syrup of ½ lb sugar to 1 pint water.	1. Pack in jars or waxed containers. Leave 1″ head space for expansion.
1. Place melon in shallow bowl. Sprinkle with lemon juice and 1 lb sugar to 5 lb melon. Mix gently. 2. Cover fruit with a prepared syrup of 14 oz sugar to 1 pint of water.	1. Pack in rigid containers. Leave 1″ head space for expansion. 2. Pack in rigid containers. Leave 1″ head space for expansion.
1. Cover fruit with a light syrup of 14 oz sugar to 1 pint of water and ¼ teaspoon ascorbic acid or 1 tablespoon lemon juice.	1. Pack in rigid containers. Leave 1″ head space for expansion.
1. Cover fruit with a light syrup of 14 oz sugar to 1 pint water. 2. As above.	1. Pack in suitable containers. Fill head space with crumpled freezer paper. 2. As above.
1. Cover fruit with a prepared syrup of 14 oz sugar to 1 pint of water and 1 tablespoon lemon juice or ¼ teaspoon ascorbic acid to prevent browning.	1. Pack in rigid containers. Fill 1″ head space with crumpled freezer paper to prevent fruit rising out of syrup.

PEARS

Choose green pears that are not fully ripened.
(*Note:* Pears have such a delicate flavour and easily damaged texture that they are not 100 per cent satisfactory to freeze.)

1. Wash, peel and core. Halve or slice.

PERSIMMONS

Choose fruit that is soft and ripe but not too strongly flavoured.
(*Note:* Whole persimmons are better when eaten before being entirely defrosted as the fruit tends to darken and turn limp when completely thawed.)

1. Wash, dry well. Remove stem ends. Leave whole.

2. Wash, peel and cut into slices.

PINEAPPLE

Choose ripe fruit (test to see if the top leaves will pull out easily).

1. Peel, core, slice or dice.

PLUMS

Choose fully ripened fruit with no blemishes.

1. Wash, cut in half and stone.

Method	*Freezing*
1. Drop pears for 1 minute into boiling syrup prepared from ¾ lb sugar to 1 pint water and ¼ teaspoon ascorbic acid or 1 tablespoon lemon juice. Cool and cover fruit with syrup.	1. Pack in rigid containers. Fill 1″ head space with crumpled freezer paper to prevent fruit rising out of the syrup.
1. Freeze before packing on a shallow tray. 2. Put fruit through a sieve and add 1 lb lump sugar to 3 lb purée.	1. Wrap each fruit in a layer of freezer paper or a plastic bag. Pack in rigid containers with crumpled freezer paper between the fruit. 2. Pack in tubs or cartons. Leave 1″ head space for expansion.
1. Freeze without sugar. 2. Cover with a prepared syrup of 1 lb sugar to 1 pint water. 3. Mix raw fruit with 1 lb sugar to 3 lb fruit.	1. Pack in suitable containers allowing ½″–1″ head space for expansion. 2. ⎱ As above. 3. ⎰
1. Cover with a prepared syrup of 1 lb sugar to 1 pint of water and 1 tablespoon lemon juice. 2. Plums can be frozen unsweetened but should not be kept for longer than 3 months.	1. Pack in suitable containers leaving 1″ head space for expansion. 2. Pack in polythene bags.

Preparation

POMEGRANATES
Choose ripe fruit.

1. Wash, cut in half. Remove the juice sacs by tapping the cells.

RASPBERRIES
Choose ripe, firm fruit with a strong flavour. Discard mushy or blemished fruit.

1. Wash fruit in iced water. Dry gently on kitchen paper.

2. Crush berries slightly with a fork.

3. Leave berries whole.

RHUBARB
Choose firm tender stalks with good colour and no tough fibres.

1. Wash and cut to required size.

STRAWBERRIES
Choose firm fruit, well coloured but not over-ripe.

1. Wash in iced water. Dry gently on kitchen paper. Lightly prick each fruit.

2. Wash fruit in iced water. Dry on kitchen paper. Leave whole or slice.

Method	Freezing
1. Cover with a prepared syrup of $\frac{1}{2}$ lb sugar to 1 pint of water.	1. Pack in suitable containers. Leave 1″ head space for expansion.
1. Freeze berries unwrapped in a single layer on a shallow tray. Do not sugar. 2. Cover berries with a medium syrup of $1\frac{1}{4}$ lb sugar to 1 pint water. 3. Place berries on a shallow dish, cover with 1 lb sugar to 4 lb berries. Shake tray gently until berries are evenly coated with sugar.	1. Pack berries in rigid containers. Leave $\frac{1}{2}$″ head space for expansion. 2. Pack berries in suitable containers. Leave 1″ head space for expansion. 3. Pack berries in rigid containers. Leave $\frac{1}{2}$″ head space for expansion.
1. Blanch in boiling water for 1 minute. Drain well. Freeze fruit without sugar.	1. Pack in suitable containers. Leave $\frac{1}{2}$″ head space for expansion.
1. Freeze berries unwrapped in a single layer on a shallow tray. 2. Place berries in a shallow dish. Cover with 1 lb sugar to 4 lb of strawberries. Shake tray to coat berries evenly. 3. Cover fruit with a medium syrup, 1 lb sugar to 1 pint of water. 4. Purée fruit.	1. Pack carefully in rigid containers, with crumpled freezer paper between layers. 2. Pack carefully in rigid containers, with crumpled freezer paper between layers. 3. Pack in suitable containers. Leave 1″ head space, for expansion. 4. Pack in tubs or cartons leaving 1″ head space for expansion.

Meat

GENERAL NOTES ON THE DEEP-FREEZING OF MEAT

Although freezing is apt to tenderize meat to a certain degree, due to the action of ice crystals which break up the fibres of the meat, it does not improve the quality or taste of the meat. Therefore it is of great importance only to freeze meat that is of the highest quality. It is also important to remember that freezing does not sterilize meat. It keeps dormant most of the enzymes and in some cases kills a certain amount of the bacteria and moulds that exist in all meat, but it is essential to make sure that meat that is to be deep-frozen is prepared in clean and sterile conditions.

Meat should be hung for the correct length of time before it is put into the deep freeze. Make sure, if you are buying your meat from the butcher, that it has been properly hung and has been chilled but not frozen.

Do not freeze greater quantities or larger joints of meat than your family can cope with. Buy when the price of meat is favourable but remember that a quick regular turnover from your deep freeze is more economic than large stocks of meat kept for months on end.

Bone meat whenever possible. Bones take up space in your deep freeze and are liable to tear protective wrappings. Use bones and spare scraps of meat to make soups and stocks. Also trim off as much excess fat as possible as fat tends to turn rancid if kept for any length of time in a frozen state.

Take great care with the packaging of all meat. A good joint of meat can be completely spoilt by freezer burn if it has not been carefully and correctly wrapped.

If you are freezing home-reared and -slaughtered meat it is well worth paying a butcher to cut it into joints for you. Unless you are an expert at butchering, the small amount you will have to pay for this service will be an economy in the long run.

PREPARATION OF MEAT FOR THE DEEP FREEZE

Large cuts for roasting, braising and boiling

Wipe over the meat with a damp cloth. Trim off any excess fat and gristle. Wrap it with a protective cover of cotton stockinette. Put it into a polythene bag. Seal, label and freeze.

Meat that is only going to be kept for a short length of time can be packed in freezer paper or aluminium foil with the joints carefully sealed with tape.

Steaks, chops, and cutlets

Wipe with a damp cloth. Trim meat. Wrap each steak or cutlet in cellophane or polythene and pack in small quantities in polythene bags or waxed containers. Seal, label, and freeze.

Offal – hearts, liver, kidneys, sweetbreads, tongue, etc

Trim off excess fat and gristle. Wash thoroughly and dry. Kidneys can be frozen in their own coating of fat. Weigh and pack in polythene bags. Seal, label and freeze. *Do not keep offal in the deep freeze for longer than 4 months.*

Bacon and sausages

Bacon and sausages should be well wrapped in quantities of 1 lb. Salted sausages and bacon should not be kept for longer than 3 months in the deep freeze. Unsalted bacon and sausages can be kept frozen for 6–8 months.

Minced and chopped meat

Discard as much fat as possible. Mince or chop meat. Weigh and pack it in small quantities in polythene bags or containers. Seal, label and freeze. Do not keep minced meat for longer than 4 months in the deep freeze.

Dog meat

Meat and scraps unfit for human consumption can be chopped, wrapped and frozen in small quantities for use as dog and cat food.

CHOOSING AND HANGING MEAT

Beef

The meat should chill to 40°F within 24 hours of being killed and should be hung 8–14 days before freezing. The flesh should be brilliant red, firm and with a fresh and light smell. The fat should be a yellowish white.

Mutton

The best mutton comes from sheep from 2–6 years old.

The meat should be chilled to 40°F immediately after slaughtering and should be hung for 6–12 days before freezing. The flesh should be a rich dark red colour with the fat white and firm. The meat should be moist and elastic but not wet or soggy.

Lamb

English lamb is usually available during the spring and early summer. The meat should be chilled to 40°F immediately after killing and should be hung for 7–10 days before freezing. The meat should be firm and elastic and of a clear pinkish colour.

Veal

The quality of veal is at its best when the animal is 3–4 months old. The meat should be chilled immediately after killing to 40°F and should be frozen as soon as possible. The meat should have a firm, moist texture and have a pale pinkish colour.

Pork

The meat should be chilled to 40°F immediately after killing and should be frozen as soon as possible. Pork should never be eaten or frozen unless it is absolutely fresh. The meat should be light pinky-white in colour, with the fat a clear white with a slight tinge of pink. The flesh should be fine-grained and compact.

As a general rule I maintain that it is far better to thaw out meat before cooking, and the best way to do this is in a refrigerator with the meat still in its original wrapping; the meat is defrosted slowly and there is no danger of its drying out as it thaws. The obvious drawback is that it takes a long time for a joint of meat to thaw out, roughly 4 hours per 1 lb of meat. I usually leave my meat to defrost in the refrigerator overnight.

It is quite possible to cook meat while still in its frozen state but up to 1½ times as long may be required to cook a frozen joint. It should be cooked at a lower temperature than thawed meat and should be carefully tested to make sure the centre of the meat is fully cooked. Frozen steaks should be cooked over a low heat to thaw. When almost thawed increase the heat to brown the meat.

As a quicker alternative to the slow method of thawing in a refrigerator, the meat can be left at room temperature, allowing about 2 hours per 1 lb of meat, or in front of an electric fan (or, while still packed, under a warm tap) when it will only take about 25 minutes a lb to thaw.

Unwrap steaks and chops and separate them to speed thawing but keep the meat well covered to prevent it drying out.

Always use all meat within 24 hours of thawing.

Poultry

Chickens, Ducks, Geese and Turkeys

GENERAL NOTES ON THE DEEP-FREEZING OF POULTRY

Deep-freezing poultry produces excellent results. One of the chief advantages is that the birds can be killed when they are at the right age or bought when they are plentiful and cheap. This applies especially to turkeys whose price fluctuates tremendously. Do be careful, when buying poultry from a butcher or store, to see that they have not already been frozen.

The birds should be completely prepared for cooking before freezing. You will find it saves time and space to joint, and even bone, birds that are not suitable for roasting but which you are going to use for casseroles, stews or pies.

Giblets cannot be stored in the deep freeze in the same way as the bird itself can, so it is important to package them separately. Giblets may be stored for 3 months.

It is possible to stuff birds for roasting before they are frozen but stuffing shortens the storage time of the bird (a stuffed bird can be stored for up to 2 months and unstuffed poultry up to 12 months). Another disadvantage of stuffing the bird before freezing is that the strong herbs and seasonings in stuffing are apt to penetrate the true flavour of the bird.

As a general rule allow ½–¾ lb of dressed weight of poultry to each person.

Note: The bones of chickens are apt to turn dark if held for longer than 3 months in the deep freeze. This is caused by the effect of ice on the bones and in no way detracts from the flavour or the nutritional value of the bird.

Preparation of poultry for the deep freeze

Poultry should be starved for 24 hours before killing to empty the crop and to clean out the insides of the bird.

If possible pluck the bird immediately after killing as the feathers come out much more easily if the bird is plucked whilst still warm. Start with the large wing feathers and the tail feathers and then pluck the rest of the bird except the head.

If it is not possible to pluck the bird at once, dip it in very hot but *not boiling water* for a minute before plucking. Dipping the bird into boiling water increases the likelihood of freezer burn. Pull out stubs with the help of a short blunt knife. Leave the bird hanging head down in a cool place for 24 hours. (If this is not done the bird will be tough when cooked.)

Cut off the head, feet and wing tips and draw the bird. Wipe inside and out carefully with a damp cloth.

To freeze for roasting

Truss the bird and tie in the legs on the body ready for cooking Do not use skewers as these will tear wrapping materials.

Package the bird in aluminium foil or freezer paper for short-term freezing, in polythene bags for medium-term freezing, and in cotton stockinette with a polythene bag over it for long-term freezing.

Seal all packages well. Label, including the weight of the bird, and freeze.

Place giblets in a polythene bag. Seal, label and freeze.

To freeze poultry for frying, casseroles, stews, and pies

Halve, quarter or fully joint the bird. Wipe over the pieces with a damp cloth, and wrap them in cellophane or moisture-proof plastic wrapping for easy separation when thawing.

Pack in polythene bags. Seal, label and freeze.

If preferred the bird can be fully boned and the bones used for stock.

CHOOSING POULTRY

Chickens

There are basically four categories of chicken:

1. *Broilers*. Young chickens of up to 2½ lb live weight, usually bred in a battery and very well fattened. The bird should be small, with a plump breast and flexible bones. Broilers are used for roasting, grilling or frying, and will serve from 1–2 people depending on the size.

2. *Capons*. Young cockerels which have been castrated by means of an injection and fattened. The flesh is tender and white and the birds weigh from 4½ lb to 5 lb live weight, being killed at between 14–16 weeks old. The breastbone should be straight and the leg and wing bones supple. There should be plenty of firm flesh on both legs and breast. Capons are used for roasting, grilling and frying.

3. *Battery hens*. Hens kept in individual cages for laying eggs, and killed before they get tough. They are usually killed at about 12 months and, according to the breed, weigh between 4–8 lb. They are not as tender as capons but are suitable for slow roasting. When buying a battery hen you may find that the skin has a strong yellow colour to it. This is due to the breed of the hen and does not affect the taste in any way.

4. *Boiling fowls*. These are old and inexpensive birds and if well fattened have endless possibilities for casseroles and slow-cooked dishes.

Ducks

Ducklings (6 weeks to 3 months old) and ducks should be prepared for the deep freeze in the same way as chickens. Their breastbones should be pliable and their beaks flexible.

Use ducklings and young ducks for roasting and old, tougher birds for braising, casseroles and pâtés. A good-sized duck should feed 4 people with ease.

Geese

Young geese and goslings have bright yellow feet and bills. In an old goose these would be reddish. The flesh should be rosy-red, and the fat pale yellow, and the legs should be supple. If you kill your own geese make sure that they are left to hang for at least 5 days.

Pluck and prepare for the deep freeze in the same way as chickens, using a taper to singe the tough stubs of quills if necessary.

Birds weighing over 10 lb are not tender enough to roast but may be boiled.

Turkeys

Hen turkeys are far more flavoursome and tender than cock birds. Choose one that has supple and smooth black legs. If you kill your own birds hang them for a week or longer. Prepare for the deep freeze as with chickens.

Game

Grouse, Partridge, Pheasant, Snipe, Wild Duck, Woodcock, Rabbits, Hares and Venison

GENERAL NOTES ON THE DEEP-FREEZING OF GAME

Like poultry, game freezes very successfully and can be kept for up to a year in the deep freeze. I do not particularly like eating roast game out of season but find it invaluable for making raised pies, pâtés, soups and casseroles throughout the summer.

It is important to make sure that the game has been properly hung before being frozen. The time of hanging varies with individual tastes. Personally I like it pretty high, and in cold weather I leave pheasants for up to a fortnight before plucking.

Prepare all game ready for eating before freezing. If you are landed with a large quantity of birds and cannot cope with them all at once it is possible to freeze them without plucking or drawing, but the obvious disadvantage of this is that it is twice as unpleasant to pluck them when thawed, wet and cold, than it is when they are fresh.

Cut tough old birds, that are no use for roasting, into joints to be used for casseroles, stews, pâtés and stock.

With pigeons, woodcock and snipe, if you are pressed for time when plucking the birds, it is possible to skin them by cutting a neat incision from the neck along the top of the backbone to the tail. Pull back the skin complete with feathers and cut off at leg and wing joints.

All game should be hung by the feet.

Grouse, Partridge, Pheasant, Wild Duck and Pigeon

Hang for the required time, 5–14 days depending on taste and weather conditions. Pluck, draw, and prepare in the same way as chickens ready for the oven.

Pack with a protective layer of stockinette and in polythene bags. Seal, label and freeze.

Snipe and Woodcock

Hang for the required time, 4–7 days depending on taste and weather conditions.

Pluck the birds. *Do not draw. Leave the heads and beaks on.*

To truss: Make a hole through the wings and breast of the bird, twist the head sideways and push the beak through the hole, pinning the head and the wings to the side of the bird.

Wrap in tin foil or stockinette and place in polythene bags. Seal, label and freeze.

Hares

Hang hares for 5–7 days head downwards with a tin or cup tied over the mouth to catch the blood.

Skin, and wipe out the inside carefully with a damp cloth.

Leave whole for roasting or cut into pieces for jugging and stews. Pack in polythene bags. Pack the blood separately in a carton. Seal, label and freeze.

Rabbits

Unlike hares, rabbits should be frozen when absolutely fresh.

Skin and draw. Wipe over the inside with a damp cloth. Cut into pieces. Pack in polythene bags. Seal, label and freeze.

Venison

Hang for 7–14 days (wipe over with milk every other day to keep the meat fresh).

Cut, or preferably get a butcher to cut, the meat into joints as for veal and beef. Pack in cotton stockinette and polythene bags. Seal, label and freeze.

I have sometimes let game hang too long, or been sent presents of venison through the post which have arrived 'stinking'. Rather than waste the game I have discovered that cooking it whilst it is still partially frozen takes away a lot of the high taste.

Fish

GENERAL NOTES ON THE DEEP-FREEZING OF FISH

Fish, almost more than any other commodity, varies considerably in price and availability depending on weather and seasonal conditions. Providing it is frozen within 24 hours of being caught, it freezes very successfully and because it adapts to so many ways of cooking and provides such a high source of protein, you should keep a permanent supply of fish in your deep freeze.

If you buy fish for freezing from a fishmonger, make absolutely sure that it is freshly caught and has not already been frozen and thawed.

Treated properly, fish frozen when really fresh will be impossible to tell from unfrozen fish. On the other hand, fish that has been allowed to get stale before freezing will never taste good and will be more susceptible to spoiling.

Whole fish can be frozen straight from the water or gutted. I find the first method most satisfactory but it does have the disadvantage that the fish must be completely thawed before being cooked and the job of gutting is even more unattractive when the fish is icy cold.

Since most fish has a strong odour it is especially important to see that it is really well wrapped.

FRESHWATER FISH

Salmon

1. Wipe over with a damp cloth, gut or leave whole. Wrap in foil or freezer paper or moisture- and vapour-proof plastic. Place in a polythene bag. Seal, label (adding the weight), and freeze.

2. Gut the fish, remove the head, tail and fins and cut cross-section slices for individual portions. Wrap each portion in moisture- and vapour-proof plastic. Pack in small quantities in polythene bags. Seal, label and freeze.

Sea trout (sometimes called Peel)

Wipe over with a damp cloth. Wrap in tin foil, freezer paper or moisture- and vapour-proof plastic. Place in a polythene bag. Seal, label and freeze.

Trout (Brown trout and Rainbow trout)

Wipe over with a damp cloth. Wrap in tin foil, freezer paper or moisture- and vapour-proof plastic. Place each trout in a polythene bag. Seal, label and freeze.

Small fish (Mackerel, Herrings, Whiting, Sprats, Bars, Whitebait, etc)

Gut, remove heads, tails and fins if necessary. Wipe over with a damp cloth. Wrap in tin foil, freezer paper or moisture- and vapour-proof plastic and (except in the case of tiny fish) place individually in polythene bags. Seal, label and freeze.

Large fish, and fish to be filleted .

Gut, remove heads, tails and fins. Remove scales by running a sharp knife under the scales from tail to head. Cut into steaks or fillets and remove the skin if necessary. Wrap each fillet or steak in moisture- and vapour-proof plastic. Pack in small quantities in polythene bags. Seal, label and freeze.

SHELLFISH

Lobster, Langoustine and Crayfish

Only freeze lobster that you have bought live. Cook it before freezing by placing the live lobster head first in fast-boiling water. Bring back to the boil and cook for 20 minutes to the lb. Allow to cool in the water.

Freeze whole and pack in a polythene bag or cut into half along the back. Remove the brain sac and the intestine. Remove all the meat from the shell and the claws and pack in small quantities in waxed cartons or polythene bags. Seal, label and freeze.

Dublin Bay and Mediterranean Prawns

Cook in boiling water. Remove the heads and pack in small quantities in polythene bags. Seal, label and freeze.

Shrimps and Prawns

Cook until pink in boiling water. Cool, shell and remove the thin black line of the intestine if it is visible. Pack in small quantities in polythene bags. Seal, label and freeze.

Crabs

Cook the crabs in boiling water. Cool. Lift off the shell with a sharp knife and carefully remove the poisonous stomach and brain sac. Twist off the legs. Remove the flesh from the main body of the crab and from the large claws. Return the flesh to the shell, pack in a polythene bag. Seal, label and freeze. Or pack the crab meat in waxed tubs or polythene bags.

OYSTERS, CLAMS AND MUSSELS

Of all the shellfish, oysters, clams and mussels are notorious poisoners. It is possible to freeze them when raw, having first cleaned their shells, but I do not recommend this and suggest always cooking oysters and mussels before freezing.

Oysters and Clams

Wash and remove from the shell, reserving the juice. Boil for 3–5 minutes in enough water and juice to cover. Cool. Pack with juice in waxed cartons.

Mussels

Scrub the shells with a stiff brush. Remove any fibrous matter sticking out from the shell. Place the mussels in a large saucepan covered with a damp cloth and place them over a medium heat until they open, about 3 minutes. Allow them to cool in the saucepan. Mussels can be frozen in their shells or removed from the shells. Freeze them in the juice. Pack in polythene bags. Seal, label and freeze.

If possible fish should be cooked when completely thawed but it may be cooked when partially frozen.

To thaw, leave the fish in its wrapping and place on a refrigerator shelf. This is much the best method, but if you are pressed for time the fish can be thawed at room temperature or by immersing it in cold water.

Dairy Produce

GENERAL NOTES ON THE DEEP-FREEZING OF DAIRY PRODUCE

Few people make their own butter these days and it is a commodity that fluctuates considerably in price. If unsalted it can be kept successfully in the deep freeze for up to 12 months. Buy when it is at rock-bottom price. The same applies to eggs.

Most dairy produce can be bought in bulk at a great saving.

Butter

No special preparation is needed to freeze butter. But as all fats are particularly easily affected by any strong odours it should be carefully sealed in polythene bags, freezer paper, or waxed containers.

Keep unsalted butter for up to 12 months, salted butter for up to 6 months.

Cheeses

Cheeses of the hard Cheddar type can be successfully frozen for up to 6 months, ie, Gloucester, Double Gloucester, Cheshire, etc.

Cream cheese with over 40 per cent butter-fat content can be kept in the deep freeze for up to 3 months. Luckily the butter-fat content of a cheese is almost always given on the wrapping.

Pack cheese in polythene bags. Seal, label and freeze.

Cream

Only freeze cream with over 40 per cent butter-fat content (commercially called 'double cream'); if the butter-fat content is lower the cream will curdle immediately it is defrosted.

Cream does not retain its full texture when defrosted and should not be used for coffee or cornflakes but only for whipping with sugar or for cooking.

Freeze cream when it is absolutely fresh. Raw or pasteurized cream can be stored for up to three months. Pack in waxed cartons or tins. Seal carefully, label and freeze.

No form of hard-boiled egg or whole cooked egg can be frozen.
Only new-laid eggs should be frozen. Since egg yolks harden when
frozen, eggs must be separated or well mixed to break up the yolk
before freezing. There are two methods of doing this:

1. The whole eggs can be broken into a bowl and mixed until
the yolks and whites are well amalgamated. They should not be
beaten.

2. The yolks and the whites can be separated. The whites can
be successfully frozen just as they are but the yolks should be
stirred with a stabilizer of sugar or salt.

Add 2 teaspoons salt to 1 pint of yolks for savoury uses.

Add 2 teaspoons sugar to 1 pint of yolks for sweet uses.

Pack in small plastic or waxed containers. Seal, label, giving
the quantity, and freeze.

To thaw: Leave the eggs in their containers and stand at room
temperature for about 40 minutes.

Note: It is useful to know that 1 tablespoon of yolks and 2 tablespoons of whites equal 1 large egg.

Margarine, Pure Lard, and Cooking Fat

These can be stored for up to 5 months in the deep freeze. Pack
in polythene bags. Seal, label and freeze.

Breads, Cakes and Pastries

Breads, rolls, cakes, and pastries seem almost to improve by being
frozen and since most shop-bought bread is of an inferior quality
these days you will find it very rewarding to bake your own and to
store it in your deep freeze.

If you are lucky enough to have found a baker who really
produces bread that is 'as your mother used to make it' buy from
him in bulk and store in your deep freeze, producing fresh crisp
bread and rolls for each meal.

When making cakes, flan cases, buns and biscuits, it is just as
easy to make double or treble the quantity, using half and freezing
the rest.

Bread, roll, and cake mixtures can be frozen before baking but the yeast and raising ingredient begin to die at the low temperature and unbaked breads or cakes should not be stored for longer than 2 weeks. In any case the results are not as satisfactory as with those ready-baked.

BREADS AND ROLLS

Fresh yeast has been used in all the recipes. If using dried yeast, follow the manufacturer's directions. Fresh yeast will keep up to 1 month in a loosely tied polythene bag in the refrigerator. Dried yeast will keep up to 6 months in an airtight tin.

Breads and rolls are particularly susceptible to dehydration and should be wrapped with extra care with an inner wrapping or moisture- and vapour-proof plastic. If carefully wrapped they can be successfully stored for up to one year. Pack in polythene bags. Seal, label and freeze.

Ways of thawing breads and rolls:

1. Thaw bread and rolls at room temperature for 2–3 hours.
2. Thaw crisp rolls and French bread for 10 minutes in a medium oven before serving.
3. Small rolls can be put straight from the deep freeze into a medium oven where they will take about 15 minutes to thaw.
4. In emergencies bread can be placed frozen in a cool oven where it will defrost in about 1 hour. (Bread defrosted in this manner tends to go stale on the second day.)
5. Frozen sliced bread can be toasted whilst still frozen and is deliciously crisp and fresh tasting.

CAKES, BISCUITS AND PASTRIES

Both cakes and pastries need careful handling when packing to avoid damaging them. I find the most satisfactory method of packing is to freeze them uncovered until they are quite hard and then to pack them in polythene bags or boxes, excluding as much air as possible. Small cakes and pastries should be individually wrapped with moisture- and vapour-proof plastic or cellophane.

One of the most frequent complaints against the freezing of cakes, biscuits and pastries is that they are apt to be soggy when they have been thawed. If the product is given ample time to thaw inside its original container and not exposed to air, this will be avoided.

Uncooked biscuit mixtures and Danish pastries can be frozen before cooking with complete success. Biscuit mixtures frozen in sausage-like shapes can be sliced whilst still frozen and placed immediately in the oven.

Cakes should not be iced or filled with anything except butter icing. Other icings tend to crumble, dry out or go soggy, and icings can easily be made while the cake is thawing.

General Notes on the Deep-freezing of Pre-Cooked Dishes

Most made-up soups, fish, meat dishes, stews, casseroles, pies and tarts can be successfully frozen and on being reheated, if properly treated, will taste just as good as if they had been freshly cooked.

To retain the full flavour of pre-cooked foods certain points must be borne in mind:

1. Nearly all seasonings with the exception of celery and garlic lose their flavour slightly during freezing. Always check for seasoning before serving.

2. Pre-cooked dishes to be served hot will have to have some additional cooking after being frozen. Always tend to undercook your casseroles, stews, etc, to allow for this.

3. Cream sauces and soups have a tendency to separate if reheated too rapidly. Avoid this by heating carefully in a bowl over boiling water and never by defrosting directly over a strong flame; or thaw completely before heating and whisk well when warming them up.

4. Quick cooling after cooking is of great importance. Cool by placing saucepan or casserole immediately the dish is cooked, over ice or in cold, running water.

5. Freeze pre-cooked dishes as soon as they are cold.

6. As always, careful packaging and sealing is of the utmost importance.

7. Be sure to check that the dish has cooked right through before serving. Nothing is so demoralizing as producing a dish that has a solid core of ice.

8. Always work in clean conditions.

PRESSURE COOKERY

For making stocks a pressure cooker is a great asset. Cooking time is cut to about one-quarter. All the flavour is retained inside the cooker and your kitchen is not pervaded by the rather sickly smell of stock. With a large family to feed the combination of pressure cooker and deep freeze is ideal for the making and storing of soups.

Stews are more complicated. Careful timing is of great importance and the manufacturers' instructions should always be followed. Three minutes too much and your stew is reduced to a soggy mush. And because most stews only take between 15–20 minutes, it is difficult to achieve the right degree of cooking to make the dish suitable for freezing and reheating.

If you are a great advocate of pressure cookery, I would advise using it for your deep freeze only for making stocks and cooking root vegetables.

SOUPS AND SAUCES

Nearly all soups and a number of sauces freeze well. Always allow room in containers for expansion when freezing liquid.

Avoid over-seasoning. Seasoning can always be added when reheating.

To save space, reduce stock by boiling and freeze in concentrated form in ice-cube moulds.

Soups

For vegetable soups, add potatoes ready cooked when reheating, as cooked potatoes toughen when frozen. This does not apply to puréed potatoes, or potatoes in soups that are cooked and then puréed.

When using milk, cream or egg yolks to thicken a soup, add them when reheating where possible. This will avoid the danger of curdling.

Do not use celery or celery salt when making soups for deep-freezing as the taste of celery becomes far more pronounced when frozen.

Do not use garlic when preparing soups for freezing, as the taste

72

goes off during deep-freezing. Put it through a garlic press and add it when reheating soups and sauces.

Always cool soups immediately after cooking by placing the saucepan over ice or in cold running water.

Pack as soon as possible in polythene bags, or waxed carton containers.

Defrost by running cold water over the container and turning the frozen soup into a saucepan or thaw in containers at room temperature. Heat gently and stir occasionally.

Sauces

Always skim fat off the surface of sauces before freezing as fat tends to turn rancid if frozen for any length of time. Follow general rules for soups.

PÂTÉS, TERRINES, FISH AND MEAT MOUSSES

Prepare for eating but do not garnish. Cool if necessary. Pack pâtés in waxed tubs or containers, pressing the meat down well. Leave mousses in their original dishes wherever possible, and pack in polythene bags. Seal, label and freeze.

To thaw, place all cold meat and fish dishes in the refrigerator, without unwrapping, overnight or for 5–8 hours, depending on size. Turn out if necessary and garnish.

COLD MEATS

Cold roast poultry or joints of meat can be frozen, but they must be packed very carefully to prevent the flesh from drying out and losing its colour. In the case of stuffed birds remove the stuffing and freeze it separately. Pack with a protective wrapping of moisture- and vapour-proof plastic and seal in polythene bags. Label and freeze.

The problem of dehydration arises even more with sliced cold meat and it is really more successful to pack the slices with a protective covering of sauce or gravy. If this is not possible separate each slice with a layer of moisture- and vapour-proof plastic before packing.

Chopped chicken, ham, and meat can be packed in polythene bags for using in salads.

All meat that is to be eaten cold should be thawed in its container on a shelf in the refrigerator.

Meat that is to be reheated can be thawed in a slow oven.

PIES

WITH MASHED POTATO TOPS

Cook almost completely, taking care not to brown the potato.

Cool quickly by placing the pie dish over ice or in running cold water.

Pack the pie in the dish it was cooked in into a polythene bag. Seal, label and freeze.

Thaw at room temperature for 5 hours and cook in a medium oven. Brown top under grill for 5 minutes or cover the frozen pie with tin foil and cook in a medium oven, removing the tin foil to brown the potato.

Note: I find it very convenient to make a number of individual pies in tin-foil dishes rather than one large one. These cook more quickly, and one can cater for the exact number.

WITH PASTRY TOPS

1. *Pies that are cooked before putting on pastry*

Cook pie and cool over ice or in cold running water.

Cover with pastry top. *Do not cut air holes.*

Pack carefully in polythene bag, taking care not to damage pastry. Seal, label and freeze.

Thaw at room temperature for 5 hours. Cut air holes and cook for the required time.

Or cut air holes and cover with tin foil while the pie is still frozen: cook in a medium oven until hot through. Brown pastry by removing tin foil.

2. *Pies that are cooked with the pastry*

Three-quarters cook the pie, being careful not to let the pastry brown. Cool immediately over ice or in cold running water.

Pack in polythene bags. Seal, label and freeze.

Thaw at room temperature and cook for the required time, or

cover the frozen pie with tin foil and cook in a medium oven, removing foil to brown the pastry.

MEAT, FISH AND VEGETABLES IN CREAM SAUCE

Cream sauces are inclined to curdle on reheating unless treated with care. Reheat any creamed dishes in a bowl over hot, *not boiling*, water. Stir occasionally to ensure even heating but be careful not to break up meat, fish, etc.

When the sauce has thawed, add seasoning and flavouring, and egg yolks or cream if necessary.

Continue heating until ready to serve.

Note: Should there be a disaster and the sauce separates, remove the meat, fish, or vegetables and keep warm. Melt 1 oz butter in a saucepan, add 1 oz flour and mix well. Gradually add the curdled sauce, stirring continually until thick and smooth.

Curdling of cream sauces after freezing is usually due to the proportion of fat used. Be sparing with fat in sauces to be frozen.

CASSEROLES AND STEWS, ETC

Cook for about three-quarters of the usual time. Cool immediately over ice or in cold running water.

Pack in suitable containers or in their original dishes in polythene bags. Seal, label and freeze.

Defrost at room temperature, reheat and finish cooking in a medium oven.

Or turn frozen casserole or stew into a heavy saucepan and heat over a low flame, stirring occasionally. *Check for seasoning before serving.*

Casseroles, stews and baked dishes can be frozen without wrapping in their original dishes. When solid, unmould and wrap in a polythene bag or in freezer paper or aluminium foil.

To heat, remove wrapping and return to original dish: heat in a moderate oven.

Note: Lightly grease baking dishes or melt a little butter in saucepans before cooking frozen dishes: this prevents sticking.

PRE-COOKED FISH DISHES, MINCED OR CHOPPED MEAT PATTIES, HAMBURGERS AND FISH CAKES

Make up ready for frying. Freeze in small quantities with each portion wrapped in a layer of moisture- and vapour-proof plastic. Seal in polythene bags or pack in boxes. Label, and freeze.

Cook whilst still frozen until heated through and nicely browned.

THE THAWING OF PRE-COOKED PUDDINGS TO BE SERVED COLD OR ICED

For cold puddings, thaw, if possible in a refrigerator, for 5 hours, or overnight. Leave wrapped whenever possible.

For iced puddings, remove from the deep freeze 10–30 minutes before serving. Keep in a refrigerator until ready to use.

SANDWICHES

Sandwiches for parties, picnics, lunch boxes and emergencies can be successfully stored in the deep freeze for up to 2 months.

To freeze: Wrap tightly in a layer of moisture- and vapour-proof plastic and put in polythene bags. Seal, label. Freeze the sandwiches away from the walls of the deep freeze. This ensures even moisture when they are defrosted.

To defrost: Remove sandwiches from the polythene bags but leave them in the inner covering. Leave at room temperature for 2½–3 hours.

When freezing sandwiches note the following points:

Do not use stale bread.

Do not be mean with butter.

Do not use fillings that include hard-boiled eggs as these go leathery during freezing.

Do not use fillings that include mayonnaise, which curdles during freezing.

Do not use fillings that include salad stuffs which go limp and tasteless during freezing, ie, lettuce, cucumber, watercress, tomatoes, etc.

Do remove the crusts from the bread.

Do soften your butter before spreading.

Do label your sandwiches carefully.

PART TWO

The Recipes

Stocks and Soups

Basic Stock

1 veal bone
2½ lb beef-soup bones with
some meat on them
6 pints water
3 medium onions stuck with a
clove apiece

1 lb assorted chopped
vegetables, including
2 carrots and a stick of
celery
Bouquet garni
Salt and freshly ground black
pepper

METHOD

1. Put the bones and meat in a heavy saucepan.
2. Pour over the cold water and add seasoning.
3. Bring slowly to the boil, skimming the surface to remove the scum that rises throughout.
4. When the stock boils, add ¾ pint of cold water and bring back to the boil. Repeat this three times, skimming the surface each time.
5. Add the vegetables: bring back to the boil and skim once more.
6. Add the bouquet garni and simmer for 3 hours.
7. Strain the stock through muslin over a hair sieve and leave to cool. Remove all fat.
(Stock from poultry carcases can be made in the same way.)

To freeze: Pour the stock into suitable containers. Seal, label and freeze.

To defrost: Place frozen stock in a saucepan and heat.

Note: This is a pure stock. An excellent stock can be made by simmering cooked bones (browned in an oven for 5 minutes), raw vegetables, bacon rind, etc, for 4–5 minutes. Strain, cool and freeze.

Marrow-bone Stock

(Cooked in a pressure cooker)

2 lb marrow bones	2 sticks celery
2 onions	Bouquet garni
1 carrot	1 quart water
1 turnip	Salt and pepper

METHOD

1. Ask your butcher to break the bones if they are too large. Put into the pressure cooker with the other ingredients.

2. Bring slowly to the boil.

3. Skim the surface. Put on the lid and bring to pressure. Reduce the heat and cook for 45 minutes. Leave until cold, strain and skim off fat.

To freeze: Pour stock into suitable containers. Seal, label and freeze.

To defrost: Place frozen stock straight in a saucepan and heat.

Basic Fish Stock

1 lb fish trimmings (preferably thick-skinned white fish)	Small bouquet garni
	Squeeze of lemon juice
2 pints water	4 peppercorns
1 onion stuck with a clove	Salt

82

1. Place all ingredients in a saucepan.
2. Bring to the boil slowly, skim and then allow to simmer gently for 30 minutes.
3. Strain immediately.

To freeze: Pour stock into suitable containers. Seal tightly, label and freeze.

To defrost: Place frozen stock straight in a saucepan and heat.

Tomato Soup

The colour of soup is very important. Nothing is so off-putting as being faced with a bowl of muddy, cloudy liquid. Tomato soups can be the most lyrical colour, and the home-made article bears no relation to the tinned variety. I serve mine with a thin slice of lemon floating in each bowl, and a dish of crisp cubes of fried bread served separately.

HOME-MADE TOMATO SOUP

1 onion	4 sprigs of parsley
2 lb ripe tomatoes	1 teaspoon of dried sage
1½ pints beef or chicken stock	½ lemon
	Salt and pepper

METHOD

1. Slice onion. Quarter tomatoes. Chop parsley. Add onion, tomatoes, parsley and sage to the stock. Season.
2. Bring to the boil and simmer for 40 minutes without a lid.
3. Rub through a fine sieve, or put in an electric blender.

To freeze: Cool the soup, pour into waxed containers allowing room for expansion.

To defrost: Put frozen soup into a saucepan and stir until hot.

To serve: Season with salt and pepper and flavour with lemon juice. Serve really hot.

Garnish with: A thin slice of lemon, grated orange rind, whipped cream flavoured with salt, pepper, and chopped chives, or sour cream.

In summer serve the soup iced with a garnish of finely chopped cucumber and garlic bread.

When tomatoes are at their cheapest, buy a lot and make and freeze plenty of this delicious soup. Do not freeze for longer than 6 months.

Home-made Vegetable Soup

This is a warming and nourishing soup that will keep your family going during the winter – so make plenty when vegetables are at their cheapest. It is important to cut or chop the vegetables into really small pieces.

2 carrots	2½ pints good stock
2 small turnips	¼ lb peas
2 leeks or 1 large onion	Salt and freshly ground black
4 green cabbage leaves	pepper
2 oz butter	2 large cooked potatoes

METHOD

1. Cut the carrots, turnips, leeks and cabbage leaves into thin strips. Melt the butter in a heavy saucepan and fry the vegetables over a medium heat for 3 minutes. Stir to prevent them sticking.

2. Pour over the stock and bring to the boil. Skim the surface to remove any scum and simmer for 15 minutes.

3. Add the peas and simmer for a further 15 minutes. Season with salt and pepper.

To serve without freezing: Add the finely chopped cooked potatoes and serve hot.

To freeze: Cool. Pack in suitable container. Seal, label and freeze.

To thaw: Turn frozen soup into a heavy saucepan. Heat over a low flame until thawed through. Add finely chopped cooked potatoes and continue to heat.

Serve: Hot.

Bortsch Soup

Bortsch, which originates from Russia, is one of the most delicious soups there is. The perfect recipe calls for a strong stock made from a duck carcase, preferably a wild duck, and raw beetroot. Since it is not always possible to obtain these ingredients I have included recipes of a more straightforward nature.

BORTSCH (*the real thing*)

1 medium onion	Salt and pepper
1 quart of strong well-	$\frac{1}{2}$ lemon
flavoured duck stock	Sherry
2 raw beetroots	Whipped sour cream

METHOD

1. Peel and chop onion. Peel and grate beetroots (I would suggest wearing rubber gloves for this as beetroot stains the hands very badly).

2. Add the onion and the beetroot to the stock and bring to the boil. Simmer for 40 minutes. Strain the soup.

To freeze: Cool, pour into waxed containers allowing space for expansion. Seal, label and freeze.

To defrost: Put frozen soup into a saucepan and heat.

To serve: Season the soup with salt, pepper, sherry, and juice of $\frac{1}{2}$ lemon. Serve very hot with a tablespoon of whipped sour cream floating on each bowl of soup.

If you cannot get real sour cream, whip ordinary cream and sour it with lemon juice and a pinch of salt.

BORTSCH (*the easy way*)

2 tins consommé
2 small tins whole baby
  beetroots
Salt and pepper

½ lemon
Sherry
Whipped sour cream

METHOD

1. Grate or shred one tin of beetroots, reserving the liquid. Combine consommé, beetroot liquid from both tins, and grated beetroot. Bring to the boil and simmer for 15 minutes. Strain soup.

2. Grate the remaining beetroot and add to soup with seasoning and juice of ½ lemon.

To freeze: Cool soup. Pour into waxed containers allowing room for expansion. Seal, label and freeze.

To defrost: Put frozen soup into a saucepan and heat.

To serve: Flavour with sherry. Serve hot with 1 tablespoon of whipped sour cream floating in each bowl of soup.

Note: Whole lemons will keep in a cool place for up to 3 months.

Cream of Spinach Soup

1 lb spinach or 1 packet of
  frozen spinach
1 oz butter
1 oz flour
1 onion
1 pint water
1 beef-stock cube
Salt and pepper
} or 1 pint
  stock

½ pint milk
½ gill cream
Lemon juice

1. Boil the spinach in the water or stock until tender. Strain the spinach and reserve the juice.
2. Chop the onion and fry in the butter until soft but not coloured.
3. Add the flour to the onion and stir over a medium heat.
4. Add the stock, stir until well blended and bring to the boil. Season with salt and pepper.
5. Add the spinach. Simmer for 15 minutes.
6. Put the soup through a sieve or purée in an electric blender.

To freeze: Pack cooked spinach soup in waxed containers. Seal, label and freeze.

To defrost: Put frozen spinach soup into a saucepan and cook over a medium heat.

To serve: Heat the milk and add to the hot soup. Adjust seasoning and add the lemon juice. Serve very hot with a spoonful of seasoned whipped cream floating on a thin slice of lemon in each bowl.

If you like the taste of nutmeg sprinkle some over the soup just before serving.

Do not keep for longer than 3 months.

Onion Soup Louise

6 medium onions	2 pints meat stock
2 oz butter	Salt and pepper
1 teaspoon Dijon mustard	$\frac{1}{4}$ pint white wine
1 tablespoon flour	Grated Gruyère cheese

METHOD

1. Peel the onions and slice thinly.
2. Fry them in the melted butter until brown, about 4 minutes.
3. Remove from the heat. Add the flour and mustard and stir until smooth and well blended.

4. Add stock slowly, stirring well. Bring to the boil and simmer for 15 minutes. Season well.

To freeze: Cool soup quickly. Pour into suitable containers. Seal, label and freeze.

To thaw: Put frozen soup into a saucepan and heat, stirring occasionally.

To serve: Add white wine. Pour the soup into earthenware or fireproof bowls. Place a slice of bread in each bowl and cover generously with grated cheese. Brown in a hot oven and serve immediately.

Jerusalem Artichoke Soup

Because they are such a tremendous bore to clean and peel, Jerusalem artichokes are not very popular as a vegetable. However, the introduction of household potato peelers has made all the difference, taking all the hard work out of their preparation. They are delicious plain, boiled or roasted, and make the most wonderful, nourishing soup.

1 lb Jerusalem artichokes	¾ pink milk
1 oz butter	2 tablespoons cream
¾ pint chicken stock	Salt and freshly ground black pepper

METHOD

1. Clean and peel the artichokes. Chop roughly and put in a heavy saucepan with the butter.
2. Cook over a gentle flame until they are soft enough to rub through a fine sieve.
3. Put the purée in a saucepan. Add the stock slowly, stirring all the time. Season and simmer for 15 minutes.

To freeze: Cool the liquid and pack in suitable containers. Seal, label and freeze.

To thaw: Put frozen soup in a saucepan and heat gently until thawed.

To serve: Heat soup and stir in milk. Simmer for 5 minutes. Check seasoning and stir in cream just before serving. Serve hot, garnished with cubes of fried bread. The soup is also good served chilled with a sprinkling of chopped parsley or chives.
Do not keep frozen for longer than 3 months.

Sweetcorn Chowder

4 rashers unsmoked bacon	½ lb cooked potatoes, diced
1 onion, chopped	Chopped parsley
1 green pepper, blanched and chopped	1 oz butter
¾ pint water	1 pint milk
Celery salt and pepper	1 lb sweetcorn kernels
1 oz flour	(frozen, fresh or tinned)

METHOD

1. Remove rind from bacon and chop into small pieces. Fry gently in a saucepan without extra fat until golden brown. Fry onion in bacon fat until brown.

2. Add the chopped green pepper and water and season with celery salt and pepper. Bring to the boil and simmer for 15 minutes.

3. In a separate saucepan, melt the butter, add the flour and stir over a medium heat until well blended. Gradually add the warm milk.

4. Add the sauce and the corn kernels to the chowder and stir well. Check seasoning.

To freeze: Pour chowder into suitable containers. Seal, label and freeze.

To thaw: Place frozen soup in a saucepan. Heat gently until thawed through.

To serve: Add ½ lb diced, cooked potatoes to the soup. Scatter parsley over the top and serve hot.

Scotch Broth

1 lb neck mutton	3 pints water
2 oz pearl barley	Salt and pepper
1 carrot ⎞	
1 turnip ⎬ peeled and finely	
2 onions ⎠ chopped	

METHOD

1. Cut meat into pieces removing all fat.
2. Wash barley in cold water.
3. Put meat, barley and water in a large saucepan. Bring to the boil and skim the surface to remove the scum that rises. Cover the pan and simmer for 1 hour.
4. Add vegetables. Bring back to the boil. Skim the surface and simmer for about 1 hour until the vegetables are cooked.
5. Take out the meat and chop it, removing the bones. Return the meat to the soup and season with salt and pepper.

To freeze: Cool the soup. Pack in suitable containers. Seal, label and freeze.

To thaw: Put frozen soup in a large saucepan. Place over a medium heat and stir gently as soup thaws.

To serve: Check seasoning and serve really hot.

Oxtail Soup

An inexpensive nourishing soup especially good in cold weather

A small oxtail
1 onion, chopped
3 carrots

2 tablespoons bacon fat
4 pints water
Salt and pepper

METHOD

1. Wash and dry the tail. Cut into small joints.
2. Place the meat in cold water, bring to the boil. Drain, rinse and dry.
3. Melt the fat and fry the onion and meat until brown.
4. Add the carrots, seasoning and water. Bring to the boil and simmer for 3–4 hours.
5. Strain the soup through a fine sieve reserving all except the largest joints. Leave the soup to get cold and then skim all the fat from the surface. Replace the bones in the soup.

To freeze: Pour soup into suitable containers. Seal, label and freeze.

To thaw: Put frozen soup into a saucepan and heat over a medium flame until really hot; check for seasoning.

To serve: Sprinkle the surface of the soup with finely chopped parsley.
Do not keep for longer than 6 months.

Soupe Chasseur

1 pheasant or partridge
2 oz butter
2 rashers bacon
Flour

1 onion, sliced
A few celery leaves
3 pints stock
Salt, pepper and a pinch of
    mace

1. Cut the pheasant or partridge into pieces. Coat them in flour and fry with bacon in the melted butter until brown.
2. Add the onions, celery and stock. Bring to the boil and skim the surface.
3. Simmer for 2 hours.
4. Strain the soup through a fine sieve. Leave to cool and re-move the fat from the surface.
5. Chop the breast meat into small pieces and add to the soup. Season with salt, pepper and mace.

To freeze: Pour the cold soup into suitable containers. Seal, label, and freeze.

To thaw: Place frozen soup in a saucepan and heat.

To serve: Check seasoning and serve really hot.

Chicken Soup with Peas

1 small boiling fowl	Salt and pepper
1 onion	$\frac{1}{2}$ lb fresh or frozen peas
2 carrots	1 oz butter
1 lemon	1 oz flour

METHOD

1. Place the fowl in a saucepan with enough water to cover.
2. Add the onion and carrots and half the lemon.
3. Bring to the boil and simmer for 2 hours, or until the chicken is really tender. Remove the bird. Chop the breast into small pieces.
4. Strain the stock. Remove as much fat as possible from the surface.
5. Melt the butter in a saucepan and add the flour. Stir over a medium heat until the flour and butter form a ball leaving the sides of the pan. Add the stock slowly, stirring all the time. It should have the consistency of thin cream.

6. Add the chicken breast, the peas, and the juice of ½ lemon to the soup. Season with salt and pepper and boil for 10 minutes.

To freeze: Cool; pour into suitable containers. Seal, label and freeze.

To thaw: Turn the frozen soup into a saucepan and heat over a medium flame, stirring occasionally, until thawed.

To serve: Serve really hot with a sprinkling of finely chopped parsley over each serving.
   Do not keep frozen for longer than 6 months.

Chilled Chicken Curry Soup

¼ lb finely chopped cooked
   chicken
1 large onion
1 tablespoon curry paste
The juice and finely shredded
   rind of ½ lemon

1 oz butter
1 tablespoon cornflour
2 pints chicken stock; or
   2 pints water and 2 chicken
   cubes
1 bay leaf
Salt and pepper

METHOD

1. Chop the onion finely and fry in the butter until soft but not brown.
2. Stir in flour and curry paste and cook for 1 minute, stirring well.
3. Add the stock slowly, stirring all the time.
4. Season with salt, pepper, lemon juice and rind, and bay leaf. Simmer for 15 minutes. Strain and add cold chicken.

To freeze: Cool; pack in suitable containers. Seal, label and freeze.

To defrost: Turn frozen soup into a saucepan and thaw slowly, stirring occasionally. Or thaw at room temperature.

To serve: Stir in some cream. Chill in a refrigerator and serve really cold, garnished with thin strips of lemon rind.

Bouillabaisse from Provence

Bouillabaisse can only be translated into English as 'Fish Soup' – a very mundane description of a heavenly dish. In Provence the soup is sometimes made with as many as twenty different types of fish. For simplicity I have included in my recipe fish that is easily obtainable in this country, but you can use any combination of fish provided that you include a fair amount of shellfish.

3 lb mixed white fish (cod, whiting, hake, haddock, eels, etc)
1 pint mussels
¾ cup olive oil
1 tablespoon tomato purée
½ teaspoon dried fennel
½ pint white wine
2 tablespoons chopped parsley

½ lb cooked lobster or prawns
1 large onion
4 ripe tomatoes (or ½ tin)
2 bay leaves
1 teaspoon saffron
Salt and ground black pepper
3 cloves garlic

METHOD

1. Finely chop the onion. Peel, seed, and chop the tomatoes.
2. Cut the fish into small pieces.
3. Fry the onion in a heavy saucepan in the olive oil until golden and transparent. Do not allow to brown.
4. Add the tomatoes, tomato purée, and herbs to the onions and simmer for 5 minutes.
5. Add the fish, pour over the white wine, and add boiling water until the fish is completely covered. Season with salt and plenty of black pepper.
6. Bring the soup to the boil, cover and continue boiling for 15 minutes. Add the mussels for the last 5 minutes of cooking.
7. Stir in the lobster and chopped parsley.

To freeze: Cool the soup and pour into suitable containers. Seal, label and freeze.

To thaw: Place frozen soup in a saucepan and heat over a slow to medium flame, stirring gently.

To serve: Fry 3 crushed cloves of garlic in a little olive oil until transparent. Add the soup and boil for 5 minutes. Serve boiling hot with a sprinkling of chopped parsley and a piece of buttered French bread floating in each bowl.

Note: If you do not intend to freeze the soup the garlic can be added at the same time as the onion.
  Do not keep frozen for longer than 1 month.

Moules Marinières

1 quart of mussels	¼ pint water
2 medium onions, finely chopped	¼ pint dry white wine
2 tablespoons butter	Bouquet garni
1 large tablespoon flour	Salt and pepper
2 tablespoons finely chopped parsley	

METHOD

1. Wash and scrub the mussels being careful to pull out the beard that sticks out from the mouth of the mussel.
2. Place the water, wine, mussels and bouquet garni in a large saucepan and bring to the boil. Cook over a fast heat for 10 minutes. Strain.
3. Remove the top shells from the mussels, checking each one to see that no beard has been left in.
4. Heat the butter in a saucepan and gently fry the onions until soft but not brown.
5. Stir in the flour until well blended. Add the liquid slowly, stirring well. Add the parsley and cook over a low flame for 5 minutes, still stirring.
6. Return the mussels to the soup. Season with salt and pepper.

To freeze: Cool quickly. Pack in suitable containers. Seal, label and freeze.

To thaw: Place the frozen soup in a large saucepan over a medium heat. Stir gently as the soup thaws.

To serve: Place the mussels in the bottom of a deep dish or tureen and cover with the liquid. Sprinkle fresh parsley over the top.
    Do not keep frozen for longer than 2 months.

Sauces

Basic White Sauce

2 oz butter   ½ pint hot milk
2 oz flour   Salt and pepper

METHOD

1. Melt the butter, add flour gradually, and stir over a low heat until the mixture forms a ball and comes away from the sides of the pan.
2. Gradually add the milk, stirring all the time until the mixture is smooth and creamy. Season with salt and pepper.
Note: For a thinner sauce add another ½ pint milk.

To freeze: Cool; pour into a suitable container. Seal, label and freeze.

To thaw: Turn into the top of a double-boiler. Heat over hot (but not boiling) water until thawed and hot through. Stir occasionally to prevent curdling.

Béchamel Sauce

Ingredients for white sauce   1 pinch of mace
1 oz carrot   1 bay leaf
1 oz onion   1 clove
½ oz turnip   2 peppercorns
1 pinch of mixed herbs

Add vegetables and herbs to the milk. Simmer gently for 20 minutes, strain and continue as for a white sauce.

Velouté Sauce

The above recipe, with milk replaced by ½ pint of stock and 2 tablespoons cream added.

Standard Brown Sauce

1 oz dripping	1 oz flour
2 oz bacon	1 pint stock
2 oz carrot	Salt and pepper
2 oz onion	Bouquet garni
1 oz turnip	

METHOD

Chop bacon and vegetables and cook until golden brown in melted dripping. Add flour, mix well until brown and gradually blend in stock. Add seasoning and herbs, bring to the boil and simmer for 5 minutes. Strain and cook, pack, label and freeze. Thaw as for white sauce.

Onion Sauce

To serve with boiled beef or mutton

2 large onions, sliced	¼ pink milk
1 tablespoon butter	Béchamel sauce
1 teaspoon Worcester sauce	

METHOD

Melt butter in a saucepan. Fry the onions over a low flame until soft and transparent. Do not allow to brown. Add the onions to a basic Béchamel sauce. Thin with ¼ pint milk. Season with Worcester sauce.

To freeze: Cool. Pack. Seal, label and freeze.

To thaw: Place in the top of a double-boiler over hot water. Stir to prevent curdling.

Parsley Sauce

To serve with fish or chicken

4 tablespoons fresh chopped parsley

½ pint Béchamel sauce
¼ pint milk

METHOD

Add parsley to a basic Béchamel sauce. Thin with ¼ pint milk.

To freeze: Cool. Pack. Seal, label, and freeze.

To thaw: Place in a double-boiler or hot water, stirring to prevent curdling. Check seasoning.

Various Sauces using a Béchamel or White Sauce Base

LOBSTER SAUCE: to serve with boiled or poached fish.

1 tablespoon lobster butter
4 tablespoons cream
2 oz diced lobster

Anchovy essence
Paprika pepper
½ pint Béchamel sauce

Pound the coral, eggs or any scarlet pieces of a lobster with a pestle and mortar, or rub through a fine sieve. Add an equal quantity of butter.

Add lobster butter and diced lobster to a basic Béchamel sauce. Cool, seal, label and freeze.

To thaw: Place on the top of a double-boiler. When hot, stir in 4 tablespoons cream. Season with anchovy essence and a pinch of paprika.

MORNAY SAUCE: a cheese sauce to serve with vegetables, poached or boiled fish, and chicken.

2 oz grated Gruyère or Parmesan cheese	1 oz butter
¼ pint cream	½ pint Béchamel sauce

Add cheese to a basic Béchamel sauce. Stir over a low heat until cheese has melted. Cool, pack, seal, label and freeze.

To thaw: Place in the top of a double-boiler over hot water. When hot, stir in ¼ pint cream and 1 oz butter. Check seasoning.

MUSHROOM SAUCE: to serve with fish or chicken or veal.

4 oz sliced mushrooms	2 tablespoons Vermouth or dry white wine
1 oz butter	
¼ pint cream	½ pint white sauce
1 teaspoon chopped dill or parsley	

Melt the butter in a saucepan. Add the mushrooms and toss them in the butter for 1 minute over a hot flame: they should not start sweating. Add them, with the dill or parsley, to a basic white sauce. Cool. Pack. Seal, label and freeze.

To thaw: Place in the top of a double-boiler over hot water. When hot, add cream and Vermouth, stirring well to prevent curdling.

Pepper Sauce

To serve with cold roast meat

2 oz butter
1 oz flour
½ pint hot stock
2 teaspoons wine vinegar
1 shallot or small onion, chopped

1 teaspoon chopped parsley
1 teaspoon chopped chives
Bouquet garni
Salt
Freshly ground black pepper

METHOD

1. Melt the butter in a saucepan. Add the flour and mix well. Cook over a medium heat until the mixture is light brown.

2. Slowly add the hot stock, stirring all the time until the sauce is smooth.

3. Add the vinegar, shallot, parsley, chives and bouquet garni. Season with salt and freshly ground black pepper.

4. Cover and simmer for 20 minutes. Strain.

To freeze: Cool. Pour into a suitable container. Seal, label and freeze.

To thaw: Turn frozen sauce into a saucepan and thaw over a moderate heat. Serve hot or cold.

Tomato Sauce

½ oz butter
½ oz flour
1 lb tomatoes or 1 large tin tomatoes, chopped
¼ pint stock

1 teaspoon mixed herbs
1 teaspoon sugar
Salt, pepper
Grated peel of ½ lemon

METHOD

1. Melt the butter in a saucepan. Add the flour and mix well. Add the stock slowly, stirring all the time. Bring to the boil and remove from the heat.

2. Add the tomatoes and herbs. Season with the salt, pepper, sugar and lemon peel.

3. Cover and simmer for 30 minutes.

4. Rub through a fine sieve.

Variations:

1. Add 1 chopped onion and 2 chopped rashers of bacon gently fried in butter to the sauce.

2. Blanch the rind of 1 orange, cut into thin strips, in boiling water for 2 minutes. Add to the sauce before serving.

3. Add 3 tablespoons sour cream to the sauce before serving.

To freeze: Cool. Pour into a suitable container. Seal, label and freeze.

To thaw: Turn frozen sauce into a saucepan and thaw over a moderate heat.

Spanish Pimento Sauce

To serve with fish

4 cloves garlic	Salt
2 red peppers	Freshly ground black pepper
½ pint olive oil	

METHOD

1. Remove the seeds from the peppers and cut into strips. Boil in salted water until they are soft. (You can use tinned peppers.)

2. Crush the garlic and pound with the peppers to a smooth paste.

3. Heat the olive oil in a saucepan. Add the garlic and pimento and cook over a medium heat for 10 minutes. Season with salt and freshly ground black pepper.

To freeze: Cool. Pack in a suitable container. Seal, label and freeze.

To thaw: Turn into a saucepan and thaw over a medium heat until hot through.

Do not store for longer than 2 weeks.

Sweet and Sour Sauce

To serve with meat, poultry or fish

½ pint pineapple juice
2 tablespoons malt vinegar
5 tablespoons brown sugar
1 dessertspoon soy sauce

1 dessertspoon cornflour
2 teaspoons water
2 carrots
¼ cucumber

METHOD

1. Mix the pineapple juice, vinegar and sugar in a saucepan. Heat over a medium heat until the sugar dissolves.

2. Add the soy sauce and the cornflour mixed with the water. Stir and cook for 3 minutes until the sauce is smooth.

3. Cut the carrots into thin strips and cook for 5 minutes in boiling water. Cut the cucumber into small dice and blanch in boiling water for 2 minutes.

4. Drain the carrots and the cucumber. Add to the sauce and mix well.

To freeze: Cool. Pack in a waxed tub or suitable container. Seal, label and freeze.

To thaw: Turn frozen sauce into a basin over hot water and heat until thawed through.

Hollandaise Sauce

To serve with fish and vegetables

4 egg yolks
1 tablespoon lemon juice
½ teaspoon salt

¼ teaspoon pepper
¼ lb unsalted butter
2 tablespoons double cream

METHOD

1. Using a wire whisk or electric beater, beat egg yolks with lemon juice. Place in a bowl over a saucepan of simmering water. Do not allow the water to touch the bowl.

2. Add 1 dessertspoonful of butter at a time. Beat into the egg yolks until each bit of butter is absorbed.

3. Beat until mixture thickens. Add cream and seasoning and stir well.

To serve without freezing: Cover the bowl with a plate and leave in a warm place until needed. Do not reheat.

To freeze: Cool. Pour sauce into suitable containers. Seal, label and freeze.

To thaw: Turn frozen sauce into the top of a double-boiler. Place over simmering water and stir until thawed.

Note: If the sauce curdles, beat in 1 dessertspoonful boiling water.

Serving suggestions: 3 chopped rashers of bacon, crisply fried, and 1 small tin of chopped asparagus, added to Hollandaise sauce, make a delicious accompaniment to spaghetti.

Apple Sauce

To serve with roast, grilled or fried pork, roast duck and roast goose. Serve sweetened with hot gingerbread

1 lb apples
¼ pint water

1 oz butter
Salt and pepper or sugar

1. Peel the apples thinly. Cut into quarters and core. Slice thinly.

2. Put apples, water and butter into a small saucepan. Bring to the boil and simmer for 20 minutes or until the apples are soft.

3. Beat with a wooden spoon until completely smooth.

To freeze: Cool. Pack in waxed cardboard tubs or containers. Seal, label and freeze.

To thaw: Melt a little butter in a saucepan. Add the frozen apple sauce and heat, stirring frequently, over a low heat. Add salt and pepper or sugar.

Cranberry Sauce

1 lb cranberries	4 oz sugar
½ pint water	1 oz butter

For a smooth sauce: Wash and sort berries. Simmer them in the water and sugar until tender. Rub through a sieve. Stir in butter until well blended.

For a thick sauce: Wash and sort berries. Boil the water and sugar together until the sugar melts. Put the berries into the syrup and simmer until they are mushy. Stir in the butter.

To freeze: Put the cooled sauce in small waxed cartons or plastic containers. Seal, label and freeze. Be sure to allow room for expansion.

To thaw: Leave at room temperature for 2–3 hours, or turn into a saucepan and cook over a low heat until thawed.

Serve: With roast turkey and cold meat.

Cumberland Sauce

To serve with cold ham, tongue and game

¼ lb redcurrant jelly
Grated rind and juice of
  1 orange
Grated rind and juice of
  1 lemon
½ pint port

2 tablespoons Worcester sauce
2 tablespoons Harvey's sauce
2 teaspoons grated horseradish
6 glacé cherries, chopped

METHOD

1. Melt the jelly in a saucepan over a low heat. Add the port and bring to the boil. Boil for 5 minutes.
2. Cool, and add the lemon and orange rind and juices, the Worcester and Harvey's sauces, grated horseradish and chopped cherries. Mix well.

To freeze: Pour into waxed tubs or jars. Seal, label and freeze.

To thaw:
To serve cold: Leave at room temperature for 1½ hours.
To serve hot: Turn into a saucepan and heat over a slow flame.

Financière Sauce

To serve with spaghetti, boiled chicken or as a filling for vol-au-vent. The truffles may be omitted

2 lambs' kidneys
2 chicken livers
½ pint stock
1 oz butter
1 tablespoon lemon juice
2 oz butter

1 oz flour
2 mushrooms ⎫ or 4
2 truffles ⎭ mushrooms
Salt
Freshly ground black pepper
Bouquet garni

1. Split the kidneys and remove the hard core. Cut into small pieces. Cut the livers into small pieces. Soak in cold water for 1 hour. Drain well.

2. Combine the stock, lemon juice and 1 oz butter in a saucepan. Add the livers and kidneys. Bring to the boil, skim and simmer slowly over a low flame. Drain and reserve the juice.

3. Melt 2 oz butter in a saucepan. Add the flour and mix well. Slowly add the stock in which the meats were cooked. Cook over a medium heat, stirring well until the sauce is smooth.

4. Add the meats, bouquet garni, mushrooms and truffles cut into thin slices. Season with salt and pepper and cook over a low heat for 1 hour.

To freeze: Cool. Pour into a suitable container. Seal, label and freeze.

To thaw: Turn frozen sauce into a saucepan. Heat over a low flame until thawed and hot through.

Spaghetti Sauce

¼ lb stewing veal, minced	3 tablespoons olive oil
2 oz smoked bacon, chopped	¼ teaspoon thyme
Large tin tomatoes	¼ teaspoon marjoram
2 tablespoons tomato purée	Salt and pepper
1 large onion, chopped	1 clove garlic, crushed
2 oz mushrooms, chopped	

METHOD

1. Heat oil in a saucepan. Add bacon and onion and fry until onions are transparent.

2. Add meat and brown.

3. Add the mushrooms, tomatoes, tomato purée and herbs. Season with salt and pepper. Cover and simmer over a low heat for 30 minutes.

To freeze: Pack in waxed cardboard tubs. Seal, label and freeze.

To thaw: Turn into a heavy saucepan. Heat over a medium heat until thawed. Add garlic and continue cooking over a low heat for 15 minutes.

Serve: Hot, over spaghetti or macaroni.

Stuffings

Forcemeat Balls

1 small onion, chopped
1 rasher bacon, chopped
½ oz butter
4 tablespoons fresh white
   breadcrumbs
1 tablespoon chopped suet

2 teaspoons chopped parsley
1 tablespoon chopped
   marjoram
Salt and pepper
2 beaten eggs
Breadcrumbs
Fat for frying

METHOD

1. Melt the butter in a saucepan. Add the onion and bacon and fry until the onion is soft.

2. Mix the onion, bacon, white breadcrumbs, suet, parsley, marjoram and seasoning together in a bowl. Bind with 1 beaten egg.

3. Shape into small balls and dip in egg and breadcrumbs.

4. Fry until crisp and brown in hot shallow fat. Drain on kitchen paper.

To freeze: Cool. Pack carefully with a sheet of freezer paper between each layer. Seal, label and freeze.

To thaw: Place frozen balls on a greased baking dish and heat in a medium-hot oven (400°F: Reg. 5) for 10 minutes or until crisp and hot through.

Serve: With jugged hare and with roast veal.

Sausage and Chestnut Stuffing for Turkey

1 lb chestnuts	1 stick celery, chopped
½ lb pork sausage meat	1 large onion, chopped
6 oz fresh breadcrumbs	2 oz butter
1 pint stock	Salt and pepper

Note: Peeling chestnuts is a miserable job. Chestnuts can be bought ready-peeled in tins.

METHOD

1. Remove the shells from the chestnuts with a sharp knife. Blanch them in boiling water for 3 minutes and peel off the inner skin.

2. Put the chestnuts, chopped celery and stock in a saucepan. Bring to the boil and cook until the chestnuts are tender and all the stock has been absorbed. Be careful not to let them boil dry. Cool.

3. Fry the onion in the butter until transparent. Cool.

4. Mix the chestnuts, sausage meat and onion together. Add enough breadcrumbs to make a firm mixture. Season with salt and pepper.

To freeze: Pack the stuffing in a polythene bag. Seal, label and freeze.

To thaw: Leave to thaw at room temperature for 2 hours or until soft.

Vegetables

Pommes Laurette

2 oz butter
¼ pint water
2½ oz flour
2 eggs

1 lb potatoes
½ oz butter
Deep fat for frying

METHOD

1. To make a choux paste: place water and butter in a saucepan, bring to the boil and remove from the heat.

2. Add the flour and beat until the mixture is smooth and comes away from the sides of the pan forming a ball. Leave to cool.

3. Beat in the eggs until the mixture is smooth.

4. Cook the potatoes until soft. Drain well and mash with the butter.

5. Mix with the choux paste.

6. Pipe the mixture through a forcing bag in rings on waxed paper.

7. Heat the fat until it is almost smoking and carefully slide in the potato rings on a spatula. Fry until golden brown.

8. Lift out and drain well on kitchen paper.

To freeze: Cool and pack carefully in waxed cardboard boxes. Separate each layer with freezer paper. Seal, label and freeze.

To thaw: Place frozen rings on a greased baking sheet. Bake in a medium-hot oven (380°F: Reg. 5) for 10 minutes until the potatoes are crisp and hot. Serve at once.

Herby Potato Balls

1 lb potatoes
6 oz flour
½ teaspoon baking powder
2 oz butter
Salt and pepper

1 beaten egg
4 tablespoons dried parsley
  and thyme for stuffing
Fat for frying

METHOD

1. Peel potatoes and boil in salted water until soft. Drain well and put through a sieve.

2. Sieve flour and baking powder. Add to potatoes with the butter and mix well until a stiff dough is formed. Season with salt and pepper.

3. Using floured hands shape into balls. Coat with beaten egg and roll in dried stuffing.

To serve without freezing: Fry potato balls in hot fat until golden brown.

To freeze: Freeze unpacked. When frozen, pack into suitable containers with a sheet of freezer paper between each layer. Seal, label and return to deep freeze.

To thaw: Fry frozen potato balls in hot fat until hot through and golden brown.

Serve: With bacon for breakfast.

Duchesse Potatoes

1 lb potatoes
1 oz butter
1 tablespoon cream

1 egg
Salt and pepper
Nutmeg (optional)

1. Peel potatoes and boil until soft. Drain well and put through a fine sieve.

2. Add butter, cream and seasoning. Mix well. The mixture should be smooth but stiff.

3. Pipe into rosettes on a greased baking tray through a star-shaped nozzle.

4. Brush with beaten egg.

5. Bake in a hot oven (410°F: Reg. 6) until light brown.

To serve without freezing: Continue baking until a golden brown.

To freeze: Cool on a cake rack. Pack carefully in waxed cardboard containers with a sheet of freezer paper between each layer. Seal, label and freeze.

To thaw: Place frozen potatoes on a greased baking sheet. Bake for 10 minutes in a hot oven (410°F: Reg. 6) until potatoes are golden brown and hot through.

French Fried or Shoestring Potatoes

2 lb potatoes   Deep fat for frying

METHOD

1. Peel potatoes and cut into small strips. Blanch for 2 minutes in boiling water. Dry well.

2. Heat fat to almost smoking point and fry potatoes until light brown. Drain well on kitchen paper.

To freeze: Cool. Pack in a rigid container. Seal, label and freeze.

To thaw: Arrange frozen potatoes on a greased baking sheet. Bake in a medium-hot oven (400°F: Reg. 5) for 5 minutes or until golden brown and crisp.

Mashed Potatoes

2 lb potatoes
1 tablespoon cream

1 oz butter
Salt and pepper

METHOD

Peel potatoes and cook in boiling water until soft. Mash or put through a sieve. Add cream and butter and season with salt and pepper.

To freeze: Cool. Pack in a suitable container. Seal, label and freeze.

To thaw: Heat potatoes in the top of a double-boiler over hot water. Cook over a medium heat stirring occasionally until hot through.

Straw Potatoes

2 lb potatoes
Juice of ½ lemon

Deep fat for frying

METHOD

1. Peel potatoes. Grate through a coarse grater. Leave to soak in cold water and lemon juice for 2 hours.
2. Drain well. Rinse in cold water. Drain again, and wipe dry in a teacloth.
3. Heat fat until almost smoking. Fry potatoes in small amounts until golden brown. Drain on kitchen paper.

To freeze: Cool. Pack in a rigid container. Seal, label and freeze.

To thaw: Place frozen potatoes on a baking sheet. Heat in a hot oven (450°F: Reg. 7) for 5 minutes until hot and crisp. Be careful not to burn.

Do not store for longer than 2 weeks.

Baked Savoury Potatoes

4 large potatoes
2 oz butter
2 tablespoons grated cheese

1 tablespoon chopped chives
Salt and pepper

METHOD

1. Scrub the potatoes. Wipe dry. Prick with a fork and rub the skins with a little melted butter.

2. Bake in a medium-hot oven (400°F: Reg. 5) for 1½ hours or until tender.

3. Cut off the top of the potatoes. Scoop out the centre and mash in a bowl with the butter, grated cheese, chives, salt and pepper.

4. Return the mashed savoury filling to the potato cases.

To freeze: Cool. Wrap each potato in aluminium foil. Pack in a polythene bag. Seal, label and freeze.

To thaw: Bake frozen potatoes in a medium-hot oven (400°F: Reg. 5) for 30 minutes or until hot through and crisp on the outside.

Note: The filling can be varied by adding chopped crisp fried bacon, parsley, or sour cream and chopped herbs.

Sweet Potatoes and Apricots

4 medium sweet potatoes
1 dessertspoon concentrated
   orange juice
1 oz butter

1 dessertspoon brown sugar
Pinch of nutmeg and pinch of
   salt
6 dried apricots, soaked and
   chopped

METHOD

1. Cook potatoes in boiling water. Peel and mash with a fork.

2. Mix potatoes with melted butter, orange juice, brown sugar, a pinch of nutmeg and salt. Stir in chopped apricots.

3. Butter a shallow casserole. Spoon in the mixture. Dot with a little butter and bake uncovered in a moderate oven (350°F: Reg. 4) for 20 minutes.

To serve without freezing: Continue baking for a further 10 minutes or until nicely browned. Cool.

To freeze: Place casserole in a polythene bag, or wrap in freezer paper or aluminium foil. Seal, label and freeze.

To thaw: Cover frozen casserole with aluminium foil. Place in a moderate oven (350°F: Reg. 4) and bake for 10 minutes. Remove cover and continue to bake for a further 10 minutes or until nicely browned.

Braised Lettuce

One of the problems of growing one's own lettuces is that they all come to their prime at the same time and inevitably half of them are wasted and go to seed. Few people seem to realize what a delicious dish hot lettuce is. Cooked with a little chopped onion and bacon, with some beef or chicken stock, it makes a perfect vegetable to go with any roast poultry or meat. It freezes well and is quick to reheat.

4 large or 6 small lettuces (preferably the crisp kind)	1 medium onion, chopped
	¼ teaspoon mixed herbs
1 oz butter	¼ pint beef or chicken stock
3 rashers bacon	Salt and pepper

METHOD

1. Melt the butter in a large saucepan. Add the chopped bacon and onion and cook over a medium heat for 5 minutes.

2. Wash and shred the lettuces. Add to the onions and bacon and cook over a medium heat for a further 5 minutes.

116

3. Add the herbs, stock and seasonings. Cover and simmer for 30 minutes.

To freeze: Cool and pack in a suitable container. Seal, label and freeze.

To thaw: Melt a little butter in a saucepan. Add the frozen lettuce and cook over a medium heat until thawed and hot through. Check seasoning.

To serve: Hot, sprinkled with chopped parsley.

Baked Cabbage

An unusual way to serve that old winter standby

1 white cabbage, shredded	1 teaspoon sugar
3 oz butter	Salt and freshly ground black
2 onions, chopped	pepper
3 green peppers	¾ lb cooked ham or tongue
6 tomatoes	

METHOD

1. Melt the butter and pour into a deep casserole dish.
2. Put in the cabbage, onions, peppers seeded and chopped, chopped tomatoes, and diced tongue or ham. Season with sugar, salt and pepper and mix well.
3. Cover tightly and cook in a moderate oven (350°F: Reg. 4) for 20 minutes. Cool.

To freeze: Pack casserole in a polythene bag, or wrap in freezer paper or aluminium foil. Seal, label and freeze.

To thaw: Return frozen casserole to a moderate oven (350°F: Reg. 4) and cook for 20 minutes or until hot through and tender.

Red Cabbage

1 medium head red cabbage
2 oz butter
1 small onion, finely chopped
4 tablespoons vinegar

4 tablespoons sugar
1 teaspoon caraway seeds
Salt and pepper

METHOD

1. Wash and slice cabbage.

2. Melt the butter in a saucepan. Add the cabbage and onion. Cook over a low heat, stirring frequently, for 5 minutes.

3. Add the vinegar, sugar and caraway seeds. Season with salt and pepper.

4. Cover and cook over a low heat for 30 minutes. See that the cabbage does not stick to the bottom of the pan. If this happens add a little water.

To freeze: Cool. Pack in a suitable container. Seal, label and freeze.

To thaw: Turn frozen cabbage into a saucepan. Cover and cook over a low heat for 40 minutes.

Spanish Peas

2 lb peas
1 oz butter
2 rashers bacon, chopped
1 oz flour
2 tablespoons tomato purée

2 tablespoons water
2 tablespoons chopped parsley
Salt and pepper
¼ lb chipolata sausages

METHOD

1. Melt the butter in a saucepan. Add the bacon and cook for 5 minutes.

2. Add the peas. Stir in the flour, tomato purée and water. Add the parsley and season with salt and pepper.

3. Cover and cook over a medium flame for 20 minutes.

4. Fry the sausages until brown. Cut into rough pieces and add to the peas.

To serve without freezing: Continue to cook over a moderate heat for a further 10 minutes or until the peas are tender but not mushy.

To freeze: Cool. Pack in a suitable container. Seal, label and freeze.

To thaw: Place frozen peas in a saucepan. Heat over a moderate flame for 20 minutes or until hot through, stirring occasionally.

To serve: Sprinkle a little chopped parsley over the top.

Stewed Okra with Tomatoes

1 rasher bacon
2 tablespoons butter
1 large onion, chopped
1½ lb okra pods cut into
   ½-inch pieces

8 tomatoes, peeled and
   chopped
½ pint boiling water
½ teaspoon sugar
Salt and freshly ground black
   pepper

METHOD

1. Melt the butter in a saucepan. Chop the bacon and fry in the butter for 3 minutes. Remove and fry the onion until golden.
2. Add the bacon, okra, tomatoes and water. Season with sugar, salt and pepper.
3. Cover and simmer for 15 minutes stirring occasionally.

To serve without freezing: Continue to simmer for a further 10 minutes.

To freeze: Cool. Pack in a suitable container. Seal, label and freeze.

To thaw: Turn frozen okra into a saucepan. Heat over a low flame stirring occasionally. When hot, cover and simmer for 10 minutes.

Cauliflower in a Cream Sauce

1 cauliflower	¼ lb grated cheese
¾ oz butter	Salt and pepper
¾ oz flour	2 oz grated Parmesan cheese
½ pint milk	2 tablespoons fine
2 tablespoons cream	breadcrumbs

METHOD

1. Remove the outer leaves from the cauliflower. Break into sprigs and cook in boiling salted water for 10 minutes.
2. Melt the butter in a saucepan. Add the flour and mix well. Slowly add the milk and stir until the sauce boils and is smooth. Add the cheese and stir until melted. Blend in the cream.
3. Add the cauliflower and season with salt and pepper.

To serve without freezing: Turn into a buttered casserole dish. Sprinkle with breadcrumbs and grated Parmesan. Bake in a medium-hot oven (380°F: Reg. 5) until golden brown.

To freeze: Pack in a suitable container. Seal, label and freeze.

To thaw: Turn frozen cauliflower into a buttered casserole. Cover and heat in a moderate oven (350°F: Reg. 3) for 20 minutes or until thawed through. Remove cover and sprinkle with breadcrumbs and grated Parmesan. Return to oven and bake in a medium heat (380°F: Reg. 5) for 10 minutes or until golden brown.

Squash or Vegetable Marrow Créole

2½ lb summer, crooked
   necksquash or small
   marrows
3 oz butter
3 tablespoons flour
3 large tomatoes

1 small green pepper
1 small onion
Salt and pepper
Breadcrumbs
Butter

METHOD

1. Peel and seed the squash or marrow unless they are young and tender. Slice thinly and parboil in boiling salted water for 3 minutes. Drain well. Place in a buttered baking dish.

2. Melt the butter in a saucepan. Add the flour and mix well.

3. Peel, seed and chop the tomatoes. Add to the butter mixture with the chopped seeded pepper and the chopped onion. Cover and cook for 5 minutes. Season with salt and pepper.

4. Pour the sauce over the squash. Sprinkle the top with breadcrumbs and dot with butter.

5. Bake in a moderate oven (350°F: Reg. 4) for 15 minutes.

To serve without freezing: Continue to bake for a further 15 minutes.

To freeze: Cool. Pack in a polythene bag, or wrap in freezer paper or aluminium foil. Seal, label and freeze.

To thaw: Cover frozen squash with a layer of aluminium foil. Bake in a moderate oven (350°F: Reg. 4) for 15 minutes. Remove cover and continue to bake for a further 15 minutes.

Note: The dish can be sprinkled with grated cheese for the last 10 minutes of cooking time.

ZUCCHINI CRÉOLE

Substitute 6 medium zucchini for the squash. Slice straight into the baking dish without boiling. Continue as above.

Creamed Cucumber

2 medium ripe cucumbers
¾ oz butter
¾ oz flour
½ pint milk
1 teaspoon chopped tarragon

1 teaspoon chopped dill
Salt and freshly ground black
 pepper
2 tablespoons cream

METHOD

1. Peel the cucumber thinly. Split and cut into 2-inch pieces.
2. Blanch in boiling water until just tender, about 5 minutes.
3. Melt the butter in a saucepan. Add the flour and stir until the mixture forms a ball and comes away from the sides of the pan. Add the milk slowly, stirring all the time until the mixture is thick and smooth.
4. Add the cucumber and the herbs. Season with salt and freshly ground black pepper.

To serve without freezing: Stir in 2 tablespoons of cream and heat through.

To freeze: Cool. Pour into suitable containers. Seal, label and freeze.

To thaw: Turn into a basin over hot but not boiling water. Heat, stirring occasionally, but be careful not to break up the cucumber.

To serve: Stir in 2 tablespoons cream, heat through and serve.

Note: Marrow and courgettes can be treated in the same way.

Cooked Cucumber

1 large cucumber
1 tablespoon vinegar
¼ oz butter
¼ oz flour
½ pint milk

1 tablespoon chopped parsley
1 tablespoon chopped chives
 or spring-onion tops
Salt and pepper

1. Peel cucumber and cut into 1-inch pieces. Boil for 10 minutes in salted water with 1 tablespoon vinegar. Drain.

2. Melt the butter in a saucepan. Add the flour and mix well. Slowly add the milk, stirring all the time. Cook until the sauce boils and is smooth.

3. Add the cucumber, parsley and chives to the sauce. Season with salt and pepper.

To freeze: Cool. Pack in a suitable container. Seal, label and freeze.

To thaw: Turn into the top of a double-boiler over hot water. Thaw over a medium flame until hot through.

Harvard Beets

1½ lb cooked beetroot
¼ lb sugar
1 tablespoon cornflour

½ teaspoon salt
½ cup mild cider vinegar

METHOD

1. Place the sugar, cornflour, salt and vinegar in the top of a double-boiler and cook over hot water.

2. Cook, stirring frequently, until the sauce thickens and is clear. Add the sliced beetroots and continue cooking for 15 minutes.

To serve without freezing: Continue cooking the beetroot for a further 15 minutes. Stir in 1 oz butter before serving.

To freeze: Cool. Pack in a suitable container. Seal, label and freeze.

To thaw: Heat in the top of a double-saucepan over hot water. When hot continue cooking for a further 15 minutes. Stir in 1 oz butter before serving.

Note: Beetroots are also delicious baked in a strong cheese sauce.

Creamed Turnips

2 bunches small turnips
2 oz butter

2 tablespoons cream
Salt and pepper

METHOD

1. Wash and peel the turnips.
2. Cook in boiling salted water for 40 minutes or until tender.
3. Force through a food mill or fine sieve.
4. Stir in the butter and mix well until melted. Add the cream.
5. Season with salt and pepper.

To freeze: Pack in a suitable container. Seal, label and freeze.

To thaw: Turn frozen turnips into the top of a double-boiler and heat over hot water. Or turn frozen turnips into a heavy pan and heat over a low flame, stirring occasionally to prevent burning.

Aubergines with Tomatoes

2–3 aubergines
Salt
1 tablespoon olive oil
2 large onions
4 large ripe tomatoes
1 tablespoon mixed herbs

1 small tin anchovy fillets
Milk
Brown breadcrumbs
1 oz butter
2 tablespoons grated cheese

METHOD

1. Split the aubergines in two. Using a sharp-pointed knife score round the edges and across the centre. Sprinkle with salt and leave to 'sweat' for 30 minutes. Drain and wipe dry.
2. Heat the olive oil in a frying-pan and fry the aubergines gently for 15 minutes. Scoop out all the flesh leaving the skin intact.
3. Soak the anchovy fillets in a little milk.
4. Peel, seed and chop the tomatoes. Fry the onions in the oil

until soft; then add the tomatoes, aubergine flesh and mixed herbs. Simmer for 5 minutes.

5. Fill the aubergine skins with the mixture. Sprinkle with breadcrumbs and decorate with anchovies.

To serve without freezing: Dot with butter, sprinkle the cheese over and bake in a hot oven (425°F: Reg. 6) for 15 minutes.

To freeze: Cool, pack in a rigid container. Seal, label and freeze.

To thaw: Place frozen aubergines in a shallow greased baking dish. Dot with butter and sprinkle grated cheese over. Cover with tin foil and bake in a moderate oven (350°F: Reg. 4) for 20 minutes. Uncover, raise heat to 425°F (Reg. 6) and bake for a further 5 minutes.

Serve: As a vegetable or as a first course.

Tomatoes au Gratin

6 large ripe tomatoes
1 tablespoon olive oil
1 tablespoon finely chopped
  parsley
3 spring onions, finely
  chopped
Salt and pepper
4 tablespoons fine
  breadcrumbs
1 oz butter

METHOD

1. Cut the tomatoes in half.

2. Heat the oil in a saucepan, add the parsley and onions, and cook gently for 2 minutes.

3. Spread this mixture on the bottom of a casserole. Place tomato halves, cut side up, on top.

4. Season with salt and pepper, cover with breadcrumbs and dot with butter.

5. Bake in a moderate oven (350°F: Reg. 3) for 30 minutes.

To serve without freezing: Continue cooking for a further 15 minutes.

To freeze: Cool. Pack in a polythene bag or wrap in freezer paper or aluminium foil. Seal, label and freeze.

To thaw: Cover dish with tin foil. Heat in a moderate oven (350°F: Reg. 3) for 20 minutes or until hot through. Remove cover and continue cooking for a further 15 minutes or until nicely browned.

Crisp Fried Onion Rings

3 large onions

Deep fat for frying

BATTER
¼ lb plain flour
3 tablespoons olive oil
¼ pint milk
White of one egg
Salt and pepper

METHOD

1. *To make the batter:* Add the olive oil to the flour and stir well. Add the milk and beat to a smooth cream. Season with salt and pepper and leave to stand for 2 hours.
2. Whip the egg white until stiff and fold into the batter.
3. Cut the onions into fairly thick slices. Separate the rings.
4. Dip the onion rings in the batter and fry in nearly smoking deep fat or oil (380°F), until golden crisp.
5. Drain really well on crumpled kitchen paper.

To freeze: When the onions are cold, pack them carefully in a rigid container with freezer paper between each layer. Seal, label and freeze.

To thaw: Place the frozen onions on a baking sheet. Heat in a medium-hot oven (400°F: Reg. 5) until thawed through and crisp.
   Do not store for over 2 months.

Note: Cutting and peeling onions under running cold water prevents tears, but be sure they are dry before dipping in the batter or the results will be disappointing.

Corn Fritters

1 tin corn kernels, or
  ½ lb cooked corn
2 eggs
6 tablespoons flour

½ teaspoon baking powder
Salt and pepper
2 oz butter

METHOD

1. Drain the corn and mash with a potato masher or put through a coarse food mincer.
2. Beat the eggs until light and add to the corn.
3. Mix in the sifted flour and baking powder. Season with salt and pepper.
4. Melt the butter in a frying-pan and when it foams put in spoonfuls of the corn mixture. Cook until light brown on both sides.

To serve without freezing: Continue cooking until golden brown.

To freeze: Drain fritters well on kitchen paper. Freeze without packing. Pack in rigid containers with a sheet of moisture- and vapour-proof paper between each layer.

To thaw: Fry frozen fritters in hot butter until hot through and golden brown.

QUICK TRICKS WITH FROZEN VEGETABLES

Brussels Sprouts with Chestnuts

1 lb frozen Brussels sprouts
½ lb chestnuts

1 oz butter
Salt and pepper

1. Cut an incision in each chestnut. Grill or bake in the oven and, when cool enough to handle, remove the shell and peel. Chop the chestnuts roughly.

2. Cook the frozen Brussels sprouts in a little boiling water until tender (be careful not to overcook). Drain well.

3. Melt the butter in a saucepan and fry the chopped chestnuts for 2 minutes over a medium flame. Season with salt and pepper and pour over the Brussels sprouts.

French Beans with Pine Kernels or Salted Almonds

2 lb frozen French beans
2 oz pine kernels or salted almonds

1 oz butter

METHOD

1. Cook the frozen beans in boiling water until tender.

2. Melt the butter in a saucepan, heat until foaming. Add the pine kernels or salted almonds. Fry the nuts for 2 minutes, shaking the pan. Pour over the beans and serve immediately.

Cauliflower à la Polonaise

1 frozen cauliflower
1 tablespoon fresh breadcrumbs
2 hard-boiled eggs
2 teaspoons chopped parsley

3 oz butter
Juice of 1 lemon
Salt and freshly ground black pepper

1. Cook the cauliflower in boiling salted water until just tender. Drain and keep hot.

2. Melt the butter in a saucepan. Cook the breadcrumbs over a medium flame until golden. Remove from the heat. Add the chopped hard-boiled eggs, parsley and lemon juice. Mix and season with salt and pepper.

3. Sprinkle the sauce over the cauliflower.

Cauliflower Fritters

BATTER
½ lb flour
2 teaspoons baking powder
1 egg
Pinch of salt
¼–½ pint water

Fat for frying
1½ lb frozen cauliflower sprigs
¼ pint oil
Juice of 1 lemon

METHOD

1. Sift the flour and baking powder into a bowl. Make a well in the centre and put in the egg, salt and a little water. Mix in the flour and beat until smooth. Add enough water to make a thick creamy consistency. Leave to stand for at least 1 hour.

2. Cook the cauliflower in boiling salted water until just tender, about 10–12 minutes. Drain and leave to marinate in the oil and lemon juice for 30 minutes.

3. Dip the cauliflower sprigs in the batter and fry in deep fat (385°F) until golden brown.

Serve: With a tomato sauce.

Note: These fritters can be frozen for 7–10 days, and thawed in a medium-hot oven (400°F: Reg. 5) until crisp.

Carrots aux Fines Herbes

1½ lb sliced frozen new carrots
1 oz butter
1 teaspoon sugar

Salt
½ tablespoon chopped parsley
½ teaspoon chopped chervil

METHOD

1. Cook the carrots in boiling water until tender, drain well.
2. Melt the butter in a saucepan and add the carrots and sugar.
Season with a little salt. Cook over a medium heat for 5 minutes.
3. Add the parsley and chervil. Mix well and serve.

Spinach with Mushrooms

2 lb frozen spinach
½ lb button mushrooms
2 oz butter

2 tablespoons grated cheese
Salt and pepper

METHOD

1. Cook frozen spinach in a little boiling salted water until
tender. Drain well and purée through a fine sieve or in an electric
blender.
2. Slice the mushrooms.
3. Melt the butter in a saucepan and when foaming add the
mushrooms and fry for 2 minutes. Lower the heat and add the
spinach.
4. Sprinkle over the cheese and mix gently so as not to break up
the mushrooms. Cook over a low heat until the cheese melts.
Season with salt and pepper.

Carrots with Cream and Lemon Juice

1½ lb frozen carrots
2 oz butter
¼ pint thick cream

Salt and pepper
1 tablespoon lemon juice

METHOD

1. Cook frozen carrots in boiling salted water until tender. Drain well.
2. Heat the butter in a saucepan and fry the carrots until golden brown. Mix in the cream over a low heat. Do not allow to boil. Season with salt and pepper.
3. Sprinkle over the lemon juice.

Carrots à la Vichy

1½ lb frozen new carrots
  or 1½ lb old carrots cut into
  Julienne strips
2 oz caster sugar

2 oz butter
1 tablespoon chopped parsley
Salt and pepper

METHOD

1. Put the frozen carrots in a saucepan with barely enough water to cover them. Add the sugar and butter.
2. Cook over a low heat until the water is absorbed and the carrots are tender. Shake the pan frequently to prevent sticking.
3. Add the chopped parsley and season with salt and pepper.

Hors d'Oeuvres

Grapefruit and Melon Cocktail

2 large ripe grapefruit
¾ lb ripe melon or 1 small
  melon

Sugar
1 tablespoon chopped mint

METHOD

1. Peel grapefruit, break into segments and remove all pith, pips and membrane. Cut segments into pieces.
2. Peel melon, cut into half and remove pips. Dice flesh or scoop into balls.
3. Mix together grapefruit and melon and sprinkle generously with sugar. Add the chopped mint and mix well.

To freeze: Pack fruit into suitable containers. Seal, label and freeze.

To thaw: Place unopened container in a refrigerator (for at least 5 hours) until thawed.
Serve really icy cold in individual glass dishes.

Note: Diced pineapple may be used instead of grapefruit.
May be stored for up to 12 months.

Orange and Prawn Cocktail

An attractive dish to look at.
Very good on a hot summer evening

Juice of 2 large oranges
½ lb prawns
1 large orange
Juice of 1 lemon
2 blanched red peppers
(or 1 small tin)

6 ripe tomatoes
1 teaspoon sugar
1 tablespoon water
Salt and pepper
Chopped chives

METHOD

1. Leave the prawns to soak in the orange juice for 2 hours.
2. Place the tomatoes, cut into quarters, with the sugar and water in a saucepan. Simmer for 15 minutes until tender. Put through a fine sieve. Season with salt and pepper.
3. Peel the orange. Break into sections and remove all pith and membrane. Chop the red peppers.
4. Drain the prawns. Add the orange juice and lemon juice to the tomato pulp. Check seasoning and pour over orange sections, prawns and chopped peppers.

To freeze: Place in suitable containers. Seal, label and freeze.

To thaw: Leave in the refrigerator for at least 5 hours, or overnight.

Serve: Chilled in individual glass dishes. Scatter a few chopped chives over the surface.

Taramasalata

(Smoked Cod's Roe Paste)

½ lb smoked cod's roe
Juice of 1 lemon
¼ pint olive oil

1 spoonful of yoghurt
Freshly ground black pepper

1. Put the cod's roe in a mortar and pound until really smooth.
2. Gradually add the lemon juice, beating all the time.
3. Very slowly add the olive oil, beating until a smooth, thick paste is formed.
4. Add the black pepper and stir in the yoghurt.

To freeze: Put the paste into a carton. Seal, label and freeze.

To thaw: Leave in a refrigerator for 4 hours, or until thawed through.

To serve: Cold, with ¼ lemon per person and fresh hot toast.

Note: A very good paste can be made in the same way with ½ lb cooked kipper fillets.
   Do not keep frozen for longer than 3 months.

Iced Camembert

1 ripe Camembert
1 demi-sel or packaged
   cream cheese
2 tablespoons hot milk

3 tablespoons whipped cream
Salt and freshly ground black
   pepper

METHOD

1. Cut the rind from the Camembert. Be careful not to waste any of the cheese.
2. Pound in a mortar or rub through a sieve until quite smooth.
3. Work the cream cheese with the hot milk until smooth.
4. Blend the cheeses together, add the whipped cream and season with salt and pepper.

To freeze: Pack in small waxed tubs or dariole moulds. Seal, label and freeze.

To serve: Dip moulds into hot water. Turn out, dust with a little paprika pepper and serve on a chilled dish with a garnish of crisp watercress. Accompany with hot salted biscuits.
Note: Can be served as a savoury.

Fruits de Mare Alexa

This is one of my favourite ways to start a dinner party. With the crab included it is definitely a rich dish, but the crab can be left out entirely and shrimps or tinned lobster substituted.

	SAUCE
4 sole fillets	1 oz flour
1 tablespoon lemon juice	¼ pint milk
½ lb fresh crab meat	2 tablespoons sherry
3 scallops	2 oz grated cheese
1 pint fresh mussels or 1 tin mussels	Salt and freshly ground black pepper
1 small tin tuna fish	Tinned pimento for decoration
1 oz butter	

METHOD

1. Poach the fillets of sole in boiling water with 1 tablespoon of lemon juice for 5 minutes. Leave to cool and remove the dark skin.
2. Clean fresh mussels and remove beards. Steam for 2–4 minutes until open. Remove the mussels from their shells.
3. Cut the black vein from the scallops and chop them into pieces. Fry them gently in 1 oz of butter over a medium flame for 3 minutes. Reserve the juice.
4. Arrange all the fish in a shallow baking dish.
5. Melt 1 oz butter in a saucepan, add the flour and mix well. Gradually add the milk, stirring continually over a medium flame until the sauce is thick and smooth. Stir in the juice from the scallops and the sherry. Season well with salt and pepper.
6. Add half the grated cheese to the sauce and pour it over the

135

fish. Decorate the surface with thin strips of tinned pimento and sprinkle with grated cheese.

To serve without freezing: Bake the fish in a hot oven (420°F: Reg. 6) for 10–15 minutes until golden brown.

To freeze: Cool. Cover the surface with a layer of moisture- and vapour-proof wrapping to prevent the surface being disturbed. Pack in a polythene bag or wrap in freezer paper. Seal, label and freeze.

To thaw: Cover frozen dish with a sheet of aluminium foil and heat in a moderate oven (350°F: Reg. 4) for 20 minutes until hot through. Brown in a hot oven for 5 minutes.

Note: This dish can be served with mashed potatoes or rice as a lunch or supper dish.

Potted Prawns, Lobster or Crab

This is a most delicious way to make a small quantity of chopped lobster go a long way.

$\frac{1}{2}$ lb prawns, lobster or crabmeat
4 oz butter
1 teaspoon freshly ground black pepper

Pinch of cayenne
1 teaspoon ground mace
Juice of $\frac{1}{2}$ lemon

1. Heat 1 tablespoon of butter in a saucepan.
2. Add the black pepper, cayenne and mace.
3. When the butter is hot, but not bubbling, add the fish and lemon juice.
4. Stir well until the fish is hot through but do not allow to brown.
5. Pack the fish into tubs or cartons.
6. Heat the remaining butter until it foams. Skim the surface

and pour over the fish. The butter should completely cover the fish.

7. Leave to cool and set hard.

To freeze: Pack, seal, label and freeze the cartons.

To thaw: Place cartons overnight in the refrigerator.

To serve: Turn out the potted fish and serve with hot toast and a garnish of parsley sprigs, with ¼ lemon for each serving.
   Do not keep for longer than 3 months.

Smoked Salmon and Crab Rolls

This is an extremely rich dish and should only be followed by a light main course. See menus.

8 slices smoked salmon	Freshly ground black pepper
¾ lb fresh crab meat	Lettuce and thin slices of
Juice of 1 lemon	lemon for garnish

1. Blend crab meat with lemon juice and freshly ground pepper. (I also add a tiny pinch of cayenne.)
2. Place 2 tablespoons crab meat on each slice smoked salmon.
3. Roll up neatly into uniform rolls. Trim edges if necessary.

To freeze: Wrap each roll in moisture- and vapour-proof paper to prevent sticking. Pack in waxed boxes. Seal, label and freeze.

To defrost: Place in a refrigerator for 5 hours, still wrapped.

To serve: Place two smoked salmon rolls on a bed of lettuce on each plate. Place two thin slices of lemon on each roll.

Note: If smoked fish or meat gets a 'dry' look wrap it for ½ hour in a muslin cloth soaked in olive oil.
   Do not keep in deep freeze for longer than 3 months.

Prawn Vol-Au-Vents

Puff-pastry vol-au-vents, depending on their size and fillings, can be used as savouries, cocktail canapés, first courses and luncheon dishes. Puff pastry takes time and patience to make, but it can be bought ready-made and successfully stored in the deep freeze for months. If you use frozen pastry leave it at room temperature for 1 hour before using.

½ lb puff pastry	¼ pint milk
1 beaten egg	¼ pint cream
½ lb shelled prawns	1 egg yolk, slightly beaten
2 tablespoons fresh dill or chives	1 dessertspoon lemon juice
	1 tablespoon sherry (optional)
2 tablespoons butter	Salt and pepper
2 tablespoons flour	

METHOD

1. Roll out the pastry to barely ¼-inch thickness. Cut into 3-inch rounds with a fluted cutter. Brush with beaten egg. Cut halfway through the centre of each round with a 1-inch cutter. Put rounds on a damp baking tray and chill for 10 minutes.

2. Bake pastry cases in a hot oven (450°F: Reg. 7) for 10 minutes until golden, crisp and well risen. Leave to cool. Remove the top and scoop away all the soft pastry from the centre of the cases.

3. To make the filling, melt the butter in a saucepan. Add the flour and stir over a low heat until well blended. Gradually add the milk and cream, stirring all the time until thick and smooth.

4. Beat in the egg yolk, sherry, lemon juice, prawns and dill; season with salt and pepper: leave to cool.

5. Fill the pastry cases with the prawn mixture.

To freeze: Pack the pastry cases carefully into waxed boxes, separating each case with a layer of freezer paper or moisture- and vapour-proof paper. Seal, label and freeze.

To thaw: The cases can be placed straight from the deep freeze into a moderate oven (330°F: Reg.3) for about 30 minutes but, to avoid any risk of the pastry being overcooked and the filling still iced, I prefer thawing the cases at room temperature for 3 hours and then heating them in a medium-hot oven (380°F: Reg.5) for 10 minutes until the filling is hot through.

Serve: Hot, allowing two cases per person.

Some Alternative Fillings for Vol-Au-Vent Cases

1. MUSHROOM filling

½ lb mushrooms, chopped	¼ pint cream
2 tablespoons butter	Dash of Worcester sauce or
2 small onions, chopped	mushroom ketchup
1 teaspoon lemon juice	Salt and pepper
2 tablespoons flour	1 tablespoon sherry (optional)
¼ pint milk	

METHOD

1. Melt butter in a saucepan. Add mushrooms, onions and lemon juice. Simmer for 5 minutes.
2. Stir in flour and mix until well blended. Gradually add milk and cream, stirring continually over a medium heat until the mixture is thick and smooth. Flavour with Worcester sauce and season with salt and pepper. Add sherry.

2. HAM AND PARSLEY filling

½ lb minced ham	¼ pint milk
2 tablespoons butter	2 tablespoons chopped parsley
2 tablespoons flour	1 teaspoon Worcester sauce
¼ pint cream	Salt and pepper

METHOD

Melt the butter in a saucepan. Add the flour and stir over a low heat until well blended. Gradually blend in the milk and cream, stirring all the time until the mixture is thickened and smooth.

Add the parsley, ham and Worcester sauce. Season with salt and pepper. Allow to cool, and fill cases.

3. CREAMED SWEETBREAD filling

1½ lb sweetbreads	2 tablespoons flour
1 quart boiling salted water	¼ pint sweetbread stock
1 tablespoon lemon juice	¼ pint cream
1 oz butter	2 teaspoons lemon juice
1 small onion, chopped	1 tablespoon sherry (optional)
¼ lb mushrooms, sliced	Salt and pepper

METHOD

1. Soak the sweetbreads in chilled water for 1 hour. Drain and place in a saucepan. Cover with the boiling water. Add lemon juice. Cover and simmer for 1 hour. Leave sweetbreads to cool in the water they were cooked in.

2. Drain sweetbreads. Reserve stock.

3. Remove membranes and tubes from the sweetbreads and cut into cubes.

4. Melt the butter in a saucepan. Fry the mushrooms and onions for 3 minutes. Add the flour and stir over a low heat until well blended. Gradually add the stock and cream until a thick smooth consistency is reached. Add sweetbreads.

5. Flavour with lemon juice, sherry, salt and pepper. Allow to cool and fill cases.

Crêpes Caravelles

(Pancakes stuffed with smoked salmon and crab)

I keep repeating the importance of labelling food well, and a typical example of what happens when this isn't done happened to me recently. I had made two batches of pancakes, stuffing one with meat sauce and one with the Caravelle mixture. Being in a hurry I didn't bother to label them. I took the one I thought was meat out of the deep freeze and served it at a dinner party.

Needless to say they were the wrong ones. To make the whole thing worse I had started the meal with smoked salmon.

PANCAKES	FILLING
2 eggs	1 oz butter
¼ pint cream	1 oz flour
1 oz melted butter	½ pint hot milk
2 oz flour	¼ lb smoked salmon
Milk	½ lb crab
Salt, pepper	Salt, pepper and 1 tablespoon
Butter for frying	chopped parsley

METHOD

1. Make the pancake batter by beating together the eggs, cream and melted butter. Add to the sifted flour and beat until smooth.

2. Add enough milk to make the mixture the consistency of thin cream. Season and leave to stand for 30 minutes.

3. Melt a little butter in an omelet pan. When it is really hot add a spoonful of batter, swirling it round until the pan is evenly coated. Cook over a hot flame for 1 minute each side. Add more milk if the batter is too thick. Stack the cooked pancakes on a plate.

4. Make a white sauce by melting the butter in a saucepan, add the flour, and stir until well blended and the flour and butter form a ball.

5. Slowly add the hot milk, stirring all the time over a medium heat until the sauce is smooth and free from all lumps.

6. Chop the smoked salmon into small pieces and add with the crab to the sauce. Season with salt, pepper and chopped parsley.

7. Spread some of the filling on each pancake and roll up. Place them in a buttered fireproof dish.

To freeze: Pack the dish in a polythene bag. Seal, label and freeze.

To thaw: Remove the frozen dish from the polythene bag. Cover with a layer of tin foil and heat in a moderately hot oven (350°F: Reg. 4) for 30 minutes until the pancakes are thawed and hot through.

To serve: Brown in a hot oven for 5 minutes and sprinkle the top with a little chopped parsley.

Prawn and Mushroom Savoury Pancakes

Savoury pancakes such as these and Crêpes Bolognaises make excellent first courses or supper dishes. They freeze well and need the minimum of preparation when serving.

PANCAKES	FILLING
2 eggs	½ lb fresh or frozen prawns
¼ pint cream	1 tablespoon chopped parsley
1 oz melted butter	¼ lb mushrooms
2 oz flour	2 oz butter
Milk	2 oz flour
Salt and pepper	½ pint thin cream or milk
Butter for frying	Salt and pepper
	1 tablespoon sherry
	2 tablespoons grated cheese

METHOD

1. *To make the pancakes:* Beat the eggs, cream and melted butter together. Add the sifted flour and beat until smooth.

2. Add enough milk to make the mixture the consistency of thin cream. Season. Leave to stand for 30 minutes.

3. Melt a little butter in an omelet pan. When it is really hot add a spoonful of batter, swirling it round until the pan is evenly coated. Cook over a hot flame for 1 minute on each side. Stack the cooked pancakes on a plate.

4. *To make the filling:* Chop the mushrooms and fry in the butter over a low flame until they are soft. Add the flour and mix well. Gradually add the thin cream or milk. Stir continually until the mixture is smooth.

5. Add the prawns to the sauce and stir in the sherry and chopped parsley. Season with salt and pepper.

6. Place a spoonful of the filling in each pancake and roll up neatly. Arrange the pancakes in a shallow baking dish.

To serve without freezing: Sprinkle the pancakes with grated cheese and bake in a hot oven (420°F: Reg. 6) for 10 minutes.

To freeze: Pack the baking dish in a polythene bag or wrap in freezer paper or aluminium foil. Seal, label and freeze.

To thaw: Sprinkle grated cheese over frozen pancakes. Cover with a layer of aluminium foil. Bake in a medium-hot oven (380°F: Reg. 5) for 10 minutes. Remove cover and continue to cook for a further 5 minutes until the pancakes are hot through and the cheese browned. Serve hot.

Stuffed Tomatoes with Crab

4 large tomatoes
1½ oz butter
3 tablespoons finely chopped green peppers
3 tablespoons finely chopped onion

1½ tablespoons flour
¾ pint milk
½ lb crab
4 oz grated cheese
Salt and pepper

METHOD

1. Cut a slice from the top of the tomatoes. Scoop out the centre without breaking the skin.

2. Melt the butter in a saucepan. Add the pepper and onion and cook over a low flame for 3 minutes.

3. Add the flour and mix until well blended. Add the milk gradually and stir until the sauce is thick and smooth.

4. Add the crab and cheese, and season with salt and pepper. Fill the tomato cases with this mixture.

5. Place the tomatoes in a greased baking dish and bake in a moderate oven (350°F: Reg. 4) for 10 minutes.

To serve without freezing: Continue to cook for a further 5–10 minutes.

To freeze: Cool and freeze unpacked. When frozen, pack in a rigid container with a sheet of moisture- and vapour-proof paper between tomatoes. Seal, label and freeze.

To thaw: Place frozen tomatoes in a greased baking dish. Cover with aluminium foil and bake in a moderate oven (350°F: Reg. 4) for 10 minutes or until hot through.

Serve: Hot. Garnished with watercress.
 Do not keep frozen for longer than 1 month.

Jellied Tomato Ring

1 pint tinned tomatoes
1 onion, finely chopped
Rind and juice of ½ lemon
1 teaspoon sage
1 bay leaf

1 teaspoon sugar
6 peppercorns
Salt
1 tablespoon gelatine
2 tablespoons water

METHOD

1. Put tomatoes, onion, lemon rind, sage, bay leaf, sugar and peppercorns into a saucepan. Season with salt. Bring slowly to the boil and simmer for 5 minutes.

2. Rub through a fine nylon sieve. Add lemon juice.

3. Dissolve the gelatine in the water. Add to the tomato pulp. Adjust the seasoning.

4. Rinse out a 1-pint ring mould with cold water. Pour in liquid and leave to set.

To freeze: Place in a plastic bag. Seal, label and freeze.

To thaw: Leave the mould in the bag for 4 hours in a refrigerator.

To serve: Turn out mould after dipping it in hot water. Fill the centre with prawns and watercress tossed in a French dressing – crab in mayonnaise, or cream cheese and chives, etc. Serve cold.

Green Peppers Stuffed with Rice and Herbs

4 large ripe green peppers
½ lb Patna rice
2 tablespoons chopped parsley
1 teaspoon marjoram or thyme

1 tablespoon lemon juice
2 tablespoons olive oil
Salt and freshly ground pepper
1 tablespoon olive oil

METHOD

1. Cook the rice in boiling water until just tender. Drain and rinse in cold water.

2. Mix the finely chopped parsley, marjoram or thyme, lemon juice, 1 tablespoon olive oil, salt and pepper with the rice.

3. Cut the peppers in half lengthways. Remove seeds and membrane from the inside of the peppers. Rinse in cold water.

4. Fill the peppers with the rice mixture.

5. Cover the bottom of a shallow baking dish with olive oil. Place the peppers in the baking dish and cover with aluminium foil.

6. Bake in a moderate oven (330°F: Reg. 3) for 1 hour. Baste with the oil every $\frac{1}{4}$ hour. Add more oil if the rice becomes dry on the surface.

To freeze: Cool peppers. Pack in waxed containers with freezer paper, or moisture- and vapour-proof plastic between the peppers. Seal, label and freeze.

To thaw: Place frozen peppers in an oiled baking dish. Cover with tin foil and heat slowly in a moderate oven for 30 minutes until peppers are hot through.

Serve: Hot as a first course or vegetable dish.
   Do not keep frozen for longer than 2 months.

Chilled Ratatouille

This can be served hot as a vegetable dish, but I much prefer it chilled, as they have it in Provence, as a first course. Because garlic is absolutely necessary for the making of ratatouille, this dish should not be kept frozen for longer than 1 month.

2 large Spanish onions	$\frac{1}{4}$ lb black olives
2 green or red peppers	2 large cloves garlic
2 large ripe aubergines	Salt, freshly ground black
2 courgettes	pepper, chopped parsley
4 large ripe tomatoes	$\frac{1}{4}$ pint olive oil
$\frac{1}{2}$ cucumber, peeled	

1. Slice the unpeeled aubergines and courgettes into thin slices. Sprinkle with salt and leave to 'sweat' in a colander for 1 hour. Drain and dry well. Remove cores and seeds from peppers, cut into thin strips. Slice onions thinly. Chop tomatoes and cucumber.

2. Heat the olive oil in a large iron casserole and fry the onions over a medium flame for 10 minutes.

3. Add the aubergines and courgettes. Cover the pan and simmer for 30 minutes.

4. Add the tomatoes, cucumber, creamed garlic and seasoning. Simmer for 45 minutes.

5. Remove the lid, add the stoned black olives and cook for 10 minutes.

6. Leave to cool and remove any excess oil from the surface.

To freeze: Pack in suitable containers. Seal, label and freeze.

To thaw: Leave in containers in a refrigerator for at least 5 hours or overnight until thawed through.

Serve: Well chilled with parsley sprinkled over the top, accompanied by hot French bread.
Do not keep frozen for longer than 1 month.

Quiche Lorraine

This is, to my mind, one of the most delicious of first courses. It can be served hot or cold and, although the true quiche of Lorraine is made of only bacon and cream and eggs, I prefer the addition of cheese and onions.

PASTRY
4 oz plain flour
2 oz butter
1 egg
Salt and pepper
Water

FILLING
1 medium onion
1 oz butter
4 rashers bacon, chopped
1 tablespoon chopped parsley
3 tablespoons grated cheese
3 egg yolks
¼ pint cream
Salt and pepper

1. *To make the pastry:* Sift the flour, salt and pepper into a bowl. Make a well in the centre and put in the butter cut in small pieces, and the egg. Mix lightly with the fingertips until the mixture is like coarse breadcrumbs.

2. Add enough cold water to make the pastry moist. Form into a ball and press flat with the palm of the hand on a floured board. Roll back into a ball and leave covered in a cold place for 2 hours.

3. *To make the filling:* Chop the onion finely and fry gently in a little butter until transparent but not brown.

4. Beat the egg yolks and cream together.

5. Add the onion, parsley, and the bacon chopped into small pieces, and season with salt and pepper.

6. Roll the pastry out as thinly as possible and line an 8-inch flan tin, pressing gently into the sides with knuckles. Pour in the custard mixture and sprinkle the top with cheese.

7. Bake in a medium-hot oven (400°F: Reg. 5) for 20 minutes. Thirty minutes if to be served without freezing.

To freeze: Leave tart to cool. Place in a polythene bag. Seal, label and freeze.

To thaw: Leave in the polythene bag at room temperature until thawed (about 3 hours). Heat in a moderate oven until warm through.

Serve: Hot or cold, cut into slices.
   Do not keep frozen for longer than 3 months.

Carnival Flan

½ lb flour	1 oz butter
6 oz butter	2 ripe tomatoes
Salt	¼ lb mushrooms
Cold water	3 eggs
Squeeze of lemon juice	Salt and pepper
4 oz ham or bacon	6 anchovies
½ onion	

1. Sift the flour and salt into a large bowl. Cut the butter into small pieces and rub it with the tips of the fingers into the flour until it looks like coarse breadcrumbs. Add enough cold water and lemon juice to make a stiff dough. Chill for ½ hour.

2. Chop the ham or bacon and the onion and fry in a little butter for 3 minutes. Add the chopped mushrooms and sliced tomatoes, and fry for a further 3 minutes.

3. Beat the eggs and season with salt and pepper.

4. Roll out the pastry as thinly as possible and line two flan tins. Place half the fried mixture in each and cover with the well-beaten eggs. Decorate with the anchovies.

5. Bake for 25 minutes in a medium-hot oven (400°F: Reg. 5). *Note:* To make the flans more savoury you can add ¼ lb grated cheese to the beaten eggs.

To freeze: Leave to cool. Pack in a plastic bag. Seal, label and freeze.

To thaw: Leave at room temperature for at least 3 hours until thawed through.

To serve: Serve cold; or heat through and serve with a tomato sauce.

Bourekakia

(Meat-filled Pastry Squares)

PASTRY
6 oz plain flour
2 oz butter
2 oz lard
4 tablespoons iced water
Pinch of salt
1 egg beaten with pinch of salt

FILLING
4 oz chicken livers
3 oz mushrooms
1 oz butter
1 tablespoon chopped parsley
Salt and freshly ground black pepper

METHOD

1. *To make the pastry:* Sift the flour and the salt, add the fats cut into pieces. Rub with fingertips until the mixture resembles coarse breadcrumbs. Add water, and mix until the pastry forms a smooth ball.

2. Leave covered in a cold place for at least 1 hour.

3. Roll the pastry between two sheets of floured waxproof paper until paper thin. Cut into 3-inch squares.

4. *To make the filling:* Chop the chicken livers and mushrooms. Melt the butter in a saucepan. When it begins to foam add the chicken livers. Cook for 1 minute. Add the mushrooms and cook for a further five minutes.

5. Add the parsley and season with salt and pepper.

6. Brush each square with melted butter. Place a spoonful of filling near one corner and bring the opposite corner over to form a triangle. Pinch edges together firmly.

7. Brush pastry squares with beaten egg.

To serve immediately: Bake in a medium-hot oven (380°F: Reg. 5) for 15 minutes until crisp and golden.

To freeze: Place unbaked pastries in waxed cardboard boxes with a layer of freezer paper or moisture- and vapour-proof plastic between each pastry. Seal, label and freeze.

To thaw: Place frozen pastries on a greased baking sheet and cook in a moderate oven (340°F: Reg. 3) for 30 minutes until crisp and golden.

Serve: Hot.

Note: Bourekakia are very good made in 2-inch squares and served hot with cocktails.
Do not keep frozen for longer than 3 months.

149

Potted Pigeon or Partridge

2 pigeons or 1 partridge
6 oz butter
A pinch of nutmeg, mace
6 crushed juniper berries

Salt and freshly ground black
  pepper
Juice of $\frac{1}{2}$ lemon
1 tablespoon brandy
6 thin rashers bacon

METHOD

1. Prepare each bird.
2. Mix together 4 oz of butter, nutmeg, mace, salt and pepper and juniper berries. Place a spoonful inside each bird and rub the rest over the outside.
3. Place birds breast down in a casserole dish. Pour over the brandy and the lemon juice. Cover with a layer of tin foil.
4. Bake in a slow oven (310°F: Reg. 2) for 2 hours until the flesh is tender. Strain the juice and leave to cool until butter solidifies on the top. Remove as much flesh as possible from the bones and chop finely.
5. Fry the bacon and line a small pot or earthenware dish with 2 rashers. Place half the meat in the bottom of the dish. Cover with 2 more rashers. Repeat, placing the last 2 rashers across the top.
6. Scrape the butter from the top of the juice and melt in a saucepan until nearly boiling. Pour over the meat.
7. Melt the remaining 2 oz of butter until foaming. Pour over the top.

To freeze: Leave to cool. Pack the dish in a polythene bag. Seal, label and freeze.

To thaw: Leave for at least 6 hours, or overnight, in a refrigerator until thawed through.

To serve: Serve cold with hot French bread or freshly made toast.
  Do not keep frozen for longer than 3 months.

Pâté de Campagne

1 lb minced pork
1 lb minced veal
½ lb minced ham or bacon
6 oz minced pork fat
½ lb minced pigs' liver
2 cloves garlic

Salt and pepper
Pinch of allspice
1 glass brandy
4 rashers fat bacon
2 bay leaves

METHOD

1. Mix together all minced meat. Season with salt, pepper and a pinch of allspice.
2. Crush the garlic and mix well with the meat.
3. Stir in the brandy.
4. Line a terrine with the bacon rashers. Press in the meat firmly. Place the bay leaves on the top. Cover with a lid and wrap the whole dish in aluminium foil to seal completely.
5. Place the terrine in a dish of hot water and bake in a moderate oven (350°F: Reg. 3) for 1½ hours.
6. Unwrap the terrine and place a weight on the pâté to press it down. Leave to get cold.

To serve without freezing: Pour a seal of aspic jelly or clarified butter over the top of the pâté. Leave to set and serve chilled with hot toast and butter.

To freeze: Wrap the terrine in freezer paper or aluminium foil or in a polythene bag. Seal, label and freeze.

To thaw: Leave to thaw still sealed in a refrigerator for 6 hours or until thawed through. Cover with a thin layer of aspic jelly or clarified butter.

Serve: Chilled, cut into slices, with hot toast and butter.
   Do not keep frozen for longer than 2 weeks.

Swedish Liver Pâté

This is a very rich, smooth pâté and a little goes a long way. The following recipe is enough for 12 servings.

1 lb calves' liver
½ lb pork belly
1 small onion, chopped
3 anchovy fillets
3 beaten eggs
3 tablespoons flour
2 tablespoons thick cream

A pinch of marjoram
A pinch of mace
2 teaspoons freshly ground black pepper
3 tablespoons brandy or dry Vermouth
¼ lb button mushrooms, sliced

METHOD

1. Cut liver and pork into small pieces. Put through a fine mincer four times until the meat is almost smooth (this can be done in an electric blender). Add the onion and anchovies to the meat and put through mincer once more.
2. Add the eggs to the meat mixture. Beat until really well blended.
3. Gradually add the flour, cream and seasonings. Add the brandy or dry Vermouth and the mushrooms, and mix well.
4. Spoon the mixture into a well-buttered 9½-inch loaf pan.
5. Cover with aluminium foil and bake, in a tin of hot water, in a moderate oven (325°F: Reg. 3) for 2 hours.
6. Cool the pâté in the pan.

To freeze: Place the pâté still in its pan in a polythene bag. Seal, label and freeze.

To thaw: Place in a refrigerator for at least 6 hours or overnight.

To serve: Turn out and garnish with sliced tomatoes or chopped aspic jelly. Serve with hot toast.

Game and Liver Pâté

½ lb calves' liver
4 oz bacon
1 shallot
A few sprigs of parsley,
  chopped
2 oz butter

Salt, freshly ground black
  pepper, and a pinch of mace
1 cold roast pheasant,
  partridge or duck

METHOD

1. Bone the pheasant and cut the meat into thin slices.
2. Chop the liver, bacon and shallot into small pieces.
3. Melt the butter in a heavy pan and fry the liver, bacon, shallot and the parsley over a low flame for 15 minutes, stirring continually.
4. Season with salt, pepper and mace.
5. Remove the meat from the pan and pound in a mortar, or use an electric blender, or put through a Mouli sieve.
6. Place a layer of the liver paste in a small terrine or pie dish.
7. Cover with a layer of the game and continue until the meat is all used, finishing with a layer of the paste.
8. Cover the dish with tin foil and place in a baking dish of water. Cook in a medium oven for 2 hours.
9. Remove tin foil. Place a weight over the pâté and leave till cold.

To freeze: Pack the pâté firmly into waxed tubs or in its original container and pack in a polythene bag. Seal, label and freeze.

To defrost: Leave the pâté in its container in a refrigerator overnight, or for about 6 hours.

To serve: Turn the pâté on to a bed of crisp lettuce leaves. Garnish with a sprig of parsley and serve with hot toast.

Hare Paté en Croûte

This pâté made in a pastry case is extremely delicious. Hare is very rich, and this recipe should be enough for 12 people if served as a first course.

PÂTÉ	STOCK	PASTRY
1 hare	Hare bones	1 lb flour
1 lb minced pork	1 onion	Salt
½ lb bacon fat	1 carrot	3 oz lard
1 glass brandy	3 pints water	5 oz butter
Salt and pepper	½ pint white wine	2 eggs
Pinch of allspice	Bouquet garni	
3 crushed juniper berries	1 oz gelatine	

METHOD

1. Save the liver and the blood of the hare. Cut off the tender flesh from the legs and back. Trim into neat fillets. Cut the rest of the flesh from the bones and mince with the liver.

2. Add the minced pork, the blood, salt, pepper, pinch of allspice and the crushed juniper berries. Stir in the brandy and mix well.

3. *Make the stock* by placing the bare bones, chopped onion, chopped carrot, water, white wine, bouquet garni and seasoning in a large pan. Bring to the boil and simmer for 2 hours. Skim and strain through a fine sieve.

4. *Make the pastry* by sieving the flour and salt on to a board. Make a well in the centre and put in the lard, butter and eggs. Mix the ingredients together with the fingertips gradually drawing in the flour. Knead until smooth and leave to chill for ½ hour. Keep one-third of the pastry aside for the top. Roll out the rest and line a raised pie mould or large loaf tin.

5. Put a good layer of the minced mixture in the bottom. Lay the hare fillets and the fat bacon cut into strips on the mince and cover with the rest of the mixture.

6. Cover with a lid of pastry. Press the edges together carefully and brush with beaten egg. Cut two air vents in the pastry to allow any air to escape.

7. Bake the pâté in a hot oven (410°F: Reg. 6) for 1½ hours. If the pastry is getting too brown cover with a layer of damp grease-proof paper.

8. Leave the pâté to cool. Fill up with 1 pint of stock mixed with 1 oz of dissolved gelatine, poured through the air vents. Leave to set and turn out carefully.

To freeze: Pack the pâté in a rigid container. Fill any spaces with crumpled freezer paper. Seal, label and freeze.

To thaw: Leave unwrapped in a refrigerator for at least 6 hours or until thawed through.

Serve: Chilled. Cut into thin slices.

Whole Chicken Pâté

This is a complicated dish but well worth the trouble. Served as a first course it should amply feed 12 people.

3½ lb chicken
½ lb minced veal
½ lb minced fresh pork
2 slices stale bread
¼ pint milk
½ lb fillet of veal
½ lb lean bacon

1 bay leaf
2 sprigs thyme
¼ lb thinly sliced salt pork
¼ pint water
¼ pint cooking brandy
Salt and pepper

METHOD

1. Ask your butcher to bone an uncooked chicken for you. This is not a thing to attempt yourself. The flesh is loosened from the skeleton through an incision made along the backbone. The wings and legs are left on. Care should be taken not to pierce the skin.

2. Chop the liver and the heart of the chicken into small pieces. Mix with the minced veal and pork.

3. Soak the bread in the milk and squeeze out excess liquid. Add to the meat. Season with salt and pepper.

4. Lay the boned chicken out as flat as possible. Spread the surface with a layer of stuffing. Cover with a layer of the ham and veal fillet cut into thin strips. Repeat these layers until the chicken is full.

5. Sew up the back and any holes of the chicken. Pat gently into its original shape.

6. Put a thin layer of salt pork in the bottom of an oval casserole or terrine large enough to take the chicken. Put in ½ bay leaf and 1 small sprig of thyme. Pour over the water and brandy.

7. Put the chicken in the terrine and cover the back with a thin strip of salt pork, ½ bay leaf and 1 sprig of thyme.

8. Sprinkle with salt and pepper. Pack any remaining stuffing round the sides of the chicken. Cover with a lid and seal with a paste made from flour and water.

9. Cook for 2½ hours in a slow oven (300°F: Reg. 2). Leave to cool without breaking the seal.

To Freeze: Pack the cooled terrine in a polythene bag or wrap in freezer paper or aluminium foil. Seal, label and freeze.

To thaw: Leave sealed terrine to thaw for 5 hours at room temperature.

To serve: Remove lid and wipe away traces of paste. Serve cold cut into slices.

Fried Bread Croûtes

1-inch-thick slices of bread   Lard for frying

METHOD

1. Cut 2-inch circles from the bread with a pastry cutter. Cut halfway through the centre of each circle with a 1-inch cutter.

2. Gently pull away the bread from the centre leaving a round cavity.

3. Melt lard in a frying-pan and fry each croûte until golden brown and crisp.

4. Drain well on kitchen paper.

Freeze filled or unfilled: Carefully pack in waxed cardboard containers with a layer of moisture- and vapour-proof paper between each layer.

To thaw: Place frozen croûtes on a baking sheet in a hot oven (410°F: Reg. 6). Fill with hot filling and serve immediately.

Fillings for Bread Croûtes

1. CANAPÉS INDIENNE

½ oz butter
2 shallots
1 teaspoon curry powder
1 tablespoon milk

1 tablespoon cream
3 oz cooked smoked haddock
1 dessertspoon chutney

METHOD

1. Melt butter in a saucepan. Add chopped shallots and fry until transparent.
2. Stir in curry powder.
3. Add milk slowly and stir well. Add cream.
4. Flake the haddock and add to the sauce with the chutney.

To freeze: Cool and fill cold fried bread croûtes. Pack in suitable containers with a layer of moisture- and vapour-proof paper between each one. Seal, label and freeze.

To thaw: Place frozen croûtes on a baking sheet. Heat in a moderate oven for 15 minutes until the bread is crisp and filling is hot through.

2. CHICKEN LIVER CANAPÉS

4 oz chicken livers
2 rashers streaky bacon
1 oz butter
1 shallot, chopped

2 tomatoes, skinned and
  seeded
2 gherkins, chopped
Cayenne pepper

METHOD

1. Chop the chicken livers and bacon into small pieces.
2. Melt the butter in a saucepan. Fry the livers and bacon for 1 minute.
3. Add the chopped shallot, tomatoes and gherkins.
4. Season with a little cayenne pepper.
5. Cook over a medium heat for 10 minutes.

To freeze: Cool. Fill cold, fried croûtes with mixture. Pack in suitable containers with moisture- and vapour-proof paper between each one. Seal, label and freeze.

To thaw: Place frozen croûtes on a baking tray. Heat in a moderate oven for 10 minutes, or until the bread is crisp and the filling is hot through.

Sandwiches and Fillings

A wide range of sandwiches can be frozen successfully for short periods. In the summer and before parties, especially, precious time can be saved by making sandwiches in advance and freezing them in large quantities.

Use fresh bread only, remove crusts before freezing and avoid salad or mayonnaise-type fillings.

To freeze: Pack sandwiches in small quantities, in moisture- and vapour-proof wrapping or in polythene bags. Seal, label and freeze.

To thaw: Thaw wrapped sandwiches at room temperature for 2–3 hours. Do not unwrap until just before sandwiches are to be eaten.
Do not freeze for longer than 2–4 weeks.

BASIC RULES FOR FREEZING AND THAWING SANDWICHES
Sandwiches for packed lunches and picnics

Here the scope is so wide and depends to such an extent on personal tastes and the ingredients at hand that I have included only a few fillings that my family seem to find particularly enjoyable:

1. White bread filled with slices of very rare cold roast beef and spread with a highly seasoned horseradish sauce.
2. Brown bread filled with slices of tongue spread with cream cheese and finely chopped pickles.
3. White bread filled with corned beef mixed with a little grated cheese and mango chutney.
4. Brown bread filled with minced chicken flavoured with curry sauce. (For curry sauce mix 2 tablespoons thick cream with 1 teaspoon curry powder, a squeeze of lemon juice and a little tomato purée.)

Some quantities to remember when making sandwiches:

1. The average sliced white loaf contains approximately 24 slices.

2. The average sliced brown loaf contains approximately 18 slices.

3. 4 oz softened butter will cover 24 slices of bread.

4. For a sandwich meal allow at least 8–10 small sandwiches per person.

5. A bowl of hot, thick soup and a plate of sandwiches make a very satisfying supper.

PARTY FILLINGS FOR SANDWICHES

1. Rye bread filled with smoked salmon. Season with a squeeze of lemon juice and freshly ground black pepper. You can often buy smoked salmon trimmings from a fishmonger: these are perfect for sandwiches and are half the price of sliced smoked salmon.

2. White bread spread with tinned pâté mixed with chopped asparagus tips.

3. White bread filled with caviare, seasoned with lemon juice and cayenne pepper.

4. Brown or rye bread filled with a mixture of chopped cold roast chicken, mustard pickle and chopped stuffed olives bound with a little thick cream and seasoned with salt and pepper.

5. White bread filled with tuna fish mixed with chopped gherkins.

6. White bread filled with a mixture of cream cheese and chopped pineapple.

7. Brown bread filled with a mixture of cream cheese and chopped anchovy fillets.

8. Brown bread filled with tinned salmon mixed with horse-radish cream.

9. White bread filled with cream cheese mixed with prawns.

CLUB SANDWICHES

Club sandwiches consist of three slices of bread sandwiching two different fillings. They look attractive and can be very substantial. According to their thickness they may have to be eaten with a knife and fork. I usually use brown bread for the outer slices and white for the inner one.

1. *1st layer:* cold roast beef spread with horseradish cream.
   2nd layer: cream cheese mixed with pickle.
2. *1st layer:* pâté mixed with chopped gherkins.
   2nd layer: tongue in fairly thick slices.
3. *1st layer:* Cheddar cheese spread with mango chutney.
   2nd layer: mashed sardines seasoned with freshly ground black pepper and lemon juice.
4. *1st layer:* slices of cold roast pork and pickles.
   2nd layer: apple sauce.
5. *1st layer:* slices of cold roast chicken.
   2nd layer: a mixture of mashed cold fried chicken liver and chopped green olives.
6. *1st layer:* slices of smoked salmon.
   2nd layer: a mixture of cream cheese and chopped black olives.

Smoked Salmon Pinwheels for Parties

These make attractive cocktail and party 'nibbles'

8 thin slices of brown bread with the crusts removed
8 slices of smoked salmon (enough to cover the bread)

3 tablespoons softened butter
Freshly ground black pepper
Lemon juice

METHOD

1. Place the bread between two slightly dampened tea towels and flatten gently with a rolling pin. This prevents the bread from crumbling when you roll it.
2. Butter the slices of bread. Cover each slice with a layer of smoked salmon. Season with pepper and lemon juice.
3. Carefully roll each piece of bread like a Swiss roll.
4. Wrap each roll in tin foil and chill in a refrigerator for $\frac{1}{2}$ hour. Unwrap and cut into thin slices.

To freeze: Place pinwheels in waxed cardboard boxes. Separate each layer with moisture- and vapour-proof paper. Seal, label and freeze.

To thaw: Leave at room temperature for 1½–2 hours.

To serve: Spread out on a large plate with a garnish of thin lemon wedges and sprigs of parsley.

Hot Toasted Ham Sandwiches

These delicious sandwiches make a quick lunch or supper dish. Keep a good store of them in the deep freeze for use in emergencies. They need no defrosting and only take about 8 minutes to cook.

4 slices of well-buttered white bread per person	1 egg
Thin slices of ham	1 cup milk
French mustard	Salt and pepper

METHOD

Spread buttered bread with mustard and sandwich with a generous filling of ham.

To freeze: Wrap each sandwich in moisture- and vapour-proof paper. Pack in polythene bags. Seal, label and freeze.

To serve: Beat egg with milk. Season with salt and pepper. Dip frozen sandwiches in egg mixture and fry for 4 minutes on each side.

Variations: Fill sandwiches with cheese slices, rare roast beef, etc.

Savoury-filled Sandwich Loaf

1 large white loaf, not too fresh
½ lb cream cheese
2 tablespoons chutney
Salt and pepper

¼ lb smoked salmon, finely chopped
½ lb butter
4 teaspoons tomato purée

METHOD

1. Cut the crusts from the loaf and slice horizontally as thinly as possible.
2. Beat the cheese with the chutney and seasoning.
3. Cream the butter and beat in the tomato paste. Mix in the smoked salmon.
4. Spread the loaf with alternate layers of cream cheese and smoked salmon butter. Press gently together.

To serve without freezing: Wrap in a cloth and leave in refrigerator for 2 hours. Garnish with cream cheese and chopped lettuce and cut in thin slices.

To freeze: Wrap loaf in moisture- and vapour-proof wrapping. Seal in a polythene bag, label and freeze.

To thaw: Leave wrapped loaf to thaw at room temperature for 1½ hours or until thawed. Spread the top with cream cheese and garnish with chopped lettuce.

Tomato and Cheese Pasties

PASTRY
8 oz plain flour
5 oz butter
3–4 tablespoons cold water
Salt
1 egg yolk
4 oz grated cheese
Pinch paprika pepper

FILLING
4 oz grated Cheddar cheese
3 spring onions, finely chopped
1 beaten egg
2 tomatoes, chopped
Salt and pepper

METHOD

1. *To make the pastry:* Sift the flour with the salt into a large bowl. Add the butter and cut with two knives into the flour. When the butter is in small pieces and well coated with flour, rub it well into the flour until the mixture looks like coarse breadcrumbs. Add the grated cheese and paprika pepper.

2. Add the egg yolk to the water. Make a well in the centre of the flour and add the cold water and egg yolk, keeping 1 tablespoon aside. Mix well with a flat knife. Press into a ball with the fingers, if necessary adding more water to form a firm dough.

3. Turn on to a floured board and knead lightly with the hands until smooth. Wrap in a cloth and chill in a cool place for at least ½ hour before rolling out.

4. *To make the filling:* Mix cheese with chopped onions and chopped tomatoes. Season with salt and pepper and bind with the beaten egg.

5. Roll out pastry to ⅛-inch thick. Cut into 3-inch rounds. Place a little of the filling in the centre of each round.

6. Fold in half and pinch edges firmly together.

To serve without freezing: Make a small slit in each pasty. Brush with milk and bake in a hot oven (425°F: Reg. 7) for 15 minutes until golden.

To freeze: Pack pasties in a suitable container, with a sheet of moisture- and vapour-proof paper between each layer. Seal, label and freeze.

To thaw: Place frozen pasties on a baking dish. Make a small slit in each one and brush with milk. Bake in a hot oven (425°F: Reg. 7) for 25 minutes until golden.

Serve: As a supper dish with a vegetable and salad, or make miniature ones to serve with cocktails.

Meat

Beef

Fillet of Beef in a Pastry Case

This is a complicated though delicious way of cooking a whole fillet of beef. The beef can only be frozen when half cooked and must be fully thawed before being returned to the oven. Deep-freezing cuts the preparation and cooking time by half.

2½ lb fillet of beef
2 tablespoons brandy
¾ lb mushrooms, finely chopped
1 tablespoon onion, finely chopped
1 tablespoon finely chopped bacon

2 oz butter
Salt and freshly ground black pepper
Puff pastry
1 beaten egg yolk
Bacon fat for larding

METHOD

1. Brush the fillet of beef with brandy. Lard the fillet with bacon fat and roast it for 15 minutes in a moderate oven (370°F: Reg. 4). Leave to cool.

2. Melt the butter in a saucepan. Add the chopped mushrooms, onion and bacon and fry for 10 minutes over a medium heat.

3. Cut the fillet into ½-inch slices three-quarters way through. Be careful not to cut right through the meat. Spread the mushroom mixture between each slice. Season the meat with salt and freshly ground black pepper.

4. Roll out the puff pastry to ⅛-inch thickness and wrap the

meat in the pastry, making a neat parcel. Seal the ends with milk or water.

To serve without freezing: Brush the pastry with cold water and bake the meat in a hot oven (440°F: Reg. 7) for 15 minutes. Brush the pastry with the beaten egg and bake for a further 5 minutes.

To freeze: Wrap the meat in a moisture- and vapour-proof wrapping and pack in a polythene bag. Seal, label and freeze.

To thaw: Leave wrapped meat to thaw in a refrigerator for at least 5 hours. Brush pastry with cold water and bake in a hot oven (440°F: Reg. 7) for 15 minutes. Brush with beaten egg and continue to bake for a further 5 minutes.

To serve: Cut through the slices with a sharp knife.

Boeuf Stroganoff

The famous Russian beef stew. Serve it as a party dish with buttered rice and a French salad.

1½ lb fillet of beef
½ lb mushrooms (leave whole if button mushrooms, chop if large)
2 onions, chopped fine
4 oz butter
1 heaped tablespoon flour

1 tin consommé
¼ pint of sour cream (or cream mixed with lemon juice)
Salt and freshly ground black pepper

METHOD

1. Beat the steak with a mallet or rolling pin until thin. Cut into strips about 2 inches long and ¼-inch wide.
2. Melt the butter in a heavy pan. Fry the onions in the butter until transparent.
3. Remove the onions and fry the meat in the butter until brown on all sides. Remove the meat and keep warm.
4. Fry the mushrooms in the juices for 2 minutes. Remove the

mushrooms. Add the flour to the juices in the pan. Stir well over a medium heat until the mixture is well blended.

5. Add the consommé and continue cooking until the mixture reaches boiling point. Add the onions, meat and mushrooms to the sauce. Season with salt and pepper.

To serve without freezing: Cover the pan and continue cooking for 15 minutes. Stir in the sour cream and serve immediately with buttered rice.

To freeze: Cool. Pack in suitable container. Seal, label and freeze.

To thaw: Turn the frozen mixture into a heavy pan. Heat over a low flame until thawed, stirring occasionally. When thawed, cook over a medium heat for 15 minutes. Add the sour cream and serve immediately.

BUTTERED RICE

Cook $\frac{1}{2}$ lb rice in boiling water until tender but still firm. Strain and rinse in cold water. Reheat in a saucepan with 2 oz melted butter, salt and plenty of ground pepper.

Rosettes of Beef

8 small slices of fillet steak
$\frac{1}{4}$ lb butter
4 tablespoons brandy
1 large onion, chopped
$\frac{1}{4}$ pint cream

$\frac{1}{4}$ pint beef bouillon or tinned consommé
Salt and freshly ground black pepper

METHOD

1. Melt the butter in a fireproof casserole with a tight-fitting lid. When hot add the beef.
2. Heat the brandy and pour over the meat. Set alight and leave to burn out over a medium heat.
3. Add the onion and cover with the cream and beef bouillon. Season with salt and freshly ground black pepper.

4. Cover tightly and bake in a moderate oven (350°F: Reg. 4) for 1 hour.

To serve without freezing: Continue cooking for a further ½ hour. Remove meat and arrange in a serving dish. Cover with the sauce.

To freeze: Cool. Pack in a suitable container. Seal, label and freeze.

To thaw: Turn into a casserole, cover and bake in a moderate oven (350°F: Reg. 4) for 40 minutes or until hot through and tender.

To serve: Remove meat and arrange on a serving dish. Pour over the sauce.

Note: If the sauce has separated or curdled: Pour a little of the butter into a saucepan. Add 1 tablespoon of flour and mix well over a medium heat. Slowly add the sauce, stirring all the time.

Steak au Poivre

4 rump steaks	¼ pint consommé
2 teaspoons black peppercorns	2 tablespoons brandy
1 oz butter	1 teaspoon cornflour
2 tablespoons oil	Pinch of salt

METHOD

1. Trim the steaks, removing all fat.
2. Crush the peppercorns with a pestle and mortar or with a rolling pin and press on to each side of the steaks so that they stick to the meat.
3. Heat the butter and oil in a large frying-pan. When the butter begins to foam add the steak and cook over a high heat for 1 minute on each side (a little longer if the steak is not to be frozen). Remove the meat from the pan and keep warm.
4. Add the consommé to the juices in the pan. Stir well over a moderate heat. Add the brandy and sprinkle in the cornflour.

Bring the sauce to the boil, stirring continually until smooth and shiny. Season with a little salt.

5. Pour the sauce over the steak.

To freeze: Cool quickly. Pack into a waxed cardboard box or suitable container. Seal, label and freeze.

To thaw: Place the frozen meat in a shallow bowl over hot water. Reheat over a medium heat until hot through.

Serve: With mashed potatoes and a green salad.

Boeuf à la Mode

A traditional French way of serving beef

3 lb rump or chuck steak	1 wineglass brandy
1 rasher fat bacon	2 carrots, chopped
2 oz butter	4 onions, chopped
1½ pints stock	Salt and pepper
¼ pint white wine	Bouquet garni

METHOD

1. Melt the butter in a large frying-pan and add the chopped bacon. When the fat is foaming add the meat and sear quickly on all sides.

2. Transfer the meat with the juices to a casserole. Add the stock, wine, brandy and vegetables. Season with salt and pepper and add the bouquet garni.

3. Cover the casserole with a tightly fitting lid and cook in a slow oven (300°F: Reg. 2) for 4½ hours.

4. Remove the bouquet garni. Skim the surface to remove as much fat as possible.

To serve without freezing: Continue to cook for a further 30 minutes. Remove the meat on to a heated dish and surround with the gravy.

To freeze: Cool quickly. Pack the meat in a suitable container well covered with the gravy. Seal, label and freeze.

To thaw: Turn the meat into a casserole dish. Cover and cook for 1¼ hours in a slow oven (300°F: Reg. 2) until hot through and tender.

Serve: With baked potatoes and a green salad.

Beef in Burgundy

1½ lb chuck steak or lean stewing steak
2 oz butter
1 large onion, chopped
4 carrots, chopped
1 oz flour

¼ pint red wine
¼ pint tinned consommé or stock
Salt and freshly ground black pepper
Bouquet garni

METHOD

1. Melt the butter in a heavy pan. When it is foaming add the steak, cut into 1-inch cubes, the onions and carrots.
2. Remove the meat and vegetables to a casserole dish.
3. Add the flour to the juices and mix well. Add the wine and consommé, slowly stirring all the time over a medium flame until the sauce is smooth. Season.
4. Pour the sauce over the meat. Add the bouquet garni, cover and cook in a moderate oven (320°F: Reg. 3) for 2½ hours.

To freeze: Cool quickly. Pack beef in a suitable container. Seal, label and freeze.

To thaw: Turn frozen beef into a casserole dish. Cover and cook in a moderate oven (320°F: Reg. 3) for 1 hour or until hot through and tender.

Swedish Beef Stew

2 lb chuck beef   3 large onions
2 beef bones   ½ teaspoon whole allspice
1½ oz butter   1 bay leaf
2 oz seasoned flour   ½ pint boiling water

METHOD

1. Cut meat into large cubes. Coat with seasoned flour.
2. Melt butter in a heavy skillet or saucepan. Add meat and brown on all sides.
3. Peel and chop onions roughly. Add to meat with bones, allspice and bay leaf. Cover with boiling water.
4. Cover and simmer over a low heat for 1 hour.

To serve without freezing: Cook for a further ½ hour until meat is really tender. Remove bones. Place meat in a serving dish and strain liquid over.

To freeze: Cool and skim off fat. Pack in a suitable container. Seal, label and freeze.

To thaw: Turn meat into a heavy skillet or saucepan. Cover and cook over a low heat for 1 hour until meat is tender. Remove bones. Place meat in a serving dish and strain liquid over.

Serve: Hot with boiled or mashed potatoes.

Sailors' Stew

2½ lb chuck or round of beef   ½ pint water
2 tablespoons butter   Dash of mushroom ketchup
4 onions, sliced   ½ lb mushrooms, sliced
Salt and pepper   1½ lb cooked potatoes
½ pint beer

1. Cut meat into slices ½-inch thick. Beat to tenderize.
2. Heat butter in a skillet or heavy saucepan. Add meat and brown over a fast heat on all sides. Remove meat and brown onions.
3. Place meat in a casserole with onions.
4. Add beer, water, mushroom ketchup and seasoning to the juices in the pan. Bring to the boil and pour over the meat and onions.
5. Cover and bake in a moderate oven for 1 hour.

To serve without freezing: Add the sliced mushrooms and cooked potatoes to the stew and cook for a further 20 minutes or until tender.

To freeze: Cool and pack in a suitable container. Seal, label and freeze.

To thaw: Turn into a casserole. Cover with aluminium foil and heat in a slow oven (310°F: Reg. 2) for 20 minutes. Add mushrooms and cooked potatoes and cook for a further 20 minutes or until meat is tender.

Curried Steak

A good way of serving beef not tender enough for grilling or frying

2 lb shin of beef
Salt and pepper
2 large onions, chopped
¼ pint boiling water
2 oz butter

SAUCE
1 tablespoon flour
1 tablespoon curry powder
    or paste
1 tablespoon sugar
¼ teaspoon dry mustard
Rind of 1 lemon, grated
2 tablespoons apricot chutney
1 tablespoon vinegar
¼ pint water

1. Cut the beef into cubes. Season with salt and pepper.
2. Melt the butter in a frying-pan and cook meat for 5 minutes, shaking well.
3. Arrange in a shallow casserole. Cover with the onions and pour over boiling water.
4. Cover and cook for ½ hour in a moderate oven (320°F: Reg. 3).
5. *To make the sauce:* Mix dry ingredients together. Add chutney, vinegar and water and mix well. Heat in a saucepan over a medium flame. Stir continuously, and cook until the sauce thickens.
6. Pour over the meat.

To serve without freezing: Return to the oven and continue cooking for a further ½ hour, or until the beef is tender.

To freeze: Cool. Pack in suitable container. Seal, label and freeze.

To thaw: Place frozen meat in a casserole. Cover with aluminium foil and cook in a moderate oven (320°F: Reg. 3) for 40 minutes or until steak is tender.

Steak and Kidney Pie

PASTRY
½ lb plain flour
3 oz butter
3 oz lard
4–8 tablespoons water

FILLING
1½ lb rump steak or skirt
½ lb ox kidney
Seasoned flour
1 onion, chopped
1 dessertspoon chopped parsley
12 oysters (optional)
Stock

METHOD

1. *To make the pastry:* Sift the flour. Rub in half the butter

with the fingertips. Mix to a firm dough with the water. Knead on a floured board until smooth.

2. Roll out. Cover two-thirds of the pastry with half the lard cut into small pieces. Fold into three. Pinch the edges together.

3. Roll out again. Repeat the process twice, using first the remaining butter and then the lard. Chill for 15–30 minutes.

4. *To make the filling:* Cut the steak and kidney into ½-inch cubes. Coat with seasoned flour.

5. Place the meat with the chopped onion and parsley in a pie dish. Cover with the stock and juice from the oysters.

6. Cover the dish with a double thickness of aluminium foil. Bake in a moderate oven for 1½ hours. Cool.

7. Add the oysters and remove excess liquid.

8. Roll out the pastry and cover the dish.

To serve without freezing: Cut two air vents in the pastry, brush with an egg beaten with a little salt. Cook in a hot oven (425°F: Reg. 6) for 40 minutes.

To freeze: Pack the pie in a polythene bag or wrap in freezer paper or aluminium foil. Seal, label and freeze.

To thaw: Cut two slits in frozen pastry. Brush with an egg beaten with a little salt. Bake in a hot oven (425°F: Reg. 6) for 55 minutes or until well browned.

Serve: Hot, with mashed potatoes and green vegetables.

Beef Rolls

2 lb beef steak in ¼-inch slices	2 oz seasoned flour
2 teaspoons French mustard	2 oz butter
8 rashers bacon	½ pint consommé or stock
4 frankfurters	4 tablespoons cream

METHOD

1. Beat the steak with a rolling pin until it is thin and flat – this also helps to tenderize it. Cut the meat into 4-inch × 2½-inch slices.

2. Spread each slice with a little mustard; cover with a rasher of bacon. Place half a frankfurter on each one and roll up tightly, securing with a toothpick. Coat each roll with seasoned flour.

3. Heat butter in a frying-pan or skillet. Brown rolls on all sides. Remove rolls and place in a deep casserole dish.

4. Heat consommé and pour over rolls. Bake in a moderate oven (350°F: Reg. 4) for ¾ hour.

To serve without freezing: Continue baking for 15 minutes. Place rolls in a warm serving dish. Remove toothpicks. Add the cream to the gravy in a saucepan and bring to the boil, stirring constantly. Pour over rolls.

To freeze: Cool and pack rolls with gravy in a suitable container.

To thaw: Turn into a shallow casserole, cover with aluminium foil and heat in a hot serving dish, taking out the toothpicks. Pour gravy into a saucepan. Add cream and bring to the boil, stirring constantly. Check for seasoning and pour over rolls.

Serve: Hot, with creamy mashed potatoes.

Cornish Pasty

1 lb plain flour	1 lb beef skirt
½ lb lard and butter mixed	½ lb potatoes
Pinch of salt	1 onion
6–8 tablespoons water	Salt and pepper

METHOD

1. *To make the pastry:* Sift the flour and salt and rub in the fat. Mix to a stiff dough with the water. Chill for 1 hour.

2. Divide into four rounds 7 inches in diameter.

3. *To make the filling:* Scrape the meat into small pieces. Peel and cut the potato into paper-thin slices. Peel and finely chop the onion. Mix together and season with salt and pepper.

4. Place a quarter of the filling in the centre of each round of pastry. Damp the edges and bring them together to form a semi-

circle. Crimp by pinching with the left hand and folding over with the right to form a rope effect.

5. Brush pasties with milk and cut a small hole in each. Cook in a hot oven (410°F: Reg. 6) for 10 minutes. Reduce heat to 350°F (Reg. 4) and continue baking for ½ hour.

To serve without freezing: Continue to cook for 15 minutes.

To freeze: Cool. Wrap each pasty in aluminium foil. Pack in a suitable container. Seal, label and freeze.

To thaw: Place frozen pasties wrapped in aluminium foil in a moderate oven (350°F: Reg. 4). Bake for 20 minutes. Unwrap and continue to cook for a further 10 minutes.

Chilli Con Carne

2 lb lean stewing beef
2 tablespoons olive oil
2 medium-sized onions, chopped
2 teaspoons chilli powder
1½ tablespoons flour

2 tins or 1 lb tomatoes
1 tin red beans
Salt
2 cloves garlic, minced

METHOD

1. Heat oil in a heavy saucepan. Fry beef and onions over a high heat until browned all over. Stir well to prevent sticking.
2. Add the chilli powder and flour and stir well.
3. Add the tinned tomatoes – or fresh tomatoes, skinned and chopped.
4. Cover and cook over a low heat for 1½ hours. Add the beans and salt.

To serve without freezing: Add the minced garlic and cook for a further 45 minutes, or until the meat is tender.

To freeze: Cool and pack into suitable containers. Seal, label and freeze.

To thaw: Turn into a heavy saucepan. Add garlic. Cover and cook over a low heat for 1 hour, stirring occasionally, until the meat is hot through and tender.

Serve: Hot with rice.

Russian Hamburgers

1½ lb minced rump or round steak
2 egg yolks
½ lb mashed cooked potatoes
4 tablespoons sour cream

1 tablespoon chopped parsley
1 medium onion, finely chopped
2 tablespoons finely chopped capers
Salt and pepper

METHOD

1. Mix steak, egg yolks, mashed potatoes and parsley together.
2. Gradually blend in cream. Mix really well.
3. Add onions and capers and season with salt and pepper.
4. Using floured hands, shape into flat cakes about 3 inches in diameter.

To freeze: Freeze uncovered. Wrap each cake in moisture- and vapour-proof paper. Pack in a suitable container. Seal, label and freeze.

To thaw: Cook frozen hamburgers in hot shallow fat until brown and hot through.

Serve: Immediately with a fried egg on each.

Cheeseburgers

1 lb minced steak – rump or chuck
4 thin slices of Gruyère or processed cheese

Salt and freshly ground black pepper

METHOD

Season the meat with salt and pepper and divide into four. Shape each portion into a flat cake with the cheese slices sandwiched in the centre of each cake.

To serve without freezing: Fry in butter for 5 minutes on each side.

To freeze: Freeze without wrapping. When solid wrap each cake in moisture- and vapour-proof wrapping; pack in a polythene bag or suitable container. Seal, label and freeze.

To thaw: Fry frozen cheeseburgers in hot butter for 8 minutes on each side.

Note: Thin slices of ham may be used instead of the cheese.

Meat Balls with Sour Cream Sauce

2 large onions, chopped
1 oz butter
1 lb finely minced beef (rump steak, round or chuck)
½ lb finely minced lean pork
¼ lb cooked mashed potatoes
2 ozs fresh white breadcrumbs
Salt and freshly ground black pepper
1 teaspoon chopped parsley
2 beaten eggs

SAUCE
1 teaspoon meat glaze (*See Note 2, p. 179*)
1 teaspoon tomato purée
3 tablespoons flour
½ pint stock
¼ pint sour cream

1. Melt the butter and fry the onions in a saucepan until golden, about 5 minutes.

2. Place the onions in a basin with the meat, potatoes, breadcrumbs, seasoning and parsley. Add the 2 beaten eggs and mix well.

3. Shape into balls. If the mixture is too dry add enough water to make it bind.

4. Fry the meat balls in plenty of hot fat or oil until well browned, shaking the pan all the time to keep them round. Keep warm.

5. *To make the sauce:* Add the meat glaze to the juices in the frying-pan. Add the flour and stir really well. Cook until the flour turns brown. Mix in the tomato purée.

6. Slowly add the stock and the sour cream. Cook, stirring all the time until the sauce is smooth. Strain over the meat balls.

To freeze: Cool, pack carefully into a suitable container. Seal, label and freeze.

To thaw: Turn frozen meat balls into a basin over hot but not boiling water. Cook over a medium heat for 30 minutes until hot through.

Serve: With a sprinkling of chopped parsley over spaghetti noodles.

Note 1: Small cocktail meat balls can be made using the same recipe. Pack carefully in a suitable container with a layer of moisture- and vapour-proof paper between each layer. Heat on a baking sheet in a medium-hot oven (400°F: Reg. 5) for 10 minutes or until hot through and crisp.

Note 2: To make a true meat glaze, 1 quart of stock, brown or white, should be reduced by boiling to 3 tablespoons.

Mexican Minced Beef

1 lb minced beef
1 tablespoon olive oil
2 large onions, chopped
1 oz flour
1 tin tomatoes

2 teaspoons Worcester sauce
1 small tin red kidney beans
½ pint strong stock
2 cloves garlic, crushed
Salt and pepper

METHOD

1. Heat oil in a saucepan. Fry onions until transparent.
2. Add meat and brown lightly.
3. Sprinkle the flour over and mix well.
4. Add the tomatoes, Worcester sauce, red beans and stock. Season with salt and pepper. Cover and cook over a low flame for ½ hour.

To serve without freezing: Add crushed garlic. Mix well and continue to cook for a further ½ hour.

To freeze: Cool quickly. Pack in a suitable container. Seal, label and freeze.

To thaw: Turn frozen meat into a heavy saucepan. Add garlic and cook over a low flame for 40 minutes or until tender.

Serve: With fluffy rice and green salad.

Farmhouse Beef Loaf

1½ lb lean minced beef
2 oz fresh white breadcrumbs
1 beaten egg
1 onion, chopped

2 tablespoons chopped parsley
1 tablespoon lemon juice
Salt and pepper
1 oz butter

METHOD

1. Mix the beef, breadcrumbs, egg, onion, parsley and lemon juice and seasonings together.
2. Spoon the mixture into a buttered loaf pan.

3. Melt the butter and pour over the top.
4. Bake the loaf in a moderate oven (350°F: Reg. 4) for 1 hour.
5. Leave to cool.

To freeze: Freeze the loaf in the pan. Turn out, wrap carefully in a polythene bag. Seal, label and freeze.

To thaw: Leave in a refrigerator for 5 hours or overnight. Cut the bag with scissors to avoid damaging the loaf and turn on to a plate.

To serve: Decorate with thin slices of tomato and cut into slices.

Note: The loaf can be reheated and served hot with a tomato sauce. Replace in the loaf pan. Cover with tin foil and heat in a moderate oven. Turn out and cover with a rich tomato sauce.

Swedish Cabbage Leaf Rolls

1 egg	Salt and pepper
1 small onion, chopped	½ pint milk
½ lb minced beef	6 large cabbage leaves
½ lb minced pork	1 tablespoon brown sugar
½ lb cooked rice	1 large tin tomatoes or
1 teaspoon Worcester sauce	tomato soup

METHOD

1. *To make stuffing:* Mix together beaten egg, onion, meat, rice and milk. Season with salt and pepper and Worcester sauce. Stir well.

2. *To prepare cabbage leaves:* Steam for 3 minutes to soften. Remove coarse stems.

3. Spoon 2 tablespoons stuffing on to each leaf and roll up firmly.

4. Place rolls in a baking dish. Sieve tinned tomatoes, mix with sugar and pour over – or, dilute tomato soup, mix with sugar and pour over rolls.

181

5. Cover and bake in a moderate oven (350°F: Reg. 4) for ¾ hour.

To serve without freezing: Continue baking for ½ hour or until tender.

To freeze: Cool. Pack in a suitable container. Seal, label and freeze.

To thaw: Turn into a greased casserole, cover and bake in a medium oven for 40 minutes or until tender.

Cottage Pie

The old 'left-over' standby, either the dreariest or, if well made, one of the most delicious of lunch dishes.

¾ lb cold meat (beef, lamb, mutton), coarsely minced, with no fat
1 dessertspoon dripping
2 medium onions, coarsely minced
2 carrots, coarsely minced
1 dessertspoon flour

½ pint stock
Tomato ketchup, Worcester sauce
Celery salt and freshly ground pepper
¾ lb boiled potatoes
Milk and butter

METHOD

1. Melt the dripping and fry the onions and carrots until they just turn transparent.
2. Add flour to the onions and stir well.
3. Mix in stock and bring to the boil. Season with celery salt and pepper. Flavour with tomato ketchup and Worcester sauce.
4. Simmer gravy for 3 minutes and pour over meat. Mix well.
5. Pour into a pie dish.
6. Mash potatoes with butter and milk. Season.
7. Cover meat with a layer of mashed potatoes. Dot with butter.

To serve without freezing: Cook in a hot oven for about 30 minutes.

To freeze: Wrap pie dish in a polythene bag. Seal, label and freeze.

To thaw: Leave the dish in the kitchen for 3 hours. Cook in a hot oven until the pie is hot and the top is crisp and brown. Or cover frozen pie with tin foil. Heat in a moderate oven (320°F: Reg. 3) for 30 minutes. Remove cover and cook for a further 5 minutes or until the top is brown and crusty.

Crêpes Bolognaises

PANCAKES	FILLING	SAUCE
2 eggs	2 tablespoons oil	1 tin Italian
¼ pint cream	1 large onion, chopped	tomatoes
1 oz melted butter	1 clove garlic, crushed	Salt and pepper
2 oz flour	½ lb minced cold meat	3 tablespoons
Milk	1 lb tomatoes, peeled	grated cheese
Salt and pepper	and chopped	
Butter for frying	6 oz tomato paste	
	¼ pint water	
	Salt and pepper	

METHOD

1. Make the pancake batter by beating together the eggs, cream and melted butter. Add to the sifted flour and beat until smooth.

2. Add enough milk to make the mixture the consistency of thin cream. Season and leave to stand for 30 minutes.

3. Melt a little butter in an omelet pan. When it is really hot add a spoonful of batter, swirling it round the pan until it is evenly coated. Cook over a hot flame for 1 minute each side. Add more milk if the batter is too thick. Stack the pancakes on a plate as each one is cooked.

4. For the filling heat the oil and fry the onion and garlic until transparent. Add the meat and continue to cook until brown.

5. Add the remaining ingredients. Cover and simmer for 30 minutes.

6. Place a spoonful of the filling in the centre of each pancake. Roll up and arrange in a shallow baking dish.

7. For the sauce put the tinned tomatoes through a fine sieve. Season with salt and pepper and pour over the pancakes.

To serve without freezing: Sprinkle the grated cheese over the surface. Bake in a hot oven (480°F: Reg. 7) until the top is brown and bubbling,

To freeze: Cool. Pack baking dish in a polythene bag (or pack pancakes and sauce in a suitable container). Seal, label and freeze.

To thaw: Sprinkle frozen pancakes with grated cheese. Cover and heat in a moderate oven (350°F: Reg. 4) for 30 minutes. Remove cover and brown in a hot oven.

To serve: Serve hot as a first course, or as a luncheon or supper dish.

Pytt i Panna

This is one of the best ways of using up the remains of a cold joint. It is easy to prepare and attractive to serve.

1 lb finely chopped cooked meat	Salt and pepper
2 onions, finely chopped	6 cooked potatoes, finely diced
6 rashers of bacon, chopped	4 eggs
2 tablespoons butter	

METHOD

1. Melt butter in a frying-pan. Add bacon and onions and fry until bacon is crisp and onions are lightly browned.

2. Add meat and fry for a further 3 minutes. Season.

To serve without freezing: Add potatoes and fry for a further 10 minutes. Transfer to a serving plate. Top with fried eggs.

To freeze: Cool and pack in a suitable container. Seal, label and freeze.

To thaw: Melt 1 tablespoon butter in a frying-pan, add the frozen meat and potatoes, and fry together for 10 minutes. Top with fried eggs.

Moussaka

(Meat and Aubergine Casserole)

1 lb minced raw beef, lamb or mutton	Salt and pepper
4 large onions, chopped	½ teaspoon sage
1 oz butter	1½ pints tomato sauce (or
2 tablespoons olive oil	sieved tinned tomatoes)
4 aubergines, sliced but not peeled	¼ pint thin cream
1 bay leaf, crumbled	1 egg

METHOD

1. Heat the olive oil and fry the aubergine until soft.
2. Fry the onions in the butter until transparent.
3. Butter a deep casserole. Fill it with alternate layers of aubergines, minced meat and onion. Season each layer with salt, pepper, sage and bay leaf.
4. Pour tomato sauce into casserole.
5. Cover and bake in a moderate oven (320°F: Reg. 3) for 45 minutes.

To serve without freezing: Beat egg with cream, season with salt and pepper and pour into casserole. Cook uncovered for a further 30 minutes in a slow oven (300°F: Reg. 1) until the custard has set.

To freeze: Cool. Cover with aluminium foil. Pack casserole in a polythene bag. Seal, label and freeze.

To thaw: Place covered casserole in a moderate oven for 20 minutes or until thawed. Pour over the beaten egg and cream and cook in a slow oven (300°F: Reg. 1) for a further 30 minutes or until the custard has set.

Note: Grated cheese can be sprinkled over the dish and browned before serving.

Meat Rolls

8 oz puff pastry
6 oz cooked meat
2 oz cooked ham
3 oz fresh breadcrumbs
1 teaspoon grated lemon rind

2 tablespoons stock
Salt and freshly ground black
    pepper
Beaten egg

METHOD

1. Mince the meat and ham. Mix with the breadcrumbs and lemon rind. Moisten with the stock and season with salt and pepper.

2. Roll out the pastry thinly. Cut into 3-inch squares. Place a little mixture on each square. Moisten the edges with water and roll up.

To serve without freezing: Brush with beaten egg and bake in a hot oven (410°F: Reg. 6) for 20 minutes or until golden brown.

To freeze: Pack frozen meat rolls in a rigid container with a sheet of moisture- and vapour-proof paper between layers. Seal, label and freeze.

To thaw: Place frozen rolls on a baking sheet. Brush with beaten egg and bake in a hot oven (410°F: Reg. 6) for 30 minutes or until golden brown.

Note: These can be made in miniature to serve with cocktails.

Left-over Beef with Piquant Sauce

A good way to freeze cold beef

Thin slices of roast or boiled
  beef

SAUCE
2 oz butter
1 oz flour
½ pint hot stock
3 tablespoons red wine vinegar

1 shallot, chopped
1 tablespoon chopped parsley
1 oz butter
2 tablespoons chopped
  gherkins
Salt
Freshly ground black pepper

METHOD

1. Melt the butter in a saucepan. Add the flour and stir well over a medium heat until the mixture turns brown. Do not burn. Slowly add the stock, stirring continually until the sauce is smooth.

2. Mix the vinegar, shallot, parsley and butter in a saucepan. Heat until the butter has melted.

3. Stir into the sauce.

4. Add the chopped gherkins and the thinly sliced meat. Season with salt and freshly ground black pepper.

To freeze: Cool. Pack in a suitable container. Seal, label and freeze.

To thaw: Turn frozen meat into a saucepan. Heat slowly until completely thawed and hot through.

Sausage Rolls

8 oz puff pastry
8 oz sausage meat

Beaten egg

1. Roll out the pastry thinly to a thin strip 3 inches wide.
2. Place the sausage meat along the centre of the pastry. Moisten the edges with water and roll up. Cut into 3-inch lengths.

To serve without freezing: Brush with beaten egg and cut two slits across each roll. Bake in a hot oven (410°F: Reg. 6) for 20 minutes until golden brown.

To freeze: Pack rolls in a rigid container with a sheet of moisture- and vapour-proof paper between layers. Seal, label and freeze.

To thaw: Brush frozen rolls with beaten egg. Cut two slits across each roll and bake in a hot oven (410°F: Reg. 6) for 30 minutes or until golden brown.

Note: These can be cut into ¾-inch rolls to serve with cocktails.

Corned Beef Pie

A cheap and easy dish very popular with children

	SAUCE
½ lb corned beef	1 oz butter
6 spring onions	1 oz flour
½ lb mashed potato	¼ pint milk
2 oz grated cheese	4 oz cheese
	Salt and pepper

METHOD

1. Melt the butter in a saucepan. Add the flour and mix well over a medium heat until the mixture forms a ball and comes away from the sides of the pan.
2. Gradually add the milk, stirring all the time. Bring to the boil.
3. Remove from the heat and add 4 oz of cheese. Stir until the cheese has melted. Season with salt and pepper.

4. Flake the corned beef, chop the onions and add to the cheese sauce. Turn into a buttered pie dish. Cover the surface with mashed potato.

To serve without freezing: Sprinkle the remaining grated cheese over the surface. Bake in a hot oven (425°F: Reg. 6) for 15 minutes until golden brown.

To freeze: Cool pie. Pack in a polythene bag. Seal, label and freeze.

To thaw: Place pie dish in a moderate oven for 20 minutes. Sprinkle with grated cheese and cook in a hot oven for a further 10 minutes or until hot through and golden brown.

Veal

Escalopes à l'Estragon

4 veal escalopes	1 teaspoon chopped fresh
3 tablespoons seasoned flour	tarragon or 2 teaspoons
2 oz butter	dried tarragon
¼ pint dry white wine	Paprika
Juice of ½ lemon	Salt and freshly ground black
2 tablespoons tomato paste	pepper

METHOD

1. Ask your butcher to flatten the escalopes. Coat them on both sides with the seasoned flour.
2. Melt the butter in a heavy pan. Fry the escalopes on both sides until brown over a fierce heat.
3. Lower the heat and add the white wine, stirring well to scrape up the juices from the pan.
4. Add the tarragon leaves, lemon juice and tomato paste and mix well. Season with salt and freshly ground black pepper.
5. Cover and simmer over a low heat for 10 minutes.

To serve without freezing: Continue to cook for a further 10 minutes. Sprinkle the surface with a little paprika and serve with mashed potatoes and a green salad.

To freeze: Cool. Pack in a suitable container. Seal, label and freeze.

To thaw: Turn frozen escalopes into a shallow dish. Cover with aluminium foil and heat in a moderate oven (350°F: Reg. 4) for 25 minutes or until hot through and tender.

Serve: With a sprinkling of paprika over the surface.

Stuffed Escalopes

8 small thin veal escalopes	4 thin slices of Gruyère
4 slices of ham	2 oz mushrooms, chopped
1 oz butter	2 tablespoons stock
2 tablespoons grated Gruyère	

METHOD

1. Melt ½ oz butter in a saucepan and lightly fry the mushrooms for 5 minutes.
2. Cover 4 slices of veal with a slice of ham, mushrooms and grated cheese. Place the other escalopes over the top and sandwich firmly together.
3. Melt ½ oz butter in a heavy pan. When it is hot put in the veal and brown on both sides for 3 minutes.
4. Place veal in a shallow baking dish. Cover each piece with a slice of Gruyère.
5. Pour the stock into the juices in the frying-pan. Stir well until the sauce bubbles.
6. Pour the sauce over the veal.

To serve without freezing: Bake covered in a medium-hot oven (400°F: Reg. 5) for 15 minutes.

To freeze: Cool. Put into a suitable container or leave in the baking dish. Pack in a polythene bag or freezer paper. Seal, label and freeze.

To thaw: Cover frozen veal with tin foil. Bake in a moderate oven (350°F: Reg. 4) for 30 minutes or until thawed through and tender.

Blanquette de Veau

1½ lb breast or neck of veal
1 carrot
1 onion
Bouquet garni
2 pints veal or chicken stock
2 oz butter
2 oz flour

6 shallots
½ lb mushrooms
Salt and pepper
2 egg yolks
2 tablespoons water
½ teaspoon lemon juice

METHOD

1. Cut the veal into ¾-inch cubes. Put into a saucepan with the carrot and the onion cut in pieces. Add the bouquet garni and stock.

2. Bring to the boil, skim the surface. Reduce the heat and simmer for 20 minutes.

3. Strain and reserve the stock. Remove the veal and keep warm.

4. Melt the butter in a saucepan. Add the flour and mix well. Slowly add the stock, stirring over a medium flame until the sauce is smooth.

5. Add the shallots, mushrooms and the seasoning to the sauce and simmer for 20 minutes. Add the veal and cook for a further 15 minutes.

To serve without freezing: Beat the egg yolks with 2 tablespoons water. Add a little of the hot sauce and mix well. Remove the blanquette from the heat and stir in the egg yolks. Do not reboil. Stir in the lemon juice and serve immediately.

To freeze: Cool. Pack into a suitable container. Seal, label and freeze.

To thaw: Place frozen blanquette in a basin over hot water. Heat until thawed through and hot – about 30 minutes. Add a little of the hot sauce to the egg yolks beaten with 2 tablespoons water. Remove the blanquette from the heat. Mix in the egg yolks. Add the lemon juice and stir well.

Serve: Immediately with a dusting of chopped parsley.

Osso Buco

(Veal Stew)

2 lb shin of veal	Salt and pepper
2 oz butter	1 tablespoon chopped parsley
¼ pint white wine	1 clove garlic, chopped
¾ lb tomatoes	Grated peel of ½ lemon
¼ pint stock	

METHOD

1. Ask your butcher to cut the shin into serving pieces 2 inches thick.
2. Melt the butter in a heavy pan. Brown the veal on all sides.
3. Arrange the veal so that the pieces stand upright. Pour the wine over and cook over a fast flame for 10 minutes. Add the peeled and chopped tomatoes and cook for a further 10 minutes.
4. Add the stock and season with salt and pepper. Cover and cook in a moderate oven (350°F: Reg. 4) for 1½ hours.

To serve without freezing: Continue to cook for ½ hour. Sprinkle the surface with chopped parsley, garlic and grated lemon peel and serve.

To freeze: Cool. Pack in a suitable container. Seal, label and freeze.

To thaw: Turn frozen veal into a casserole. Cover and cook in a moderate oven (350°F: Reg. 4) for 40 minutes or until hot through and tender.

Serve: Hot, with chopped parsley, garlic and grated lemon peel over the top.

Sweet and Sour Veal

1 lb veal	¼ pint stock
1 medium tin pineapple titbits	1 tin bean sprouts
1½ oz butter	¼ lb mushrooms, sliced
1 medium onion, chopped	2 tablespoons cornflour
3 stalks of celery, chopped	2 tablespoons soy sauce
Salt and pepper	1 teaspoon monosodium glutamate

METHOD

1. Cut the veal into 1½-inch cubes.
2. Melt butter and brown veal on all sides.
3. Add onion, celery, salt, pepper, stock and pineapple juice.
4. Cover and simmer over a low heat for 1 hour or until veal is tender.
5. Add pineapple, bean sprouts and mushrooms.
6. Mix cornflour with soy sauce and monosodium glutamate. Stir into veal mixture. Cook over a low heat until thickened.

To freeze: Cool. Pack into a suitable container. Seal, label and freeze.

To thaw: Turn into a saucepan. Heat over a medium flame until thawed through.

Serve: Hot over a bed of fluffy rice.

Veal and Ham Pie

(Untraditional)

8 oz plain flour
3 oz butter
3 oz lard
4–8 tablespoons cold water
1½ lb shoulder of veal or
  pie veal
4 oz ham

1 tablespoon chopped onion
1 tablespoon chopped parsley
Pinch of sage
Grated rind of ½ lemon
Salt and pepper
Firm jelly stock

METHOD

1. *To make the pastry:* Sift the flour. Rub in half the butter with the fingertips. Mix to a firm dough with the water. Knead on a floured board until smooth.

2. Roll out. Cover two-thirds of the pastry with half the lard cut into small pieces. Fold into three. Pinch the edges together.

3. Roll out again. Repeat the process twice, using first the remaining butter and then the lard. Chill for 15–30 minutes.

4. *To make the filling:* Cut the veal into 1-inch cubes. Cut the ham into strips.

5. Arrange the meat, ham, onions, parsley, sage and lemon rind in a pie dish. Season with salt and pepper. Fill nearly to the top with stock.

6. Roll out the pastry, cover the dish, cut two air vents and brush over with 1 egg beaten with a little salt.

7. Bake in a hot oven (425°F: Reg. 7) for 40 minutes. Cover the whole pie with dampened greaseproof paper. Return to a moderate oven (350°F: Reg. 4) for a further 1½ hours.

Leave to get cold.

To freeze: Pack pie in a polythene bag or wrap in freezer paper or aluminium foil. Seal, label and freeze.

To thaw: Leave in refrigerator overnight or for at least 8 hours until thawed.

Serve: Cold, with salad.

Veal Meat Balls with Tomato Sauce

1 lb finely minced veal
2 oz minced pork fat
1 small onion, chopped
1 teaspoon chopped parsley
1 teaspoon chopped thyme
5 oz stale white breadcrumbs
Milk
¼ pint cold water
Salt and paprika
Flour
Fat for frying

SAUCE
1 oz butter
½ oz flour
¼ pint stock
1 teaspoon mixed herbs
1 lb tomatoes or 1 large tin
   tomatoes, chopped
3 tablespoons sour cream
8 black olives
1 lemon
Salt and pepper
Sugar

METHOD

1. Soak the bread in milk until soft.
2. Mix the bread with the finely chopped onion, veal, fat, parsley and thyme. Season with salt and paprika.
3. Beat the mixture well, slowly adding the water. Continue to beat until the mixture is almost smooth.
4. Shape the meat into small balls. Roll in flour.
5. Heat the fat and fry the balls over a hot flame until brown.
6. *To make the sauce:* Melt the butter in a saucepan. Add the flour and mix well. Add the stock slowly, stirring all the time, and bring to the boil.
7. Add the tomatoes and herbs. Season with salt, pepper and sugar. Cover and simmer for 30 minutes. Rub through a fine sieve.

To serve without freezing: Place the meat balls in a baking dish, cover with the tomato sauce and bake in a moderate oven (325°F: Reg. 4) for 15 minutes. Stir in the sour cream, and garnish with the stoned olives cut into halves and the lemon in quarters.

To freeze: Cool and pack veal balls with the tomato sauce in a suitable container. Seal, label and freeze.

To thaw: Place frozen veal balls in a baking dish. Cover and heat in a moderate oven (325°F: Reg. 4) for 30 minutes. Remove the cover and stir in the cream.

To serve: Garnish with halved stoned olives and the lemon cut into quarters.

Mock Escalopes of Veal

A good way of tenderizing tough veal

½ lb veal	Salt and pepper
1 small onion	Beaten egg and breadcrumbs
1 tablespoon parsley	Fat for frying
2 eggs	

METHOD

1. Mince veal, onion and parsley together through a fine mincing blade.
2. Mix with 2 beaten eggs. Season with salt and pepper.
3. Using floured hands shape the meat into flat cakes about 3 inches in diameter. Place on waxed paper and leave to chill for ½ hour.
4. Coat cakes in beaten egg and breadcrumbs.

To freeze: Freeze cakes unpacked. Wrap each in a piece of moisture- and vapour-proof paper. Pack in a suitable container. Seal, label and freeze.

To thaw: Fry frozen cakes in hot shallow fat until golden brown and hot through.

Cold Veal in Tarragon Sauce

Slices of cold veal
SAUCE

2 oz butter	2 tablespoons chopped
1 oz flour	tarragon
¼ pint chicken or veal stock	1 teaspoon lemon juice
¼ pint dry white wine	Salt and pepper

1. Melt the butter in a saucepan. Add the flour and mix well over a medium heat until the mixture turns brown.

2. Add the stock and wine, stirring continually until the sauce is smooth. Add the lemon juice and tarragon, and season with salt and pepper.

3. Add the veal and simmer over a low heat for 15 minutes.

To serve without freezing: Simmer for a further 15 minutes. Serve immediately.

To freeze: Cool. Pack in a suitable container. Seal, label and freeze.

To thaw: Turn frozen veal into a heavy pan. Heat over a medium flame, stirring occasionally to prevent sticking. When hot, cover and simmer for 15 minutes.

Serve: Immediately, with the meat arranged on a serving dish and the sauce poured over.

Lamb

Lamb and Cabbage Casserole

3 lb shoulder of lamb	Salt
1 small white cabbage	Freshly ground black pepper
1 oz fat	Parsley
4 rashers lean bacon	

METHOD

1. Cut the lamb into 1-inch cubes. Chop the bacon into small bits. Shred the cabbage.

2. Melt the fat in a frying-pan. Fry the bacon in the fat for 5 minutes. Remove the bacon and brown the meat on all sides.

3. Remove the meat and brown the cabbage in the pan.

4. Arrange alternate layers of meat and cabbage in a casserole with some of the bacon in each layer. Season with salt and freshly ground black pepper. Cover and cook in a moderate oven (350°F: Reg. 3) for 45 minutes.

To serve without freezing: Continue to cook for a further 15 minutes, or until the lamb is tender. Serve with a garnish of chopped parsley.

To freeze: Cool. Pack the casserole in a polythene bag, or wrap in freezer paper or aluminium foil. Seal, label and freeze.

To thaw: Cover frozen casserole and thaw in a moderate oven (350°F: Reg. 3) for 30–40 minutes until the casserole is hot through and the meat tender.

Serve: With a garnish of chopped parsley.

Turkish Lamb Stew

Easy and spicy

2 lb lamb
1 green pepper, seeded and sliced
4 tomatoes, peeled and sliced
3 large onions, sliced
1 teaspoon chopped fennel or dill
1 teaspoon chopped sage

2 bay leaves
Salt and pepper
1½ pints meat stock
4 potatoes, peeled and diced
2 cloves garlic, chopped

METHOD

1. Put all the ingredients except the potatoes and garlic into a large stewpan. Cover and bring to the boil. Skim the surface to remove scum.

2. Simmer for 1¾ hours.

To serve without freezing: Add garlic and chopped potatoes and continue cooking for 45 minutes or until the meat is tender.

To freeze: Cool and pack into a suitable container. Seal, label and freeze.

To thaw: Put frozen stew into a heavy pan. Heat over a medium heat until thawed. Add potatoes and garlic, cover and simmer for a further 45 minutes until lamb is tender.

Lancashire Hotpot

2 lb lamb chops (8)	½ pint rich stock
2 large onions	1½ lb potatoes
4 oz mushrooms	½ oz melted butter
2 lambs' kidneys	Salt and pepper
8 oysters – fresh or tinned	

METHOD

1. Trim the chops, removing fat and gristle. Use trimmings for stock.
2. Slice the mushrooms, the onions and the kidneys. Clean the oysters.
3. Butter a deep casserole. Place the chops and kidneys with the oysters in the dish. Cover with the onions and mushrooms. Pour in enough stock to cover. Season with salt and pepper.
4. Cover the dish and bake in a moderate oven for 2 hours.

To freeze: Cool, pack in a suitable container, or leave in the casserole dish and pack in a polythene bag. Seal, label and freeze.

To thaw: Place the frozen casserole in a moderate oven. Parboil the potatoes for 20 minutes. Drain and slice and arrange in a layer over the frozen casserole. Pour over ½ oz melted butter. Cover with a piece of buttered paper and bake for 35 minutes or until the meat is hot through and tender. Remove the paper and brown the potatoes for 5 minutes.

Serve: Straight from the casserole dish.

Spécialité Lamb Cutlets

An unusual and special way of cooking lamb cutlets

8 cutlets from best end neck
of lamb
Butter for frying
6 oz mushrooms, chopped
½ oz butter
2 oz minced ham

1 dessertspoon chopped
parsley
2 teaspoons tomato purée
Pinch of salt and pepper
1 dessertspoon hot water
¼ lb puff pastry
1 beaten egg

METHOD

1. Ask your butcher to trim the cutlets so that the end of each bone is scraped clean. Fry them until tender in butter.

2. In a bowl, mix together the mushrooms, butter, ham, parsley, tomato purée, salt and pepper and hot water.

3. Roll out the pastry and cut into eight, 6-inch oval pieces.

4. Spread a spoonful of filling on each piece. Place a cutlet on top. Spread more filling on the cutlet.

5. Moisten the edges of the pastry with water and fold over, pinching the edges together. The meat of the cutlet should be completely encased but 1½ inches of bone should be left sticking out of the pastry parcel.

To serve without freezing: Brush with beaten egg and bake in a hot oven (410°F: Reg. 6) for 25 minutes.

To freeze: Wrap each cutlet carefully in moisture- and vapour-proof paper. Pack in suitable containers. Seal, label and freeze.

To thaw: Brush frozen pastry with beaten egg. Place on a baking sheet and bake in a medium-hot oven (380°F: Reg. 5) for 40 minutes, until hot through and golden brown.

Pork

Fillet of Pork with Prunes

2½ lb fillet of pork   Salt
1 tin prunes   Freshly ground black pepper
4 rashers bacon

METHOD

1. Stone prunes and reserve liquid.
2. Using a sharp knife, make incisions through meat and stuff with prunes.
3. Season meat with salt and pepper and wrap in bacon rashers.
4. Place meat in a shallow casserole. Bake in a moderate oven (350°F: Reg. 5) for 45 minutes. Add prune juice and continue to bake for a further 10 minutes, basting frequently.

To serve without freezing: Continue to bake for a further 20 minutes.

To freeze: Cool. Skim fat. Pack in suitable container. Seal, label and freeze.

To thaw: Turn into shallow casserole. Cover with aluminium foil. Bake in a slow oven (310°F: Reg. 2) for 30 minutes. Remove foil, increase heat (to 350°F: Reg. 4) and bake for a further 25 minutes, basting frequently.

Serve: Hot, cut into serving pieces. This is also delicious cold.

Crisp Sweet and Sour Pork

½ lb lean pork
2 tablespoons flour
1 egg
Salt and pepper
Deep fat for frying

SAUCE
1 small tin pineapple titbits
1 large carrot
1 green pepper
1 tablespoon olive oil
1 tablespoon cornflour
2 teaspoons soy sauce
1 tablespoon brown sugar
2 tablespoons vinegar
1 tablespoon chopped sweet
pickles

METHOD

1. Cut the pork into 1-inch cubes. Beat the egg and add to the flour. Season with salt and pepper. Coat the pork with the thick batter and fry in deep fat until lightly browned.

2. *To make the sauce:* Drain the pineapple and reserve the juice.

3. Chop the carrot and green pepper and fry in the olive oil for 2 minutes. Add the cornflour, stir in the pineapple juice and mix well until smooth.

4. Add the remaining ingredients. Bring to the boil and simmer for 3 minutes.

Note: The carrot and pepper should be *crunchy.*

To serve without freezing: Return the pork to the deep fat and fry until crisp and golden brown. Serve, surrounded by the sweet and sour sauce, with boiled rice.

To freeze: Cool. Pack the pork in a suitable container, separating the pieces with moisture- and vapour-proof wrapping. Pack the sauce in a waxed tub. Seal, label and freeze.

To thaw: Turn frozen sauce into a thick pan and heat over a low flame until thawed and hot through. Place frozen pork on a greased baking sheet and bake in a hot oven (420°F: Reg. 6) for 10–15 minutes until golden brown. Serve as above.

Do not keep frozen for longer than 1 month.

Pork with Apples and Ginger

1 tablespoon olive oil
2 lb pork, cut into 1-inch cubes
3 tart apples
2 tablespoons chopped sweet
  ginger

2 beef bouillon cubes
¾ pint water
½ teaspoon freshly ground
  black pepper

METHOD

1. Heat the oil in a heavy saucepan over a high heat.
2. Add the pork and brown quickly.
3. Peel, core and chop apples. Spread apples and ginger on the bottom of a casserole. Place pork on top.
4. Dissolve bouillon cubes in water and pour over pork. Season.
5. Cover and bake in a moderate oven (350°F: Reg. 4) for 45 minutes.

To serve without freezing: Remove cover and increase heat to 400°F (Reg. 5) and bake for a further 15 minutes until pork is browned and crisp.

To freeze: Cool and skim off surface fat. Freeze in casserole, or remove from casserole when frozen. Pack, seal, label and freeze.

To thaw: Cover casserole with aluminium foil. Bake in a slow oven (310°F: Reg. 2) for 30 minutes. Remove foil, increase heat to 400°F (Reg. 5) and bake for a further 15 minutes.

Serve: With spiced red cabbage.

Pork Chops and Rosemary

Rosemary is one of the most versatile of herbs. Delicious with lamb, chicken and fish, but best of all with pork.

4 pork chops
1 tablespoon olive oil
1 large onion, chopped
½ lb tomatoes, chopped and
 peeled

2 teaspoons rosemary
1 glass port
Salt and pepper
1 clove garlic

METHOD

1. Heat the olive oil in a frying-pan. Brown the chops on both sides. Remove and place in a shallow casserole.

2. Fry the onion in the oil until transparent. Add the tomatoes, rosemary and seasoning. Pour in the port and stir until bubbling.

3. Pour the sauce over the chops.

To serve without freezing: Add 1 crushed garlic clove and bake in a moderate oven (350°F: Reg. 4) for 20 minutes or until the chops are tender.

To freeze: Skim off any excess fat. Cool. Pack in a suitable container. Seal, label and freeze.

To thaw: Place frozen chops in a shallow baking dish. Add 1 crushed clove of garlic. Cover with aluminium foil and bake in a moderate oven (350°F: Reg. 4) for 30 minutes. Remove the cover and bake for a further 5 minutes.

Barbecued Spare Ribs of Pork

2 lb spare ribs
¼ pint sweet sherry
1 tablespoon lemon juice
1 tablespoon oil
1 small onion, chopped
¼ pint water
2 tablespoons white wine
 vinegar

1 tablespoon Worcester sauce
2 tablespoons lemon juice
2 tablespoons brown sugar
¼ pint chilli sauce
Salt
Pinch of paprika pepper

METHOD

1. Ask your butcher to cut the spare ribs into pieces for serving. Rub with salt and paprika, and marinate overnight in the sherry and 1 tablespoon lemon juice. Turn to make sure they are well soaked.

2. Heat the olive oil in a saucepan. Add the onion and cook until brown.

3. Add the other ingredients. Cover and simmer over a low heat for 20 minutes.

4. Place spare ribs in a pan. Cover with aluminium foil and bake in a very hot oven (480°F: Reg. 9) for 15 minutes.

5. Remove foil, cover with the sauce and continue baking in a moderate oven (350°F: Reg. 4) for 45 minutes, basting frequently.

To serve without freezing: Continue to bake for a further 30 minutes, basting frequently.

To freeze: Cool and skim fat. Pack into a suitable container. Seal, label and freeze.

To thaw: Turn into a shallow pan. Cover with aluminium foil. Bake in a slow oven (300°F: Reg. 2) for 20 minutes. Remove foil. Separate ribs with a fork and continue baking for a further 30 minutes, basting frequently.

Serve: Hot, with mashed potatoes or rice.

Home-made Baked Beans

Once you have made these you will wonder why you ever considered eating the tinned ones.

1 lb large white beans
¾ lb lean salt pork
1 large onion

8 fluid oz golden syrup or
black treacle
1 teaspoon dry mustard

METHOD

1. Wash beans and soak for at least 12 hours in ¾ pint water, then drain.

2. Put the beans in a saucepan with enough water to cover. Simmer for 20 minutes or until skins begin to split and loosen.

3. Cut salt pork into 1-inch cubes and blanch in boiling water for 2 minutes.

4. Chop the onion and put in the bottom of a deep casserole. Add the pork and the beans, the treacle and mustard and mix well. Fill the casserole with water, cover and bake in a slow oven (300°F: Reg. 2) for 9 hours. Add more water as the beans swell.

5. Remove the cover and bake for another ½ hour.

To freeze: Cool. Pack into suitable containers. Seal, label and freeze.

To thaw: Turn frozen beans into a saucepan and heat over a medium flame until thawed through and hot.

Note: These quantities are enough for 10 people. Because salt pork develops an off-flavour if stored for too long in the deep freeze, these beans should not be kept for longer than 2 months.

Sausages and Cabbage

1 lb pork chipolata sausages
1 oz bacon fat
3 tablespoons flour
1 pint hot stock

Salt and pepper
Bouquet garni
1 medium white cabbage

METHOD

1. Prick the sausages with a fork and fry in the bacon fat until well browned on all sides.

2. Quarter the cabbage and boil in salted water for 15 minutes. Drain and shred.

3. Remove the sausages and add the flour, mix well and slowly add the stock, stirring all the time until the sauce is smooth.

4. Add the bouquet garni to the sauce. Season with salt and pepper.

5. Add the cabbage and sausages to the sauce. Cover and simmer for 15 minutes.

To serve without freezing: Continue to simmer for a further 15 minutes. Arrange the cabbage on a dish and place the sausages round it. Remove the bouquet garni and pour over the sauce.

To freeze: Cool. Pack in a suitable container. Seal, label and freeze.

To thaw: Turn frozen cabbage and sausages into a heavy pan. Heat over a medium heat until thawed through. Cover and simmer for 15 minutes. Remove bouquet garni and serve as above.

Bean and Bacon Pie

A cheap, easy supper dish for children

1 large tin baked beans	1 lb cooked potatoes
1 oz butter or fat	Milk
1 small onion, chopped	Salt and pepper
4 oz streaky bacon, chopped	

METHOD

1. Melt the butter in a pan. Fry the onion and the bacon in the fat until the onion is light brown.

2. Mix the onion and the bacon with the beans and pour into a small casserole dish.

3. Mash the potatoes with a little milk. Season with salt and pepper and spread over the casserole.

To serve without freezing: Bake in a medium-hot oven (400°F: Reg. 5) for 20 minutes until the potato is browned.

To freeze: Cool. Pack the casserole in a polythene bag, or wrap in freezer paper or aluminium foil. Seal, label and freeze.

To thaw: Cover frozen casserole with aluminium foil. Heat in a moderate oven (350°F: Reg. 4) for 20 minutes until hot through. Increase heat to 400°F (Reg. 5) and cook for 20 minutes until the potato is brown.

Mousse de Jambon

1½ lb cooked lean ham
2 tablespoons tomato purée
Pinch paprika pepper
⅓ pint double cream

½ oz gelatine
5 tablespoons water
Salt and pepper

METHOD

1. Mince the ham. Add the tomato purée and paprika.
2. Put the mixture through a fine sieve, or purée in an electric blender.
3. Whip the cream. Melt the gelatine in a little water and add both slowly to the ham mixture, stirring well. Season with salt and pepper.
4. Turn into a mould and leave to set.

To freeze: Pack mould in a polythene bag. Seal, label and freeze.

To thaw: Leave mould wrapped in a refrigerator until thawed – about 4 hours.

To serve: Turn out and serve on a bed of chopped aspic jelly.

Ham Rolls with Creamed Spinach

8 thin slices of smoked ham or
  Italian Parma ham
½ lb grated Gruyère cheese
1 lb fresh spinach
1 oz butter

3 tablespoons flour
½ pint milk
Salt and pepper
½ teaspoon lemon juice

1. *To make the creamed spinach:* Boil the spinach in a little water until tender. Drain well and chop finely.

2. Melt butter in a saucepan over a medium heat. Add the flour and stir well until the butter and flour form a ball. Add the milk slowly, stirring continually until a thick smooth cream is formed.

3. Add the spinach and season with salt, pepper and lemon juice.

4. Place a spoonful of spinach on each slice of ham and roll up. Put them in a baking dish and cover with the remaining spinach.

To freeze: Place the dish in a polythene bag. Seal, label and freeze.

To thaw: Remove the dish from the plastic bag, cover with tin foil and heat in a moderate oven (330°F: Reg. 3) for 30 minutes until hot through. Or thaw at room temperature and heat through in a hot oven (410°F: Reg. 6) for 10 minutes.

To serve: Remove tin foil, sprinkle the cheese over the surface and brown quickly under the grill. Serve immediately.

Braised Ham with Mushroom Sauce

2½ lb processed ham or gammon
2 oz butter
1 small onion, sliced
1 small carrot, sliced
Bouquet garni
¼ pint dry white wine
¼ pint chicken stock
¼ pint water

SAUCE
½ lb mushrooms, chopped
2 tablespoons butter
1½ tablespoons flour
2 tablespoons double cream
¼ pint stock from ham
Juice of ½ lemon
½ lb cooked small green peas
Pepper

METHOD

1. In a heavy pan melt the butter and lightly brown the sliced onion and carrot.

2. Add the ham, bouquet garni, wine, chicken stock and water. Simmer over a low heat for 1 hour 5 minutes (about 15 minutes to the lb).

3. Leave the ham to cool for 15 minutes in the liquid. Remove ham and strain the stock.

4. *To make the sauce:* Skim the fat from the stock and boil fiercely until it is reduced by two-thirds.

5. Melt butter in a saucepan. Fry mushrooms for 5 minutes. Stir in flour and gradually add ½ pint stock, stirring all the time until the sauce is smooth.

6. Add the cream and continue stirring.

7. Add the cooked peas to the sauce with the juice of ½ lemon. Season with pepper.

To serve without freezing: Carve the ham into thick slices. Arrange in a baking dish and pour over sauce.

To freeze: Slice ham into thick slices. Pack in a suitable container. Pour over cooled sauce. Pack, seal, label and freeze.

To thaw: Turn into a shallow bowl over a saucepan of hot water. Cook over a medium heat until hot and thawed through. Remove ham and arrange in a shallow dish. Pour over sauce.

Serve: At once.

Offal

Liver and Bacon

1½ lb calves' liver cut into ½-inch thick slices
½ lb bacon
2 oz mushrooms (optional)
3 large onions

1 oz butter
1 tablespoon flour
⅛ pint cider
½ pint stock
Salt and pepper

1. Heat butter in a heavy pan. Fry the liver over a high heat until brown on all sides – about 5 minutes. Remove and keep warm in a casserole dish.
2. Chop bacon into small strips, slice onions and mushrooms, fry in the butter for 2 minutes.
3. Add the flour and mix well.
4. Gradually stir in the stock and cider, stirring all the time until the gravy is smooth. Season. Bring to the boil and pour over the liver.
5. Cover and cook in a moderate oven (350°F: Reg. 3) for 30 minutes.

To serve without freezing: Cook for a further 20 minutes, or until the liver is tender.

To freeze: Cool, pack in a suitable container, seal, label and freeze.

To thaw: Turn frozen liver into a casserole dish. Cover with aluminium foil and bake in a moderate oven (350°F: Reg. 3) until the liver is hot through and tender – about 40 minutes.

Calves' Liver in Tin-foil Cases

4 slices calves' liver
2 oz butter
Olive oil
8 thin rashers bacon

1 tablespoon chopped parsley
1 tablespoon finely chopped onion
Salt and pepper

METHOD

1. Melt the butter in a frying-pan. When it begins to foam put in the liver and fry until browned – about 2 minutes each side.
2. Cut four pieces of aluminium foil twice the size of the liver. Spread with a film of olive oil. Lay 1 rasher of bacon on each. Sprinkle with parsley and onion. Season with a little salt and pepper.

3. Cover with 1 slice of liver. Sprinkle over a little more onion, parsley and seasoning and lay 1 rasher of bacon on top.

4. Fold over the aluminium foil to make a neat parcel. Pinch the edges firmly together.

5. Bake in a moderate oven (350°F: Reg. 4) for 15 minutes.

To serve without freezing: Continue baking for a further 15 minutes. Serve in the aluminium-foil cases.

To freeze: Cool. Do not unwrap. Pack in a suitable container. Seal, label and freeze.

To thaw: Place frozen cases in a moderate oven (350°F: Reg. 4). Bake for 30 minutes.

Serve: In the aluminium cases.

Louella's Lamb Kidneys

12 lambs' kidneys	$\frac{1}{2}$ pint stock
2$\frac{1}{2}$ oz butter	Salt
2 tablespoons flour	Paprika pepper
1 small onion, finely chopped	2 tablespoons medium dry
or grated	dry sherry
	1 tablespoon chopped parsley

METHOD

1. Wash the kidneys in cold water. Remove skin and membrane. Cut each in half.

2. Melt the butter in a saucepan. Fry the kidneys over a high heat for 5 minutes, stir frequently.

3. Lower the heat and stir in the flour and onion. Add the stock slowly and stir until the sauce is smooth. Bring to the boil and remove from the heat.

To serve without freezing: Season with salt and a pinch of paprika. Blend in 2 tablespoons sherry. Garnish with chopped parsley.

To freeze: Cool. Pack in a suitable container. Seal, label and freeze.

To thaw: Turn frozen kidneys into a heavy saucepan. Heat over a medium flame. stirring occasionally until hot through. Season with salt and a pinch of paprika. Blend in sherry.

To serve: Dust with chopped parsley. Serve in a ring of mashed potato or on toast.

Stuffed Veal Hearts with Apples

2 veal hearts
1½ oz butter
6 oz dry white breadcrumbs
2 oz melted butter
1 medium onion, finely chopped

1 tablespoon finely chopped celery
2 teaspoons dried sage
Salt and pepper
6 cooking apples
½ pint claret or other red wine

METHOD

1. Cut all tubes, fat, membranes and hard skin from the hearts.
2. Melt the butter in a frying-pan and quickly brown the hearts on all sides.
3. Mix together breadcrumbs, melted butter, onion, celery and sage. Season with salt and pepper.
4. Fill the centres of the hearts with the stuffing.
5. Peel and core the apples.
6. Arrange the hearts in a deep casserole with the apples. Pour over the wine and cover.
7. Bake in a moderate oven (350°F: Reg. 4) for 1 hour.

To serve without freezing: Continue cooking for 20 minutes or until tender.

To freeze: Cool. Pour off liquid. Slice hearts and apples and arrange in aluminium foil, or shallow baking dish. Pour over the liquid. Seal, label and freeze.

To thaw: Cover frozen hearts with aluminium foil. Place in a moderate oven (350°F: Reg. 4) for 30 minutes, or until hot through and tender.

Individual Sweetbread Tarts

11 oz flour
¼ teaspoon salt
4½ oz soft butter
Water to mix
2 pairs sweetbreads
4 oz butter
1 lb mushrooms
4 tablespoons thick cream

Juice of ½ lemon
Salt and freshly ground black
  pepper

SAUCE
1 oz flour
¼ pint milk

METHOD

1. *To make the pastry:* Sieve the flour and salt on to a marble slab or cold surface. Make a well in the centre and put in the butter cut in small pieces. Mix in using the fingertips. Add enough water to make a smooth paste. Wrap in a floured cloth and leave to rest in a cool place for 2 hours. Roll out to ½-inch thickness.

2. Line individual tartlet tins with the pastry. Prick well with a fork and bake in a medium-hot oven (400°F: Reg. 5) for 10 minutes. Leave to cool in the tins.

3. *To make the filling:* Wash the sweetbreads. Place them in a saucepan of cold water and bring to the boil. Drain and rinse at at once in cold water. Cut out the membranes. Dry well.

4. Cut the sweetbreads into small pieces and coat with flour. Fry in 2 oz butter for 3 minutes until golden, remove from pan, add a further 2 oz butter and fry the chopped mushrooms for 5 minutes.

5. Make a thick sauce by melting 1 oz butter in a saucepan. Add 1 oz flour and mix well. Slowly add the milk, stirring continually over a medium heat until the sauce is thick and smooth.

6. Add the mushrooms and the sweetbreads to the sauce. Stir in the cream. Mix well and season with salt, pepper and lemon juice.

7. Spoon the mixture into the tart cases.

To serve without freezing: Reheat in a medium-hot oven (400°F: Reg. 5) for 5 minutes.

To freeze: Pack the tarts carefully in a rigid container with a sheet of moisture- and vapour-proof paper between each layer. Seal, label and freeze.

To thaw: Arrange frozen tartlets on a baking sheet and heat in a moderate oven (325F: Reg. 3) for 10–15 minutes until hot through.

Serve: With a garnish of thin lemon slices.

Sweetbread Balls

1 pair sweetbreads	Salt and pepper
¼ lb mushrooms, chopped	1 beaten egg
2 oz butter	Breadcrumbs
2 oz flour	Deep fat for frying
½ pint milk	

METHOD

1. Soak the sweetbreads in warm water for 1 hour. Drain and put into boiling salted water with 2 teaspoons lemon juice. Boil for 10 minutes. Drain and plunge into cold water. Drain and wipe dry. Cut into small pieces.

2. Melt the butter in a saucepan. Add the flour. Stir over a medium heat until the mixture forms a ball and leaves the sides of the pan. Slowly add the milk, stirring continually until the sauce is smooth.

3. Add the sweetbreads and chopped mushrooms to the sauce and season with salt and pepper. Simmer for 15 minutes. Cool.

4. Form the mixture into small balls. Dip in beaten egg and roll in breadcrumbs.

To freeze: Freeze balls unwrapped. When frozen pack in a suitable container with a sheet of moisture- and vapour-proof paper between each layer. Seal, label and freeze.

To thaw: Fry frozen balls in almost smoking deep fat for 5 minutes or until golden brown.

Serve: With rice and a tomato sauce.

Pressed Ox Tongue

4–6 lb ox tongue
1 onion, chopped
1 carrot, chopped

1 head of celery
Bouquet garni
10 black peppercorns

METHOD

1. Wash the tongue well in cold water. Place it in a large pan and cover with cold water. Bring slowly to the boil.
2. Throw away the water. Cover the tongue with fresh water and bring to the boil again. Skim the surface and add the chopped vegetables, bouquet garni, and peppercorns.
3. Cover and simmer for about 3 hours.
4. Test for tenderness by seeing if the bones at the root of the tongue are easy to remove.
5. Cool in the liquid. Take out the tongue. Remove the bones, fat and gristle from the root, and skin.
6. Cool the tongue in a tongue press or cake tin with a removable bottom. Place a plate over the top and a heavy weight on that.
7. Leave to set for 12 hours in a cool place. Turn out.

To freeze: Wrap tongue well in freezer paper. Seal in a polythene bag. Label and freeze.

To thaw: Leave in a refrigerator overnight.

To serve: Cut in thin slices across the top.

Tongue Véronique

1 lb thinly sliced ox tongue
1 oz butter
Bouquet garni
2 shallots
1 carrot
A few mushrooms
¾ oz flour

1 teaspoon tomato purée
1 pint beef stock
1 glass sherry
¼ lb grapes, skinned and halved
1 oz shredded almonds
Salt and pepper

METHOD

1. Dice the shallots and carrot and brown in the melted butter.
2. Add the flour, stir well and allow to brown.
3. Add the chopped mushrooms, tomato purée, stock, and bouquet garni. Simmer for 30 minutes.
4. Strain the sauce, return to the pan and add the sherry. Continue simmering until slightly thickened. Season with salt and pepper. Add the grapes and almonds. Pour over the sliced tongue.

To freeze: Cool and pack the tongue well covered with the sauce in a suitable container.

To thaw: Place the frozen tongue in a baking dish, cover and heat in a moderate oven (320°F: Reg. 3) for about 35 minutes, or until hot right through.

To serve: Serve hot with a garnish of chopped parsley on a bed of mashed potatoes.

Home-made Brawn

2 lambs' heads
¾ lb lean stewing steak
Small bunch parsley
Sprig of thyme

2 bay leaves
6 black peppercorns
Salt

217

1. Leave heads to soak overnight. Wash well in salted water. Remove all skin and surplus fat from heads.

2. Place the heads in a large saucepan. Add seasoning and herbs. Cover with water. Bring to the boil and simmer for 1 hour.

3. Remove the heads from the stock. Cut off all the meat. Dice into small cubes.

4. Cut the steak into small dice. Add all the meat to the stock and simmer for 1½–2 hours until the meat is really tender.

5. Strain off the stock and arrange the meat in a dish or mould.

6. Boil the stock until it is reduced to ¾ pint; skim off any fat. Strain over the meat and leave to set.

To freeze: Leave in mould, packed in a polythene bag. Seal, label and freeze.

To thaw: Leave covered in refrigerator for at least 5 hours until thawed through.

To serve: Turn out and serve chilled, cut in slices, with salad.
Do not keep for longer than 2 months.

Poultry

Chicken

Chicken Pie

This serves 6

1 roasting chicken
Seasoned flour
2 oz butter
4 rashers bacon
4 spring onions
8 carrots

1 tablespoon chopped parsley
1 teaspoon sage
½ pint stock
Salt and pepper
Shortcrust pastry for top

METHOD

1. Cut the chicken into serving pieces. Coat in seasoned flour. Melt the butter in a heavy pan and sauté the chicken with the onion bulbs for 10 minutes.
2. Chop the onion tops, the bacon and the carrots, and simmer in the stock for 15 minutes.
3. Arrange the chicken and vegetables in a pie dish, pour over the stock and sprinkle with chopped parsley and sage. Season with salt and pepper.
4. Bake in a moderate oven (350°F: Reg. 4) for 45 minutes.
5. Roll out the pastry and cover the pie.

To serve without freezing: Cut air vents in the pastry. Brush with milk and bake for a further 30–45 minutes in a medium-hot oven (380°F: Reg. 5)

To freeze: Cool. Pack the pie in a polythene bag, or wrap in freezer paper or aluminium foil. Seal, label and freeze.

To thaw: Cut air vents in frozen pastry. Brush with milk and bake the pie in a medium-hot oven (380°F: Reg. 5) for 50–60 minutes.
Serve hot or cold.

Chicken with Brandy

1 chicken	¼ pint brandy
2 oz butter	2 teaspoons curry paste
1 oz flour	Salt and pepper
½ pint double cream	2 cloves garlic

METHOD

1. Cut chicken into eight pieces.
2. Melt the butter in an iron casserole. Sauté the chicken for 5 minutes over a medium flame.
3. Add the flour and stir well.
4. Add the curry paste, cream and brandy. Season with salt and pepper.
5. Cover and bake in a medium-hot oven (380°F: Reg. 5) for 35 minutes.

To freeze: Cool quickly. Pack in a suitable container. Seal, label and freeze.

To thaw: Place frozen chicken in a double-boiler and heat for about 30 minutes.

To serve: Add 2 minced cloves of garlic. Continue cooking for a further 20 minutes until the chicken is tender and hot through.
Serve the casserole hot with a sprinkling of parsley over the surface.

Chicken Créole

1 roasting chicken
3 oz butter
3 onions
2 oz flour
6 tomatoes
6 red peppers

1 teaspoon chopped parsley
1 teaspoon thyme
1 bay leaf, chopped
1 pint chicken stock
Salt and freshly ground black
    pepper

METHOD

1. Joint the chicken into serving pieces. Melt the butter in a large pan and fry the chicken until brown on all sides over a fierce heat.

2. Chop the onions and add to the chicken. Cook over a medium heat for 2 minutes.

3. Stir in the flour and cook until it begins to brown.

4. Peel, seed, and chop the tomatoes and peppers and add to the chicken with the herbs. Cover and sauté gently for 20 minutes.

5. Add the stock and mix well. Season with salt and pepper. Cover and simmer for a further 30 minutes.

To serve without freezing: Continue to simmer for a further 15 minutes or until the chicken is tender.

To freeze: Cool. Pack in a suitable container. Seal, label and freeze.

To thaw: Turn frozen chicken into a heavy saucepan. Thaw over a low heat for 30 minutes until hot through and tender. Stir occasionally to prevent the chicken sticking to the pan.

Serve: On a bed of boiled rice.

Chicken with Peas

1 boiling fowl
2 large onions, chopped
2 oz butter
2 oz flour
1 pint chicken stock

1 glass white wine
1 teaspoon saffron
1 tablespoon chopped parsley
Salt and pepper
2 lb peas

METHOD

1. Cut the chicken into serving pieces. Melt the butter in a large pan, add the chicken and the onions and fry until a golden brown.

2. Stir in the flour and slowly add the stock. Mix well.

3. Add the white wine, saffron and parsley, and season with salt and pepper.

4. Cover and simmer over a low heat for 1 hour. Add the peas and continue to simmer for a further 10 minutes.

To serve without freezing: Continue cooking for a further 10 minutes or until the chicken is tender and the peas cooked.

To freeze: Cool. Pack in a suitable container. Seal, label and freeze.

To thaw: Turn frozen chicken into a heavy pan. Thaw over a medium heat for 30 minutes or until the chicken is hot through and tender.

Serve: Hot on a bed of mashed potato.

Chicken Marengo

The dish that Napoleon Bonaparte feasted on after the Battle of Marengo, when the French defeated the Austrians in 1800. It was invented by Napoleon's chef, using only the ingredients he had to hand at the time. Originally, the dish contained crayfish but these have since been replaced by mushrooms in most recipes.

This dish does need a certain amount of preparation after defrosting.

1 chicken	½ lb mushrooms
2 tablespoons olive oil	1 clove garlic
1 oz flour seasoned with salt and pepper	1 tablespoon butter
1 pint chicken or veal stock	4 heart-shaped bread croûtons fried in butter
½ cup white wine	4 small eggs fried in butter

METHOD

1. Joint chicken into eight pieces. Toss pieces in seasoned flour.
2. Melt the oil in a heavy pan and fry the chicken until golden brown.
3. Add the stock and wine to the chicken and stir well.
4. Bring to boiling point, reduce heat and simmer for 30 minutes.

To freeze: Cool the chicken. Seal, label, and freeze.

To thaw: Thaw at room temperature. Heat over low flame in a heavy pan. Melt the butter and fry sliced mushrooms and crushed garlic clove for 3 minutes and add to chicken. Continue cooking for 15 minutes (or heat frozen chicken in a double-boiler until defrosted and then transfer to heavy pan).

To serve: Serve in a shallow dish, with fried breadcrumbs and fried eggs.

Chicken Mexicana

1 large chicken	1 pint boiling water
2 medium onions, chopped	½ lb ripe green olives
2 bay leaves	¾ pint medium dry sherry
2 teaspoons chilli powder	2 cloves garlic, minced
1 teaspoon oregano	

1. Cut the chicken into eight pieces. Place in a large casserole with the onions, chilli powder, bay leaves, and oregano.

2. Add 1 pint boiling water. Cover and bake in a moderate oven (350°F: Reg. 4) for 45 minutes.

To serve without freezing: Add the minced garlic, sherry and green olives. Return to the oven and bake for a further 20 minutes.

To freeze: Cool quickly. Pack in a suitable container. Seal, label, and freeze.

To thaw: Place frozen chicken in a casserole. Cover and heat in a moderate oven for ½ hour until thawed. Add minced garlic, sherry and green olives. Cook for a further 20 minutes.

Serve: Hot with crisp rolls and a green salad.

Chicken Caesar

1 3-lb chicken	½ lb mushrooms
¼ lb butter	Bouquet garni
2 tablespoons flour	5 tablespoons brandy
¼ lb diced bacon	1 pint red wine
10 shallots	Salt and pepper

METHOD

1. Cut the chicken into serving pieces.

2. Melt the butter in a deep frying pan. Add the bacon and onions and fry for 5 minutes. Add the mushrooms cut into quarters and fry for a further 5 minutes.

3. Remove all the ingredients from the pan. Add the chicken to the fat and fry for 10 minutes until golden brown. Add the bacon, onions and mushrooms and continue cooking for 5 minutes.

4. Sprinkle the flour and mix well. Pour the brandy over and set alight.

5. Season with salt and pepper. Add the bouquet garni and pour the wine over.

6. Cover and simmer for 20 minutes. Remove bouquet garni.

To serve without freezing: Continue to simmer for a further 15 minutes or until chicken is tender.

To freeze: Cool quickly and pack in a suitable container. Seal, label, and freeze.

To thaw: Turn frozen chicken into a heavy pan. Thaw over a low heat until hot. Cover and simmer for 15 minutes until tender.

Serve: With fried bread croûtons.

Poulet à l'Estragon

1 chicken	Water as required
2 oz butter	2 tablespoons thick cream
1 oz flour	2 tablespoons chopped fresh
Salt and pepper	tarragon
1 onion	1 tablespoon Vermouth
1 carrot	Lemon juice
1 glass white wine	Bouquet garni
½ pint chicken stock	

METHOD

1. Poach chicken with a bouquet garni, chopped onion and carrot, stock and water if necessary and 1 wineglass white wine. The chicken should be just covered with liquid. Reserve stock for sauce.

2. Melt butter in a saucepan, add flour and stir well. Slowly add stock and lemon juice. Bring to the boil and simmer for 10 minutes.

3. Add cream and tarragon. Season with salt and pepper. Simmer for a further 10 minutes.

4. Cut chicken into thin slices and add to sauce. Heat through.

To serve without freezing: Arrange chicken on a shallow dish with a ring of rice. Add Vermouth to sauce and pour over chicken.

To freeze: Cool. Pack into a suitable container. Seal, label, and freeze.

To thaw: Turn into the top of a double-boiler over hot water. Cook until thawed through and hot.

To serve: Arrange chicken on a shallow dish. Blend in Vermouth to sauce and pour over chicken.

Chicken à la King

1 cooked chicken
3 tablespoons flour
2 oz butter
½ pint cream
½ pint chicken stock
2 teaspoons lemon juice

6 button mushrooms
½ green pepper, chopped
1 pimento, chopped
2 egg yolks
Salt and pepper

METHOD

1. Melt the butter in a saucepan, add the flour and stir well.
2. Blend in the stock slowly, stirring all the time until the mixture is smooth and thick.
3. Add the cream (reserving 2 tablespoons) and lemon juice.
4. Add the mushrooms, chopped seeded green pepper and chopped pimento. Simmer for 10 minutes.
5. Remove the meat off the chicken and cut into small dice. Add to the sauce and simmer for a further 10 minutes. Season.

To freeze: Cool and pack in a suitable container. Seal, label, and freeze.

To thaw: Place frozen chicken in a double-boiler over hot water. Heat over a medium flame until thawed and hot through.

To serve: Blend in 2 egg yolks, beaten with a little cream, and garnish with chopped parsley and small triangles of fried bread.

Chicken Louis

2 lb fresh spinach
4 oz butter
1 lb cooked chicken
4 oz grated Gruyère cheese
2 oz flour

¾ pint milk
Salt and freshly ground black pepper
A pinch of grated nutmeg

METHOD

1. Clean the spinach and trim the stalks. Cover with cold water and bring to the boil. Boil for 4 minutes.

2. Drain the spinach and squeeze as dry as possible.

3. Add 2 oz of butter and a pinch of nutmeg to the spinach and heat until the butter has melted. Mix well.

4. Melt 2 oz of butter in a saucepan. Add the flour and stir well. Slowly add the milk stirring constantly over a medium heat until the sauce is smooth. Add 2 oz cheese and season with salt and pepper.

5. Chop the chicken into small dice and add to the sauce.

6. Arrange half the spinach in a shallow baking dish. Spoon over half the chicken mixture. Sprinkle with half the grated cheese and dot with butter. Repeat with remaining spinach and chicken. Sprinkle the surface with the remaining cheese.

To serve without freezing: Heat in a hot oven (450°F: Reg. 7) for 10 minutes until the dish is hot through and the surface browned.

To freeze: Cool quickly. Pack in a polythene bag, or wrap in freezer paper. Seal, label, and freeze.

To thaw: Cover frozen dish with aluminium foil. Heat in a medium hot oven (380°F: Reg. 5) for 20 minutes or until hot through. Remove aluminium foil and brown in a hot oven (450°F: Reg. 7) for 5 minutes.

Note: The baking dish can be lined with aluminium foil so that the chicken can be removed from the dish when frozen.

Tinker's Pie

½ lb puff pastry
1½ lb cooked chicken, turkey or rabbit meat
1½ oz butter
1 oz flour
2 oz mushrooms

1 egg
¾ pint chicken stock
4 rashers bacon
2 tablespoons cream
1 tablespoon chopped parsley
Salt and pepper

METHOD

1. Shred the meat. Chop the mushrooms and the bacon.

2. Melt 1 oz butter in a saucepan. Add the flour and mix well. Gradually add the stock, stirring over a medium heat until the mixture is smooth and thick. Add the parsley and the meat.

3. Melt the remaining ½ oz butter and fry the mushrooms and bacon for 5 minutes. Drain and add to the chicken mixture. Season with salt and pepper.

4. Stir in the cream and put the mixture in a pie dish. Cover with puff pastry.

To serve without freezing: Brush the pastry with beaten egg. Bake in a hot oven (420°F: Reg. 6) for 30 minutes or until the pastry is golden brown.

To freeze: Pack pie dish in a polythene bag, or wrap in freezer paper or aluminium foil. Seal, label, and freeze.

To thaw: Brush frozen pastry with beaten egg. Bake in a hot oven (420°F: Reg. 6) for 40 minutes or until the pastry is golden brown.

Chinese Spring Rolls

¼ lb plain flour
½ pint water
½ teaspoon salt
1 onion
1 oz butter

8 oz cooked shredded pork or
    chicken
8 oz shrimps
8 oz bean sprouts
1 tablespoon soy sauce

METHOD

1. Make a thin batter by combining the flour, water and salt. Beat until smooth.

2. Grease an omelet or pancake pan. Add a tablespoon of the batter and cook for about 2 minutes on one side only. Remove from pan and repeat until the batter has been used up.

3. Finely chop the onions and fry in 1 oz butter until transparent. Add the meat, shrimps and bean sprouts and fry for a further 3 minutes. Season with a little salt and soy sauce.

4. Place some filling on the centre of each pancake. Fold two sides to the middle. Fold over the other sides to form a parcel. Seal the edges of the pancakes with water.

To serve without freezing: Deep-fry stuffed rolls until crisp and golden brown.

To freeze: Freeze rolls without packing. When solid, pack in a suitable container with moisture- and vapour-proof paper between each layer. Seal, label, and freeze.

To thaw: Drop frozen rolls into hot fat. Deep-fry until crisp and golden brown.

Note: The pancakes can be deep-fried until a light brown before freezing. Drain well. Cool and freeze. Thaw by placing rolls on a baking sheet. Heat for 10 minutes in a hot oven until hot through and golden brown.

Serve: With sweet and sour sauce.

Chicken Kromeskies

½ lb cooked chicken
1½ oz butter
1½ oz flour
⅜ pint milk
¼ oz butter
2 oz mushrooms
1 egg yolk
Salt and pepper
8 rindless rashers bacon
Deep fat for frying

BATTER
4 oz plain flour
2 egg yolks
1 tablespoon oil
¼ pint milk
1 egg white
Pinch of salt

METHOD

1. *To make the batter:* Sift the flour with a pinch of salt. Make a well in the centre. Put in the egg yolks and oil. Add the milk and mix well until the mixture is smooth. Beat for 1 minute.

2. Leave to stand for ½ hour. Beat the egg white and fold into the batter before using.

3. *To make the croquettes:* Mince the chicken through a coarse blade. Chop the mushrooms and fry gently in ¼ oz butter.

4. Melt 1½ oz butter in a saucepan. Add the flour and stir well. Add the milk and continue stirring over a medium flame until the mixture is thick and smooth.

5. Mix the chicken and the mushrooms into the sauce. Add the egg yolk and continue mixing over a medium flame until the mixture leaves the side of the pan. Season with salt and pepper.

6. Shape the mixture into eight croquettes on a floured board. Wrap each in a rasher of bacon and dip in the batter.

7. Cook in deep fat until a golden brown.

To freeze: Drain well on kitchen paper and leave to cool. Pack in a suitable container with a layer of moisture- and vapour-proof paper between the croquettes. Seal, label and freeze.

To thaw: Place frozen croquettes on a baking sheet in a hot oven (410°F: Reg. 6) for 15 minutes or until hot through.

Serve: With a garnish of crisp fresh parsley and tomato sauce.
   Do not keep for longer than 1 month.

Duck

Duck with Olive Sauce

1 duck or 2 wild duck
1 tablespoon cornflour
¼ pint stock
Juice of 2 oranges
1 tablespoon sherry

1 small tablespoon
  marmalade
3 teaspoons Worcester sauce
Salt and pepper
¼ lb stoned green olives

METHOD

1. Roast the duck or wild ducks in a medium-hot oven (400°F: Reg. 5) allowing 15 minutes to the lb.

2. Hold the ducks end up on the oven tin to drain out the juices. Remove and cut into serving portions.

3. Add the cornflour to the juices in the pan and mix well over a medium heat.

4. Add the stock slowly, stirring continually

5. Add the orange juice, sherry, marmalade, and Worcester sauce. Mix well and season with salt and pepper.

6. Strain the sauce into a clean pan and add the olives. Simmer for a further 10 minutes. Pour the sauce over the duck.

To serve without freezing: Reheat in a moderate oven for 10 minutes.

To freeze: Cool quickly. Pack duck in a suitable container and cover with the sauce. Seal, label, and freeze.

To thaw: Turn frozen duck into a bowl over hot water. Thaw over a medium heat until the duck is hot through.

Serve: With mashed potatoes and green peas.

Duck in Red Wine Sauce

1 cold roast duck, sliced
2 oz butter
2 oz flour
¼ pint stock
¼ pint red wine
1 onion, chopped

1 tablespoon chopped parsley
1 tablespoon orange juice
Grated rind of 1 orange
Bouquet garni
Salt and pepper

METHOD

1. Melt the butter in a saucepan. Add the flour and mix well. Slowly add the stock, red wine and orange juice, stirring continually until the sauce is smooth.

2. Add the onion, parsley, orange rind, bouquet garni and the sliced cold duck. Season with salt and pepper.

3. Simmer for 45 minutes.

To serve without freezing: Continue to simmer for a further 15 minutes. Remove the bouquet garni and serve on rounds of toasted bread.

To freeze: Cool. Skim off any excess fat. Pack in a suitable container. Seal, label and freeze.

To thaw: Turn frozen duck into a heavy pan. Thaw over a medium heat, stirring occasionally to prevent sticking. When hot, cover and simmer for 15 minutes.

Serve: On rounds of toasted bread.

Duck with Orange Sauce

1 duck
2 oranges
1 lemon
3 tablespoons wine vinegar

1 tablespoon flour
1 tablespoon brown sugar
4 tablespoons chicken stock
Salt and pepper

METHOD

1. Roast the duck in a moderate oven (325°F: Reg. 3) for 25 minutes to the lb. Prick the skin to release the fat and baste well

during cooking. Drain the fat from the pan but reserve the juices.

2. Place the duck on a rack so that all the fat can drain off. Cut into six pieces.

3. Using a coarse grater, grate the rind from 2 oranges and 1 lemon. Blanch in boiling water for 1 minute and drain.

4. In a saucepan, simmer the vinegar with the sugar for 10 minutes. Add the juice of the oranges and lemon, simmer for 2 minutes, and add the rinds.

5. Over a medium heat mix the flour with the juices from the duck and stir until smooth and thick. Slowly mix in the chicken stock and orange sauce. Season with salt and pepper and pour over the duck.

To freeze: Cool. Pack in a suitable container. Seal, label, and freeze.

To thaw: Turn frozen duck into the top of a double-saucepan over hot water. Cook for 30 minutes or until hot through.

Serve: With traditional green peas and a garnish of thin orange slices.

Turkey

Blanquette of Turkey

Now that turkeys are being produced in more reasonable sizes they make economical family dishes for other occasions than Christmas and Thanksgiving. But the problem of the left-overs still arises. This recipe solves that problem.

1 lb chopped cooked turkey	¼ pint turkey stock, or chicken consommé
1 oz flour	3 tablespoons water
2 oz butter	1 tablespoon lemon juice
¼ pint thin cream	Salt and pepper
¼ lb mushrooms	

233

1. Melt butter in a saucepan. Add flour and mix until mixture forms a ball and leaves the side of the pan.

2. Slowly add cream and stock. Stir well over a medium heat until sauce is smooth.

3. Chop mushrooms and simmer in the water and lemon juice over a low heat for 5 minutes.

4. Add the mushrooms and liquid to the cream sauce. Stir in the chopped turkey. Season.

To serve without freezing: Simmer the blanquette over a low heat until the turkey is heated through.

To freeze: Cool and pour into a suitable container.

To thaw: Place frozen blanquette into the top of a double-saucepan over hot water. Heat through, stirring occasionally to avoid curdling.

Serve: Hot, on toast or with mashed potatoes.

Game

A FEW NOTES ON ROASTING AND CARVING GAME

GAME IN SEASON

Grouse:	*From* August 12th *to* December 10th
Partridge:	*From* September 1st *to* February 1st
Pheasant:	*From* October 1st *to* February 1st
Wild Duck:	*From* September 1st *to* January 31st
Pigeon:	No close season
Snipe:	*From* August 12th *to* January 31st
Woodcock:	*From* October 1st *to* January 31st

GROUSE

To roast: Rub the birds with butter and a little salt. Place in a roasting tin in a hot oven. Cook for 30–35 minutes, basting well.

To carve: Using a very sharp knife or a pair of game scissors, cut each bird in two along the backbone.

To serve: Place each half, leg upwards, on a slice of buttered toast. Serves 2.

PARTRIDGE

To roast: Rub the birds with butter and a little salt. Place in a roasting tin in a hot oven. Cook for 25–35 minutes, basting well.

To carve: Either cut the bird in half (as with a grouse) or cut into three portions by cutting off the leg and wing together from both sides and cutting off the breast in thin slices.

To serve: Serve with gravy and bread sauce. Accompany the bird with game chips and baby Brussels sprouts. Serves 2–3.

PHEASANT

To roast: Rub the bird with butter and a little salt. Cover the breast with a slice or two of bacon (pheasant is very apt to dry out during cooking and the bacon provides extra fat). Place in a roasting tin in a hot oven. Cook for 40–60 minutes, basting well.

To carve: Slice the breast thinly. Cut off the legs and wings.

To serve: Serve with gravy, a bread sauce, and fresh breadcrumbs fried in bacon fat. Accompany the bird with game chips or Smith's crisps, and Brussels sprouts. Serves 4.

WILD DUCK

To roast: Rub the bird with butter and roast in a hot oven, basting well, for 20–25 minutes if liked underdone, 30–35 minutes if well done.

To carve: Cut slices from the front to the back of the breast. Cut the leg and wing off together.

To serve: Serve with gravy and an orange salad, game chips and young peas. Serves 2–3.

SNIPE

To roast: Place the bird on a piece of buttered white bread in a roasting tin. Rub with butter and cover with a strip of bacon. Roast in a hot oven for 15 minutes.

To serve: Serve on buttered toast, 1 bird per person, as a savoury.

Note: The brains of the snipe are considered to be a great delicacy. Slice off the top of the head and scoop out the brains.

WOODCOCK

To roast: Roast in a hot oven as for snipe for 20 minutes. Serve one as a savoury.

PIGEON

To roast: Roast as a small chicken (older birds should be casseroled).

To serve: Serve with gravy and bread sauce.

West Country Pigeon or Squab

2 large or 4 small pigeons
 or squab
2 oz butter
8 shallots
¾ pint beef consommé
2 oz stoned raisins

¼ pint water
1 oz butter
1 oz flour
Salt and pepper
2 tablespoons sherry

METHOD

1. Melt the butter in a large pan. Add the pigeons and brown on all sides over a fierce heat. Remove the pigeons and keep warm in a casserole dish. Add the shallots to the butter and brown.

2. Add the consommé to the shallots and bring to the boil. Pour over the pigeons. Season with salt and pepper. Cover and cook in a moderate oven (325°F: Reg. 3) for 40 minutes.

3. Soak the raisins in the water for ½ hour.

4. Add the raisins and the water to the pigeons. Baste well and continue cooking for a further 15 minutes or until the birds are tender. Remove the birds and split in half. Cut away the backbone with a pair of scissors.

5. Melt the butter in a saucepan. Add the flour and stir well over a moderate heat. Slowly mix in the sauce and cook, stirring continually until the sauce is thick and smooth.

To serve without freezing: Add the sherry to the sauce and pour over the pigeons.

To freeze: Cool quickly and pack the pigeons, covered with the sauce, in a suitable container. Seal, label, and freeze.

To thaw: Turn the frozen pigeons into the top of a double-boiler over hot water. Heat until thawed through. Stir in the sherry and continue cooking until hot through.

Pigeon Pie

2 oz butter
4 plump young pigeons
4 spring onions
4 thin slices fillet, rump or
   round steak
¼ lb mushrooms
1 tablespoon chopped parsley
1 tablespoon flour
½ pint white wine
Salt and pepper

PASTRY
8 oz plain flour
Salt
6 oz butter
1 egg yolk
2 tablespoons iced water

METHOD

1. *To make the pastry:* Sift the flour and salt together. Rub in the butter with the fingertips until the mixture resembles coarse breadcrumbs. Beat the egg and mix with 1 tablespoon of the water. Add to the butter and flour and work into a stiff dough. Add the rest of the water. Leave to chill in a refrigerator for 1 hour.

2. Melt the butter in a pan. Fry the pigeons and chopped onions until golden brown on all sides. Place in a deep buttered pie dish.

3. Fry the steak and mushrooms for 5 minutes. Add to the pigeons. Sprinkle with parsley.

4. Add the flour to the juices in the pan and mix until the flour browns. Slowly add the wine. Season with salt and pepper. Pour over the pigeons and steak.

5. Cover and bake in a medium hot oven (380°F: Reg. 5) for 45 minutes.

To serve without freezing: Roll out pastry, cover pie dish. Brush with beaten egg and cut two air vents. Bake for a further 20 minutes in a medium-hot oven.

To freeze: Cool pie. Roll out pastry and cover. Do not make air vents. Pack in a polythene bag or wrap in freezer paper. Seal, label, and freeze.

To thaw: Cut two slits in the frozen pastry. Brush with beaten egg and bake in a medium-hot oven (380°F: Reg. 5) for 40 minutes or until pigeons are hot through and pastry is golden brown.

Pheasant Normande

1 pheasant	3 eating apples
1 oz butter	½ pint stock
4 shallots or 1 large onion	Bouquet garni
1 glass Calvados	2 tablespoons thick cream
Seasoned flour	Salt and pepper

METHOD

1. Cut the pheasant into 4 pieces. Coat well in seasoned flour.
2. Melt the butter and brown the pheasant on all sides. Add the chopped shallots (or onion) and cook over a medium flame until golden.
3. Pour the Calvados over and set it alight.
4. Add the stock, the peeled, cored and sliced apples and the bouquet garni. Season with salt and pepper. Bring to the boil. Cover and cook slowly for 50 minutes.
5. Remove the pheasant and put the juices through a fine sieve.

To serve without freezing: Heat the cream and add to the juices. Pour over the pheasant.

To freeze: Pour the juices over the pheasant. Cool quickly, and pack in a suitable container. Seal, label, and freeze.

To thaw: Turn the frozen pheasant into the top of a double-boiler over hot water. Cook over a medium heat until hot. Remove the pheasant pieces to a hot serving dish. Heat the cream and add to the sauce. Check seasoning and pour over the pheasant.

Serve: Hot with mashed potatoes and Julienne carrots with parsley.

Partridge or Pheasant with Red Cabbage

A delicious way to deal with old birds

2 old partridges or 1 old pheasant
2 tablespoons flour
1 lb red cabbage, chopped
1 onion, chopped
2 rashers bacon, chopped
1 cooking apple, peeled or chopped

2 tablespoons olive oil
2 tablespoons cider
1 tablespoon brown sugar
Salt and freshly ground black pepper
Bouquet garni

METHOD

1. Cut birds into serving portions. Coat with seasoned flour.
2. Heat 1 tablespoon oil in a deep casserole. Fry the birds until brown on all sides. Remove and keep warm.
3. Add the remaining oil and bacon and fry for 1 minute. Add cabbage, onion and apple and fry for a further 3 minutes until the onions are transparent, turning all the time.
4. Pour over them the cider, sugar and seasoning and mix well.
5. Place the birds on top of the vegetables. Add the bouquet garni. Cover tightly and bake in a slow oven (310°F: Reg. 2) for 2½ hours.

To serve without freezing: Cook for a further ½ hour or until the meat is tender. Remove bouquet garni.

To freeze: Cool quickly. Skim fat. Pack in suitable containers. Seal, label, and freeze.

To thaw: Turn into a casserole. Cover and bake in a slow oven for 1 hour or until casserole is hot and the meat is tender.

To serve: Remove bouquet garni and serve piping hot with mashed potatoes.

Devilled Rabbit

Since myxomatosis became so widespread throughout the world rabbits have been treated with a certain amount of suspicion. However, they are beginning to be bred on a commercial scale again and many butchers now sell them. It would be a pity to disregard them completely, as they are one of the cheapest and most tasty forms of meat available.

1 plump rabbit	1 tablespoon French mustard
¼ lb salt pork	1 teaspoon Worcester sauce
1 oz dripping	Bouquet garni
1 tablespoon vinegar	Salt and pepper
6 medium onions, sliced	4 tablespoons cream
1 oz flour	1 tablespoon chopped parsley
1¼ pints stock	

METHOD

1. Cut the rabbit into serving pieces. Soak for 8 hours in water with 1 tablespoon of vinegar and 1 teaspoon of salt. Drain, rinse in fresh water, and wipe dry.
2. Melt the dripping and fry the rabbit until brown on all sides. Remove and add the chopped pork and the onions. Fry until golden.
3. Add the flour and mix well. Slowly stir in the stock and bring to the boil, stirring all the time.
4. Add the rabbit, bouquet garni, mustard and Worcester sauce. Season with salt and pepper. Cover tightly and simmer for 20 minutes.

To serve without freezing: Simmer for a further 10 minutes or until the rabbit is really tender. Stir in the cream and the parsley and serve immediately.

To freeze: Cool quickly and pack in a suitable container. Seal, label, and freeze.

To thaw: Turn the frozen rabbit into a heavy saucepan. Cook over a low heat for 30 minutes until hot and tender. Stir occasionally to prevent sticking. Stir in the cream and the chopped parsley.

Serve: At once.

Rabbit Chasseur

1 tender rabbit	$\frac{1}{2}$ pint chicken stock
1 tablespoon vinegar	2 teaspoons tomato purée
2 oz butter	1 teaspoon mixed herbs
2 shallots	Salt and pepper
1 oz flour	2 oz mushrooms
1 glass white wine	

METHOD

1. Cut the rabbit into serving pieces. Soak for 8 hours in water with 1 tablespoon vinegar and 1 teaspoon salt. Drain. Rinse in fresh water, and dry.

2. Heat the butter and fry the rabbit until golden brown on all sides. Add the chopped shallots. Cook for 3 minutes over a medium heat.

3. Add the flour. Stir well and cook until the flour colours. Slowly add the wine, stock and tomato purée. Blend until smooth.

4. Add herbs and season with salt and pepper. Cover and simmer for 40 minutes.

To serve without freezing: Add the chopped mushrooms and continue to simmer for a further 20 minutes or until the rabbit is tender.

To freeze: Cool quickly and pack in a suitable container. Seal, label, and freeze.

To thaw: Turn frozen rabbit into a heavy pan. Thaw over a low heat until hot through. Add the chopped mushrooms and continue to cook for a further 20 minutes, or until the rabbit is tender.

Serve: With a dusting of parsley garnished with fried-bread triangles.

Jugged Hare

One of the most classic English dishes. Serves 6

MARINADE

¾ pint cheap red wine
4 tablespoons olive oil
1 onion, sliced
Bouquet garni of bay leaf, thyme, marjoram and parsley
6 crushed juniper berries
2 thinly pared strips of orange peel
Salt and freshly ground black pepper

1 hare cut into pieces (reserve the blood)
1 tablespoon bacon fat
2 onions, chopped
2 carrots, chopped
1 teaspoon allspice
Juice and rind of 1 lemon
Stock to cover
1 glass port
1 tablespoon marmalade
1 oz butter
1 oz flour

METHOD

1. *To make the marinade:* Put wine, onion, bouquet garni, juniper berries, orange rind, salt and pepper into a pan. Bring to the boil and simmer for 5 minutes.
2. Cool and add olive oil.
3. Pour marinade over hare. Leave for at least 12 hours, turning occasionally.
4. *To cook the hare:* Dry hare well. Melt bacon fat in a pan and brown the hare on all sides.
5. Pack meat into a deep casserole with vegetables, bouquet garni, spices, lemon juice and rind. Pour over enough stock to

cover. Finish with two layers of aluminium foil so that the dish is completely sealed.

6. Cook in a slow oven (300°F: Reg. 2) for 3 hours.

7. Remove hare. Strain juices into a saucepan.

8. Mix the flour and butter together and add to the gravy. Bring to the boil and stir well until thickened.

9. Lower the heat, stir in the blood, port and marmalade. Pour over the hare.

To serve without freezing: Reheat in a moderate oven until hot through.

To freeze: Cool. Pack in a suitable container. Seal, label, and freeze.

To thaw: Place in a casserole. Cover with tinfoil and heat in a moderate oven (350°F: Reg. 4) until hot through.

Serve: With forcemeat balls.

Casserole of Venison

2 lb venison (preferably breast)
¼ lb salt pork
2 oz butter
2 oz flour
1 pint water
½ pint red wine

Salt
Black pepper
Bouquet garni
3 large onions, chopped
¼ lb mushrooms
1 clove garlic

METHOD

1. Melt the butter in a heavy pan. Cut the pork into small dice. Fry until brown. Remove and keep warm.

2. Cut the venison into 1-inch cubes. Fry in the fat until well browned. Remove and keep warm.

3. Add the flour to the fat and mix well. Slowly add the water and wine, stirring over a medium heat until the sauce is smooth.

Add the onions, bouquet garni and the meat. Season with salt and pepper.

4. Cover and simmer over a low heat for 1 hour.

To serve without freezing: Mince the clove of garlic, add with the mushrooms to the meat, and simmer for a further 30 minutes. Arrange the meat, mushrooms and onions in a serving dish and strain the sauce over.

To freeze: Cool. Pack in a suitable container. Seal, label and freeze.

To thaw: Turn the frozen meat into a heavy pan. Heat over a low flame until thawed through. Add the minced clove of garlic and the mushrooms. Cover and simmer for 30 minutes.

To serve: Arrange the meat, onions and mushrooms in a serving dish. Strain over the sauce.

Left-over Venison with Pepper Sauce

This rather hot sauce goes well over the remains of cold venison, and is one way of solving the problem of an over large joint of this rich meat.

Cold roast venison	½ tablespoon chopped parsley
2 oz butter	½ tablespoon chopped chives
1 oz flour	Bouquet garni
½ pint hot stock	1 teaspoon coarsely ground
2 teaspoons red wine vinegar	black pepper
1 small onion, finely chopped	Salt

METHOD

1. Cut the cold venison into thin slices.

2. *To make the sauce:* Melt the butter in a saucepan. Add the flour and mix well. Slowly add the stock, stirring all the time over a medium heat until the sauce is thick and smooth.

3. Add the remaining ingredients and simmer for 25 minutes. Strain over the sliced venison.

To serve without freezing: Reheat the meat in the sauce and serve.

To freeze: Cool quickly. Pack the meat well covered by the sauce in a suitable container. Seal, label and freeze.

To thaw: Turn the frozen meat into a bowl over hot water. Place over a medium heat until hot through.

Serve: With a garnish of fresh watercress.

Fish

Frozen Salmon or Sea Trout

To thaw: Remove fish from the deep freeze and thaw in its wrapping on a shelf in the refrigerator or at room temperature.

When fully thawed, gut the fish and wipe it well with a damp cloth.

To cook: Place the fish in a fish kettle or large pan. Cover it with cold water, adding 1 tablespoon vinegar, 1 tablespoon olive oil, 1 bay leaf, 4 peppercorns and a pinch of salt to each quart of water. Cover the pan and bring slowly to the boil. Simmer for 5 minutes only. Remove the pan from the heat and leave the fish to cool in the water.

Note: This the only way I know of cooking salmon that does not tend to over-cook and dry the fish.

Sole in Cider Sauce

4 oz butter
3 tablespoons chopped parsley
8 sole fillets
2 tablespoons dry
 breadcrumbs

$\frac{1}{2}$ pint dry cider
Salt and freshly ground black
 pepper
4 tablespoons double cream

METHOD

1. Well butter a shallow baking dish with 2 oz butter. Sprinkle with half the parsley.
2. Lay the sole in the dish. Cover with parsley and the bread-

crumbs and dot with the remaining butter.

3. Season with salt and pepper and pour the cider over the fish.

4. Bake in a moderate oven (350°F: Reg. 4) for 10 minutes.

To serve without freezing: Continue to bake for a further 10 minutes. Just before serving pour the cream over.

To freeze: Cool. Pack in a polythene bag or wrap in freezer paper. Seal, label and freeze.

To thaw: Cover frozen dish with a sheet of aluminium foil. Heat in a moderate oven (350°F: Reg. 4) for 20 minutes or until hot through. Just before serving pour over the cream.

Sole Walewska

One of the Emperors amongst fish dishes

2 lb Dover sole, filleted	6 peppercorns
4 crayfish tails	Salt
4 slices of truffle	1 oz butter
½ pint water	¾ oz flour
Bouquet garni	4 tablespoons thin cream
½ onion, chopped	1 oz grated Parmesan cheese
1 small carrot, chopped	

METHOD

1. Place fillets in a buttered fireproof dish. Cover each fillet with a crayfish tail and a slice of truffle.

2. Place fish bones in a saucepan with the water, bouquet garni, onion, carrot, peppercorns and salt. Bring to the boil and simmer for 20 minutes.

3. Strain 4 tablespoons of the fish stock over the sole. Cover with buttered paper and poach in a moderate oven for 10 minutes. Drain off the liquid.

4. Melt the butter in a saucepan. Add the flour and mix well over a medium heat. Gradually add the remaining fish stock. Remove from the heat and stir in the cream and the cheese. Pour over the fish.

To freeze: Cool and pack baking dish in a polythene bag, or wrap in freezer paper or aluminium foil. Seal, label and freeze.

To thaw: Leave at room temperature to thaw, about 3–4 hours. Place under a hot grill until hot through and well browned on the surface.

Serve: With a dusting of chopped parsley as a first or main course.

Mullet Florentine

2 lb spinach
2 oz butter
2 oz flour
½ pint milk

12 oz cooked mullet or white fish
Salt and freshly ground black pepper
4 oz grated Gruyère cheese

METHOD

1. Wash the spinach and trim the stems. Cover with cold water and bring to the boil. Boil for 4 minutes. Rinse in cold water and drain well, pressing to remove any excess water.

2. Melt the butter in a saucepan. Add the flour and mix well. Slowly add the milk, stirring all the time over a medium heat until the sauce is thick and smooth.

3. Flake the fish with a fork and add to the sauce. Season with salt and pepper.

4. Arrange the spinach in a shallow baking dish. Pour over the sauce and sprinkle grated cheese over the surface.

To serve without freezing: Reheat in a hot oven (450°F: Reg. 7) until well browned.

To freeze: Cool and pack in a polythene bag or wrap in freezer paper. Seal, label and freeze.

To thaw: Cover the frozen dish with a sheet of aluminium foil and heat in a medium-hot oven (380°F: Reg. 5) for 20 minutes or until hot through. Remove the foil and brown the surface in a hot oven (450°F: Reg. 7) for 5 minutes.

Note: The baking dish can be lined with aluminium foil so that the fish can be removed from the baking dish when frozen.

Stuffed Baked Mackerel

4 small mackerel	1 shallot or small onion,
2 oz butter	chopped
1 tablespoon chopped parsley	Juice of ½ lemon
1 tablespoon chopped	Salt and pepper
chives	Olive oil

METHOD

1. Clean the mackerel, leaving on the heads and tails. Cut incisions along each side of the fish.

2. Soften the butter, blend in the parsley, chives, shallot or onion and 1 teaspoon lemon juice. Season with salt and pepper.

3. Stuff the filling into the sides of the mackerel.

4. Wrap each fish in a piece of aluminium foil well oiled with olive oil. Wrap up so that the fish are completely sealed in.

5. Bake in a moderate oven (350°F: Reg. 4) for 30 minutes.

To serve without freezing: Continue cooking for a further 15 minutes. Unwrap and remove fish carefully on to a serving dish. Pour over the juice from the paper and a little lemon juice.

To freeze: Cool wrapped fish. Pack in a polythene bag. Seal, label and freeze.

To thaw: Place wrapped fish in a moderate oven (350°F: Reg. 4) for 30 minutes. Unwrap and remove fish carefully to a serving dish, pour over the juice from the paper and a little lemon juice.

To serve: Garnish with sprigs of fresh parsley.

Filleted Plaice Florentine

2 lb spinach
Pepper and salt
Grated nutmeg
1½ oz butter
6 large or 8 small plaice
   fillets

1 oz flour
1 dessertspoon lemon juice
¼ pint thin cream
2 tablespoons grated Parmesan
   cheese.

METHOD

1. Cook spinach and drain well. Chop and mix with ½ oz butter and season with salt, pepper and a little grated nutmeg.
2. Poach fillets in a little water for 6 minutes, retain the stock.
3. Melt 1 oz butter in a saucepan, add flour and stir well. Make a thin sauce by adding thin cream, some of the fish liquid and lemon juice. Flavour with salt and a little nutmeg and 1 tablespoon grated Parmesan cheese.
4. Place fish on a bed of spinach in a shallow baking dish. Cover with sauce.

To serve without freezing: Dust surface with grated Parmesan. Place on top shelf of hot oven (400°F: Reg. 6) until top is lightly browned.

To freeze: Cool, pack in baking dish in a polythene bag. Seal, label and freeze.

To thaw: Thaw at room temperature for 3 hours.

To serve: Dust surface with grated Parmesan cheese. Place on the top shelf of a hot oven (400°F: Reg. 6) until hot through and the top golden brown.

Note: Cod fillets or other cheap fish can be used instead of plaice.

Somerset Plaice

2 large plaice fillets
2 tomatoes, sliced
1 large onion, chopped
2 oz butter

2 tablespoons flour
1 dessertspoon chopped
   parsley
Pepper and salt
About ½ pint dry cider

METHOD

1. Butter a shallow baking dish. Arrange fillets of plaice and cover with the chopped onion and tomatoes.
2. Melt butter in a saucepan, add flour and stir well. Mix in cider gradually, stirring all the time. Add parsley and season with salt and pepper.
3. Pour sauce over fish and bake in a medium-hot oven (400°F: Reg. 5) for 10 minutes.

To serve without freezing: Continue cooking for a further 10 minutes, or until plaice fillets are tender.

To freeze: Cool, pack, seal, label and freeze.

To thaw: Leave at room temperature for 3 hours.

To serve: Bake in a medium-hot oven (400°F: Reg. 5) for 10 minutes.

Fritto Mare

1½ lb plaice fillets
Deep fat, or oil for frying

BATTER
¼ lb plain flour
3 tablespoons olive oil
¼ pint milk
1 egg white
Salt and pepper

METHOD

1. Make the batter by stirring the olive oil into the flour. Add the milk and stir to a smooth cream. Season with salt and pepper and leave to stand for 2 hours.
2. Whisk the egg white until stiff and fold into the batter.
3. Cut the fillets into small strips about ¼ inch wide and 1½ inches long.
4. Dip the fish in the batter and fry until golden crisp in smoking hot oil (380°F).
5. Drain on crumpled kitchen paper.

To freeze: Allow the fish to cool. Pack in waxed boxes with each layer of fish separated by a sheet of freezer paper or moisture- and vapour-proof paper. Seal, label and freeze.

To thaw: Place the frozen fish, each piece separated, on a baking sheet. Heat in a medium-hot oven (400°F: Reg. 5) until thawed through and crisp. About 12–15 minutes.

To serve: Serve immediately while still crisp with a bowl of sauce tartare (mayonnaise with chopped capers and gherkins).

Note: Small pieces of cod, haddock or shell fish can be prepared in the same way.
   Do not save for longer than 2 months.

Fish Mousse

¾ lb plaice fillets
1 small tin pimentoes
¾ pint mayonnaise
1 tablespoon tomato ketchup

1 teaspoon Worcester sauce
1 oz gelatine melted in 1
   tablespoon hot lemon juice
1 egg white

METHOD

1. Steam the fish fillets over boiling water for 15 minutes until tender. Leave to cool.

2. Remove any black skin from the fillets and break into pieces. Chop the pimentoes.

3. Add tomato ketchup and Worcester sauce to mayonnaise. Season if necessary.

4. Add fish and pimentoes to mayonnaise.

5. Mix in the gelatine.

6. Whip the egg white until firm and fold into the mixture.

7. Pour into a mould.

To freeze: Place mould in a polythene bag. Seal, label and freeze.

To thaw: Leave mould, still in the polythene cover, in the refrigerator for at least 6 hours or overnight.

To serve: Unmould mousse by dipping the mould in hot water. Garnish with crisp lettuce leaves and thin tomato slices. Serve very cold.

Note: A few prawns can be added to the mousse mixture before folding in the whipped white of egg.
   Do not keep frozen for longer than 3 months.

Cod au Gratin

1½ lb cod fillet
1 oz butter
1 oz flour
½ pint milk
3 oz grated cheese

2 teaspoons made mustard
  or ¼ teaspoon dry mustard
Salt and pepper
1 tablespoon golden
  breadcrumbs

METHOD

1. Cut the cod fillet into even pieces and arrange in a buttered fireproof dish.
2. Melt the butter in a saucepan. Add the flour and the mustard. Stir over a medium heat until the mixture forms a ball and comes away from the sides of the pan. Gradually add the milk, stirring all the time. Heat until the mixture boils.
3. Add the grated cheese, reserving 1 tablespoon, and season with salt and pepper.
4. Pour the sauce over the fish. Dust with a mixture of breadcrumbs and grated cheese and dot with butter.
5. Bake in a moderate oven (350°F: Reg. 4) for 20 minutes.

To freeze: Cool. Pack in a polythene bag or in aluminium foil. Seal, label and freeze.

To thaw: Cover frozen fish with aluminium foil. Heat in a moderate oven (350°F: Reg. 4) for 20 minutes or until hot through.

Fish Pie

1½ lb cooked potatoes
1 tablespoon cream
1 oz butter
¼ lb cooked cod, bream or
  any white fish
¼ lb tinned salmon

2 oz butter
2 oz flour
¾ pint milk
2 tablespoons finely chopped
  parsley
Salt and pepper

1. Melt 2 oz butter in a saucepan. Add flour and stir well until the mixture forms a ball and leaves the side of the pan.

2. Gradually add the milk, stirring all the time over a medium heat until the mixture is smooth and creamy.

3. Add the fish and the drained salmon to the sauce. Mix in the chopped parsley. Season with salt and pepper.

4. Turn into a buttered casserole dish.

5. Mash the potatoes with 1 tablespoon cream and 1 oz butter. Spread over the fish.

To serve without freezing: Bake in a medium-hot oven (400°F: Reg. 5) until pie is hot and top is browned – about 20 minutes.

To freeze: Cool. Pack in freezer paper, aluminium foil or a polythene bag. Seal, label and freeze.

To thaw: Place frozen pie, covered with aluminium foil, in a moderate oven (350°F: Reg. 4), and bake for 20 minutes or until pie is thawed through. Remove foil, and brown top in a hot oven for 5 minutes.

Variations for Fish Pie:

1. Add 2 oz chopped cooked mushrooms and 1 chopped blanched pimento to the sauce with the fish.

2. Add 2 oz of grated cheese to mashed potato with the butter and cream.

Fish Fingers

1½ lb cod fillet	Breadcrumbs
2 beaten eggs	Fat for frying
Seasoned flour	

METHOD

1. Cut the fillet into fingers 3 inches long by ¾ inch wide.
2. Dip each finger into beaten egg. Coat with seasoned flour.

Dip again into beaten egg and coat generously with breadcrumbs.

To freeze: Freeze fish fingers unpacked. Pack when frozen in a suitable container with a sheet of moisture- and vapour-proof paper between each layer. Seal, label and freeze.

To thaw: Fry frozen fish in hot shallow fat until golden brown and cooked through.

Serve: Immediately, with parsley sauce.

Note: Fish fingers are always popular with children. Compare the cost of making your own with that of the commercial variety. Buy cod when it is plentiful and cheap – make sure it is absolutely fresh – and freeze a lot at a time.

Fish Cakes

Delicious served for breakfast or supper

½ lb cooked potatoes
½ lb any white fish or salmon for special occasions, flaked
1 oz butter
1 beaten egg

1 tablespoon finely chopped parsley
Salt and pepper
Beaten egg
Breadcrumbs
Fat for frying

METHOD

1. Put potatoes through a fine sieve.
2. Mix potatoes and fish.
3. Beat in butter and 1 beaten egg.
4. Add chopped parsley and season with salt and pepper. Chill.
5. Using floured hands, shape mixture into flat cakes about 2 inches in diameter.
6. Coat with beaten egg and breadcrumbs.

To serve without freezing: Fry fish cakes in hot shallow fat.

To freeze: Freeze cakes without packing. Pack frozen cakes carefully in waxed cardboard containers with a sheet of freezer paper between each layer.

To thaw: Fry frozen cakes in hot shallow fat until golden brown and cooked through.

Fish Stew

2 lb boned firm white fish (hake, halibut, cod, whiting, etc)
1 tablespoon chopped parsley
1 small onion, chopped
3 tablespoons olive oil
1 tin drained tomatoes, or 3 large tomatoes, peeled, seeded and chopped

Wineglass dry white wine
Salt and pepper
Pinch of thyme
2 cloves of garlic, crushed

METHOD

1. Heat olive oil in a heavy pan. Add chopped onion and parsley. Cook gently until onion turns transparent. Do not brown.
2. Cut fish into 2-inch pieces.
3. Add the fish and fry over a low flame for 5 minutes.
4. Add tomatoes, wine, salt, pepper and pinch of thyme. Cover and simmer for 5 minutes.

To serve without freezing: Add garlic and continue to simmer for 20 minutes.

To freeze: Cool. Pack in a suitable container. Seal, label and freeze.

To thaw: Turn frozen fish into a heavy pan. Heat over a low flame until juice is thawed. Add garlic, cover and simmer for 20 minutes.

Serve: With boiled new potatoes.

Fillets of Fish with Lemon Sauce

2 lb haddock, bream or cod
  fillets
Juice of ½ lemon
1 oz butter
½ pint prawns
Salt and pepper

SAUCE
2 oz butter
1½ oz flour
1½ pint fish stock
¼ pint cream
Salt and pepper
Juice of ½ lemon
1 egg yolk

METHOD

1. Roll up the fish fillets and place in a buttered baking dish. Add lemon juice, seasonings, and enough water to cover.

2. Cover and bake in a moderate oven (350°F: Reg. 3) for 30 minutes or until fish is tender. Remove fillets and strain stock.

3. Fry prawns in melted butter for 3 minutes. Drain, keep warm.

4. *To make the sauce:* Melt the butter and add the flour. Stir until the mixture forms a ball and comes away from the sides of the pan. Gradually add the fish stock and lemon juice and prawns. Season with salt and pepper.

To serve without freezing: Beat egg yolk with a little of the sauce. Stir in the rest of the sauce and the cream. Pour over the fish fillets.

To freeze: Cool fish and sauce. Pack with the fish well covered by the sauce. Seal, label and freeze.

To thaw: Heat in a shallow bowl over hot but not boiling water. Stir occasionally, but be careful not to break up fish.

To serve: Remove fish to a buttered serving dish. Keep hot. Add a little sauce to the beaten egg yolk. Add the rest of the sauce and the cream, and heat through, stirring well. Pour over the fish and serve.

Baked Fish with Tomato Sauce

A 3-lb fish: turbot, halibut, etc
Seasoned flour
4 oz butter
½ green pepper, chopped and seeded
2 tablespoons finely chopped celery
1 medium onion, chopped

1 large tin tomatoes
1 tablespoon Worcester sauce
1 tablespoon tomato purée
Juice of 1 lemon
2 bay leaves
Salt and freshly ground black pepper

METHOD

1. Clean the fish and leave whole. Coat with seasoned flour. Place in a greased baking dish just large enough to take the fish.

2. Melt the butter in a saucepan. Add the pepper, celery and onion and cook over a low heat for 5 minutes.

3. Add the tomatoes, Worcester sauce, tomato purée, lemon juice and bay leaves. Season with salt and pepper. Cover and simmer for 30 minutes or until the celery is tender.

4. Put the sauce through a food mill or fine sieve. Pour over the fish.

5. Bake in a moderate oven (350°F: Reg. 4) for 30 minutes. The fish should be covered by the sauce, but if it is not, baste frequently,

To serve without freezing: Continue to bake for a further 15 minutes.

To freeze: Cool. Pack in a suitable container or freeze the fish unpacked in the baking dish. When solid unmould and pack in a polythene bag. Seal, label and freeze.

To thaw: Place frozen fish in a baking dish. Cover with aluminium foil and bake in a moderate oven (350°F: Reg. 4) for 30 minutes.

Smoked Haddock Flan

PASTRY
8 oz plain flour
5 oz butter
Pinch of salt
1 teaspoon lemon juice
2–3 tablespoons cold water
1 egg yolk

FILLING
½ lb flaked cooked smoked
   haddock
2 large tomatoes
1 oz butter
1 large onion, chopped
2 eggs
½ pint milk or thin cream
Salt, pepper and nutmeg
Grated cheese

METHOD

1. *To make the pastry:* Sift the flour and salt. Add the butter cut in small pieces and rub into the flour with the fingertips until the mixture resembles coarse breadcrumbs.

2. Mix in the egg yolk beaten with the water and lemon juice. Mix with the hands into a firm dough. Chill in a refrigerator for 1 hour.

3. Roll out, and line a flan ring. Press a piece of waxed paper into the flan and fill with rice or dried beans. Bake in a hot oven (425°F: Reg. 6) for 15 minutes. Remove paper and beans and bake for a further 5 minutes. Leave to cool.

4. *To make the filling:* Peel, seed and chop tomatoes. Arrange with the fish in the baked flan shell.

5. Melt the butter in a saucepan. Add onion and cook until transparent. Add cream or milk and cook until at boiling point.

6. Remove from heat and mix in beaten eggs, salt, pepper and a little grated nutmeg. Pour over fish and tomatoes. Sprinkle the surface with cheese.

7. Bake in a moderate oven for 20 minutes.

To serve without freezing: Continue baking for a further 10 minutes or until pie is set and brown.

To freeze: Cool. Pack between two cardboard plates. Secure with waterproof tape. Pack, seal, label and freeze.

To thaw: Bake frozen pie in a moderate oven (325°F: Reg. 4) for 25 minutes or until hot through and brown.

Serve: Hot, cut into wedges.

Lobster Thermidor

2 small boiled lobsters
2 oz butter
½ teaspoon finely chopped
   onion
Pinch of cayenne pepper
½ glass dry white wine
½ lb mushrooms, finely
   chopped
1 tablespoon tomato purée

SAUCE
2 oz butter
2 oz flour
½ pint hot milk
Salt and pepper
2 tablespoons grated
   Parmesan cheese

METHOD

1. Cut the lobsters in half and take out the meat. Clean the shells carefully. Remove the meat from the claws and chop all the meat into small dice.

2. Heat the butter in a saucepan, add the lobster meat, onion, cayenne and wine. Simmer over a medium heat for 5 minutes stirring all the time.

3. Add the chopped mushrooms, tomato purée and mix well.

4. Fill the lobster shells with the meat mixture, packing it down well.

5. Make a white sauce by melting the butter in a saucepan. Add the flour and mix well until the mixture forms a ball and leaves the sides of the pan. Add the hot milk slowly, stirring all the time. Season lightly with salt and pepper.

6. Pour the white sauce over each lobster so that the meat is covered.

To serve without freezing: Cover with grated cheese. Heat thoroughly in a hot oven (420°F: Reg. 6) and then put under a hot grill for 2 minutes.

To freeze: Cool. Wrap each lobster half in moisture- and vapour-proof paper. Pack in a polythene bag or a container. Seal, label and freeze.

To thaw: Unwrap lobsters. Place in a baking dish. Cover with aluminium foil and heat in a medium-hot oven (400°F: Reg. 5) for 20 minutes or until lobsters are hot through. Remove foil, sprinkle with cheese and brown under a hot grill for 2 minutes.

Lobster Newburg

To my mind the most delicious of hot lobster dishes,
but unfortunately expensive

2 cooked 1-lb lobsters	2 oz butter
1 tablespoon flour	1 cup single cream
½ cup sherry	3 egg yolks
Salt and pepper	Paprika pepper
A few drops of tabasco sauce	Chopped parsley

METHOD

1. Cut the lobsters in half down the centre of the back using a sharp knife.

2. Remove the brain sac and the intestine (thin black line) from each side. Take out the meat from the shell and cut into small cubes.

3. Melt the butter in a saucepan.

4. Blend in flour.

5. Gradually add the cream and sherry, stirring all the time, until the sauce reaches boiling point. Season with salt, pepper, paprika and tabasco sauce.

6. Cover and cook over a low heat for 5 minutes. *Do not allow to boil.*

7. Beat the egg yolks.

8. Gradually stir the hot sauce into the egg yolks.

9. Mix in the lobster.

To freeze: Cool and pack into a polythene or waxed container. Seal, label and freeze.

To defrost: Turn the frozen lobster into a basin or double-boiler. Place over hot water, cover and cook until thawed. Remove cover and stir continually until heated through.

To serve: Heat the lobster until really hot over low heat, stirring continually. Serve on a bed of buttered rice with a sprinkling of chopped parsley over the top.

Do not freeze for longer than 1 month.

Lobster Mousse

1 lobster
½ pint mayonnaise
½ pint thick cream
1 egg white
Juice of 1 lemon

2 tablespoons water
1 tablespoon tomato ketchup
1 oz gelatine
Salt and pepper

METHOD

1. Split the lobster. Remove the brain sac. Chop the flesh from the body and claws into small pieces.
2. Dissolve the gelatine in the lemon juice and water over a medium flame. Leave to cool.
3. Add the tomato ketchup and lobster to the mayonnaise. Mix in the gelatine.
4. Whip the cream and fold into the mixture.
5. Whip the egg white until stiff and fold into the mixture. Season with salt and pepper.
6. Pour into a jelly mould and leave to set.

To serve without freezing: Leave in a refrigerator until set. Turn out and garnish with watercress.

To freeze: Pack the mould in a polythene bag. Seal, label and freeze.

To thaw: Leave the mould in a refrigerator for at least 4 hours. Unmould.

To serve: Garnish with watercress.

Note: The mousse can be made with one 6-oz tin lobster meat.

Baked Crab or Tinned Salmon with Mushrooms

1 lb dressed crab or 2 tins
  salmon
½ lb mushrooms
1 oz butter
1 oz flour

½ pint milk
¼ lb fresh breadcrumbs
¼ lb grated cheese
Salt and pepper

METHOD

1. Slice the mushrooms and fry in the melted butter for 15 minutes over a medium heat.
2. Add the flour and mix well.
3. Slowly add the milk, stirring continually, and cook for 1 minute.
4. Add the crab or salmon to the sauce. Season with salt and pepper.

To freeze: Cool and pour into suitable containers. Seal, label and freeze.

To thaw: Turn the frozen mixture into a buttered casserole dish. Cover with tin foil and heat in a moderate oven (325°F: Reg. 3) for 20 minutes.

To serve: Remove tin foil, cover with breadcrumbs, sprinkle over the cheese and continue baking in a hot oven (410°F: Reg. 6) for a further 15 minutes.

Devilled Crab

1 lb fresh, frozen or tinned
  crab meat
5 oz butter
1 small onion, chopped
3 oz flour
1 teaspoon Worcester sauce
1 teaspoon dry mustard

1 pint milk
Salt and pepper
2 beaten egg yolks
1 tablespoon chopped chives
1 tablespoon made English
  mustard
Breadcrumbs

265

1. Melt 4 oz of the butter in a saucepan and fry the onions until they soften and turn transparent. Mix in the flour, dry mustard and Worcester sauce.

2. Stir well and slowly add the milk, stirring all the time until the sauce is thick and smooth. Stir in the chives and crab meat and seasonings. Cook for 5 minutes over a medium heat.

To serve without freezing: Remove from the heat and stir in the beaten egg yolks. Pour into a shallow baking dish. Spread the top thinly with the made mustard, sprinkle with breadcrumbs and dot with 1 oz butter cut into small pieces. Bake in a moderate oven (350°F: Reg. 5) for 15 minutes until the top is brown.

To freeze: Cool the mixture and pour into a suitable container. Seal, label and freeze.

To thaw: Turn into a saucepan and stir over a moderate heat until the mixture is hot through. Remove from the heat and stir in the beaten egg yolks. Pour into a shallow baking dish, spread the top with made mustard, sprinkle with breadcrumbs and dot with 1 oz butter. Bake in a moderate oven for 15 minutes.

Scampi Provençale

1 lb scampi
1½ oz butter
Seasoned flour
2 shallots, chopped
1½ glasses white wine
Bouquet garni
½ oz flour

2 tomatoes, peeled and
  chopped
A few chopped mushrooms
1 clove garlic
2 teaspoons tomato purée
¾ pint stock

METHOD

1. Simmer the shallots and the bouquet garni in the wine until it is reduced by half. Remove bouquet garni.
2. Melt 1 oz of the butter, add the flour, stir well, and allow to

brown. Mix in the stock and add the mushrooms, the minced garlic, tomato purée and tomatoes. Simmer for 20 minutes.

3. Add the shallots and wine and simmer for a further 15 minutes.

4. Roll the scampi in seasoned flour and sauté for 5 minutes in melted butter. Pour the sauce over and mix well.

To freeze: Cool and pack into suitable containers. Seal, label and freeze.

To thaw: Turn frozen scampi into a double-saucepan. Thaw over a medium heat, stirring occasionally.

To serve: Serve really hot, on a bed of rice.
 Do not freeze for longer than 1 month.

Coquilles St Jacques

	SAUCE
8 scallops	1 oz flour
1 small onion, finely chopped	1 oz butter
1 large tomato, peeled and chopped	¼ pint milk
¼ lb mushrooms, thinly sliced	Salt, pepper and a pinch of paprika
2 oz butter	

Ask your fishmonger to open and clean the scallops and to give you the shells. Clean them well, dry and store until needed.

METHOD

1. First make the sauce. Melt the butter in a small saucepan over a medium heat. Add the flour and stir well until the flour and butter form a soft ball and leave the sides of the pan.

2. Add the milk slowly, stirring all the time until the mixture bubbles and is quite smooth. Add the seasoning and remove from the heat.

3. Wash the scallops and put in a saucepan. Cover with cold

salted water. Bring to the boil and simmer for 6 minutes. Drain
and chop.

4. Cook the scallops, onion, tomato and mushrooms in the
butter over a medium heat for 3 minutes.

5. Add the sauce and mix well.

To freeze: Cool the mixture. Pack in suitable containers. Seal,
label and freeze.

To thaw: Place frozen scallops in a double-boiler over water. Stir
gently as the mixture thaws.

To serve: Fill the scallop shells with the hot mixture. Place under a
hot grill to brown the top. Sprinkle with chopped parsley and
serve piping hot.

Note: To make the scallops stretch further, pipe a ring of mashed
potato round the edge of the shells.

The scallops can be placed on the shells before freezing and then
heated in a medium oven until they are hot through before brown-
ing under the grill.

Do not freeze for longer than 2 months.

Scallops with Mushrooms

8 scallops	½ pint thin cream
¼ lb mushrooms	1 dessertspoon dry Vermouth
3 oz butter	Salt and pepper
1 oz flour	Breadcrumbs

METHOD

1. Melt 2 oz butter in a saucepan. Chop the mushrooms and
fry gently in the butter for 5 minutes.

2. Add the flour and mix well. Slowly stir in the cream over a
low flame. Continue stirring until the sauce is smooth.

3. Add the Vermouth and season with salt and pepper.

4. Stir in the scallops cut into quarters. Pour into a shallow

buttered casserole. Sprinkle breadcrumbs over the surface and dot with remaining 1 oz butter.

4. Cover. Bake in a medium-hot oven (375°F: Reg. 5) for 10 minutes.

To serve without freezing: Remove cover and continue to bake for a further 10 minutes.

To freeze: Cool. Pack casserole in a polythene bag or wrap in freezer paper or aluminium foil. Seal, label and freeze.

To thaw: Cover frozen casserole with aluminium foil and cook in a medium-hot oven (375°F: Reg. 5) for 20–30 minutes. Remove cover for last 10 minutes to brown the surface.

Clam and Courgette Casserole

Tinned minced clams can be bought in most delicatessen shops, but fresh clams or cockles could be substituted

6 courgettes	4 tablespoons chopped
1 tin minced clams	parsley
6 rashers bacon	Salt and pepper
	Butter

METHOD

1. Thinly slice unpeeled courgettes.
2. Fry bacon until crisp. Leave to cool and crumble into small pieces.
3. Butter a casserole dish. Fill it with alternate layers of courgettes, clams and juice, bacon and parsley. Season with salt and pepper. Dot the surface with butter.
4. Bake in a moderate oven (350°F: Reg. 4) for 20 minutes.

To serve without freezing: Bake for a further 10 minutes.

To freeze: Cool quickly. Pack in casserole in a polythene bag. Seal, label and freeze.

To thaw: Cover frozen casserole and thaw in a moderate oven for about 30 minutes until hot right through.

Serve: Hot with a mixed salad.

Sardine Rolls

	PASTRY
2 tins sardines	8 oz flour
Salt and pepper	5 oz butter
Lemon juice	3–4 tablespoons water
1 tablespoon chopped parsley	1 egg yolk
	4 oz grated cheese
	Salt and paprika pepper

METHOD

1. *To make pastry:* Sift the flour with the salt into a large bowl. Add the butter and cut with two knives into the flour. When the butter is in small pieces and well coated with flour rub it well into the flour until the mixture looks like coarse breadcrumbs. Add the grated cheese and paprika pepper.

2. Keeping 1 tablespoon water aside, add the egg yolk to the remainder. Make a well in the centre of the flour and add the cold water and egg yolk. Mix well with a flat knife. Press into a ball with the fingers, if necessary adding more water to form a firm dough.

3. Turn on to a floured board and knead lightly with the hands until smooth. Wrap in a cloth and chill in a cool place for at least ½ hour before rolling out.

4. Roll out pastry to 8-inch thickness and cut into oblongs 2 inches by 3 inches.

5. Drain sardines and place one in the centre of each piece of pastry. Sprinkle over a little chopped parsley. Season lightly with salt and pepper and a little lemon juice. Damp the edges of the pastry and roll up.

To serve without freezing: Brush rolls with milk and bake in a hot oven (400°F: Reg 6) for 10–12 minutes until golden brown.

To freeze: Freeze uncooked rolls before packing. When solid, pack in a suitable container with a sheet of moisture- and vapour-proof paper between each layer.

To thaw: Place frozen rolls on a baking sheet. Brush with milk and bake in a hot oven (400°F: Reg. 6) for 15–20 minutes until golden brown.

Pastries

Shortcrust Pastry

½ lb plain flour
5 oz butter

3–4 tablespoons cold water
Salt or sugar

METHOD

1. Sift the flour with the salt or sugar into a large bowl. Add the butter and cut with two knives into the flour. When the butter is in small pieces and well coated with flour, rub it well into the flour until the mixture looks like coarse breadcrumbs.

2. Make a well in the centre and add the cold water, keeping 1 tablespoonful aside. Mix well with a flat knife. Press into a ball with the fingers, if necessary adding more water to form a firm dough.

3. Turn on to a floured board and knead lightly with the hands until smooth. Wrap in a cloth and chill in a cool place for at least ½ hour before rolling out.

Note: For a richer pastry: Add 1 egg yolk to the water and mix well before adding to the flour.

For a cheese pastry: Add 1 egg yolk to the water before mixing into the flour. Add 4 oz cheese and a pinch of paprika pepper to the flour.

Flaky Pastry

½ lb plain flour
3 oz butter
3 oz lard

4–6 tablespoons cold water
Pinch of salt

METHOD

1. Sift the flour and salt into a large bowl. Rub in half the butter with the fingertips. Mix to a firm dough with the water. Knead on a floured board until smooth.

2. Roll out. Cover two-thirds of the pastry with half the lard cut into small pieces. Fold into three. Pinch the edges together firmly with the fingertips.

3. Roll out again. Repeat twice, using first the remaining butter and then the lard. Fold up and chill for a least 30 minutes.

Puff Pastry

½ lb plain flour
½ lb butter

¼ pint iced water
1 teaspoon lemon juice

METHOD

1. Sift the flour with the salt into a large mixing bowl. Rub in 1 oz butter with the fingertips and mix to a firm dough with the water. Knead on a floured board until smooth. Chill for 15 minutes.

2. Roll out into an oblong on a floured board. Dust with flour and place the softened butter in the centre. Spread out with a knife. Fold in half. Turn and fold in half again.

3. Roll out again and fold in three. Turn until the open edge is in front of you. Roll out and again fold in three. Wrap in a cloth and chill for 15 minutes.

4. Repeat the rolling, folding and chilling process six times or until all the butter has been absorbed into the pastry. Chill for a final 15 minutes before using.

To freeze the foregoing types of pastry: Wrap in a layer of moisture- and vapour-proof paper. Pack in a polythene bag, or wrap in freezer paper or aluminium foil. Seal, label and freeze.

To thaw: Leave in a refrigerator or at room temperature until the pastry is soft enough to work. 1 hour at room temperature should be enough. Do not allow it to get warm. Unpack carefully, brush frozen pastry with beaten egg or milk as required and bake in a hot oven.

Note: Pastry cases, vol-au-vent cases, etc, can be frozen before baking.

Tart Pastry

For sweet and savoury tarts and tartlets

11 oz plain flour	¼ teaspoon salt or 1 oz caster
4½ oz soft butter	sugar
	Water to mix

METHOD

1. Sift the flour on to a marble slab or cold surface. Make a well in the centre and put in the butter cut into small pieces. Add the salt or sugar.

2. Mix the butter into the flour with the fingertips, adding enough water to give a smooth workable paste.

To use without freezing: Wrap the pastry in a floured cloth and leave to rest in a cool place for 2–3 hours.

To freeze: Pack pastry in a polythene bag. Seal, label and freeze.

To thaw: Leave pastry in its wrapping in a refrigerator or at room temperature until it is soft enough to work. Do not allow to get warm.

METHOD

1. Leave pastry to rest for 2–3 hours in a cool place. Roll out very thinly on a floured board to a thickness of about $\frac{1}{8}$ inch.
2. Line a tart tin or cut into rounds with a pastry cutter to line individual tartlet tins.
3. Prick the pastry all over with a fork and bake for 12–15 minutes in a medium-hot oven (400°F: Reg. 5).
4. Leave to cool in their tins before turning out.

To freeze: Pack in waxed boxes or rigid containers. Seal, label and freeze.

To thaw: Leave in containers at room temperature until thawed, about 15–60 minutes.

Note: If the pastry has become a little soft it can be crisped by heating for 5 minutes in a medium-hot oven. Tarts that are to be served hot can be filled whilst still frozen.

Choux Pastry

4 oz flour
$\frac{1}{2}$ teaspoon salt
2 oz butter

$\frac{1}{4}$ pint water
4 eggs

METHOD

1. Heat the water with the butter to boiling point.
2. Stir in the flour and cook, stirring all the time, until the mixture forms a soft ball of dough.
3. Remove from the heat and beat in the egg a little at a time.
4. Use as required.

To freeze: Wrap in a layer of moisture- and vapour-proof paper. Pack in a polythene bag. Seal, label and freeze.

To thaw: Leave in refrigerator or at room temperature until the pastry is soft enough to use.

Sweets

Baked Spiced Apples

4 large cooking apples
4 tablespoons brown sugar

4 tablespoons mincemeat
4 tablespoons water

METHOD

1. Wash the apples. Using a knife, hollow out the centre round the core, or use an apple corer and enlarge the hole.
2. Trim the flesh from around the core and mash with the mincemeat and brown sugar.
3. Fill the centre of the apples with the mincemeat mixture, pressing down firmly.
4. Place in a baking dish with the water. Sprinkle with a little brown sugar and bake in a moderate oven (320°F: Reg. 3). Baste frequently to prevent burning and cook for about 1 hour until tender but still firm.

To freeze: Freeze unpacked. When frozen pack into a rigid container with a sheet of moisture- and vapour-proof paper between apples.

To thaw: Thaw in a refrigerator for at least 4 hours or at room temperature for approximately 1½ hours.

Serve: Cold in the summer, or heat through in a moderate oven to serve as a cold-weather pudding.

Curried Fruit Salad

This unusual sweet is delicious hot or cold; the curry tastes very subtle, and is impossible to recognize unless you know what it is.

1 lb red gooseberries
½ lb raspberries
¼ lb redcurrants or any
  mixture of fresh fruit in
  season

¼ lb sugar
Juice of 1 lemon
2 teaspoons curry paste

METHOD

1. Place gooseberries and raspberries with sugar in a heavy pan: simmer for 5 minutes. Add redcurrants and simmer for a further 3 minutes.

2. Strain fruit and return the juice to the pan. Add curry paste and lemon juice and cook over a medium heat until curry is completely dissolved. Cool and pour over fruit.

To freeze: Cool. Pack in a suitable container. Seal, label and freeze.

To thaw: Leave fruit salad packed at room temperature for about 2 hours.

To serve hot: Turn frozen fruit salad into a heavy pan. Thaw over a low heat until hot through.

Tipsy Apples in Spiced Syrup

12 small, crisp, flavoursome
  dessert apples
½ lb sugar
1 pint water
Grated rind of 1 lemon

1 tablespoon lemon juice
1 cinnamon stick
3 cloves
4 tablespoons rum

278

1. Put sugar and water in a saucepan. Bring to the boil.
2. Add the lemon rind and juice, cinnamon and cloves. Continue to boil for 5 minutes.
3. Remove cinnamon and cloves. Add the whole apples, peeled and cored. Simmer in the syrup for 15 minutes.

To serve without freezing: Simmer for a further 10 minutes until the apples are soft. Leave to cool for 15 minutes. Place apples on a baking dish. Pour over 4 tablespoons warm rum and set alight. Serve whilst still flaming.

To freeze: Leave to cool. Pack carefully with syrup. Seal, label and freeze.

To thaw: Turn frozen apples into a shallow pan. Heat gently over a moderate heat for 20 minutes. Leave to cool in syrup for 15 minutes.

To serve: Pour over 4 tablespoons warm rum. Set alight and serve flaming.

Note: Fresh peaches and brandy can also be prepared in the same way, using 4 peaches, and brandy in the place of rum.

Plums Baked in Port

1 lb firm Victoria or cooking plums
3 tablespoons vanilla sugar
2 tablespoons water
3 tablespoons port

METHOD

1. Wipe plums and remove the stems. Cut a slit in each one.
2. Pack the plums in a baking dish. Sprinkle over the sugar and add the water and port.
3. Bake uncovered in a slow oven (210°F: Reg. 2) for 40 minutes, until tender but not mushy.

To freeze: Cool. Pack in a suitable container. Seal, label and freeze.

To thaw: Leave plums wrapped at room temperature for 2 hours until thawed. Serve cold with ice-cream, or warm in a slow oven and serve hot with a milk pudding.

Fruit Pie

1 lb plain flour
2 lb prepared fruit (apples, rhubarb, blackberries or blackcurrants, etc)
10 oz butter

6–8 tablespoons water
2 teaspoons salt
¼ lb sugar
3 tablespoons cream

METHOD

1. *To make the pastry:* Sift the flour with the salt into a large bowl. Add the butter and cut with two knives into the flour. When the butter is in small pieces and well coated with flour, rub it well into the flour until the mixture looks like coarse breadcrumbs.

2. Make a well in the centre and add the cold water, keeping 1 tablespoonful aside. Mix well with a flat knife. Press into a ball with the fingers, adding more water if necessary, to form a firm dough.

3. Turn on to a floured board and knead lightly with the hands until smooth. Wrap in a cloth and chill in a cool place for at least ½ hour before rolling out.

4. Divide pastry into two. Roll out half and line a pie plate.

5. Fill with fruit. Sprinkle fruit that tends to discolour with 2 teaspoons lemon juice. Sprinkle ¼ lb sugar over.

6. Roll out remaining pastry. Cover the fruit and press the edges together firmly.

To cook without freezing: Make two slits in the pastry. Brush with a little of the cream and bake for 45 minutes in a hot oven (420°F: Reg. 6). Pour in the remaining cream through one of the slits, using a funnel, for the last 10 minutes of cooking time.

To freeze: Pack pie between two cardboard plates. Pack, seal, label and freeze.

To thaw: Cut two slits in the frozen pastry. Brush with a little cream and bake in a hot oven (420°F: Reg. 6) for 55 minutes. Pour remaining cream through one of the slits, using a funnel, for the last 10 minutes of baking time.

Serve: Hot or cold, with the surface of the pie dusted with caster sugar.

Treacle Tart

PASTRY
4 oz plain flour
2 oz butter
2 oz vanilla sugar
2 egg yolks

FILLING
4 tablespoons golden syrup,
    or 2 tablespoons black treacle
    and 2 tablespoons golden
    syrup
1 oz butter
2 tablespoons cream
Grated rind of 1 lemon
1 dessert apple, peeled and
    grated

METHOD

1. *To make pastry:* Sift the flour on to a board. Make a well in the centre.

2. Mix egg yolks, butter and sugar together in a bowl.

3. Pour into the well in the flour. Mix the flour in gradually with the fingertips. When it is blended knead for 1 minute and form into a ball.

4. Wrap in a floured cloth and leave in refrigerator for at least 1 hour.

5. *To make filling:* Put the syrup in a saucepan and melt over a low heat.

6. Remove from the heat and mix in the butter.

7. Add cream, lemon rind and grated apple, and stir well.

8. Roll out the pastry thinly and brush the bottom with a little melted butter. Fill with the syrup mixture. You can decorate the top with thin strips of the pastry trimmings.

9. Bake in a moderate oven (350°F: Reg. 4) for 30 minutes or until the filling is set. Prick the bottom with a knitting needle or skewer after 15 minutes.

To freeze: Cool on a cake rack. Pack between two cardboard plates, secure with waterproof tape, and pack in freezer paper in a polythene bag. Seal, label and freeze.

To thaw: Leave unpacked at room temperature for 3 hours or until thawed.

Serve: Cold or reheat for 10 minutes in a moderate oven.

Mince Pies

½ lb mincemeat	1 egg yolk
8 oz plain flour	2 tablespoons iced water
6 oz butter	1 teaspoon sugar

METHOD

1. *To make the pastry:* Sift the flour and sugar together. Rub in the butter with the fingertips until the mixture resembles coarse breadcrumbs. Beat the egg yolk with 2 tablespoons water. Add to the flour and work into a stiff dough, adding the rest of the water. Cover and leave to chill in a refrigerator for 1 hour.

2. Roll out the pastry and cut into twelve large and twelve small rounds with floured pastry cutters. Press larger rounds into patty tins.

3. Fill with a spoonful of mincemeat. Cover with smaller pastry rounds and press edges firmly together. Brush with milk and make a small slit in the top of each pie.

4. Bake in a hot oven (420°F: Reg. 6) for 5 minutes. Reduce heat to medium hot (400°F: Reg. 5) and continue baking for 10 minutes.

To serve without freezing: Bake for a further 5 minutes or until pies are golden brown. Dust with icing sugar.

To freeze: Cool. Pack in suitable containers with a layer of freezer paper between pies. Seal, label and freeze.

To thaw: Remove pies from freezer and leave for 10 minutes. Place on a baking sheet in a medium-hot oven and heat for 15 minutes or until hot through and golden brown.

Serve: With brandy butter.

Almond Pie

	TOPPING
2 eggs	¼ lb almonds
8 oz sugar	2 oz butter
1 teaspoon vanilla essence	3 tablespoons sugar
5 oz flour	1 tablespoon cream
1½ teaspoons baking powder	1 tablespoon flour
4 tablespoons cream	
¼ lb melted butter	

METHOD

1. Beat the eggs, sugar and vanilla essence until light and fluffy.
2. Sift the flour with the baking powder. Fold into the egg mixture with the cream. Stir until well blended.
3. Add the melted butter and mix until smooth. Pour the mixture into a well-greased and floured Pyrex pie plate.
4. Bake in a moderate oven (325°F: Reg. 3) for 30 minutes until the centre of the cake is firm.
5. *To make the topping:* Blanch the almonds. Remove the skins and slice. Place the almonds, butter, sugar, cream and flour in a small saucepan and cook over a medium heat until the mixture bubbles.
6. Remove from the heat and stir well. Pour the topping over the pie.

To serve without freezing: Return the pie to a medium-hot oven (375°F: Reg. 5) for 5–10 minutes until the top is brown. Serve warm, cut into wedges.

To freeze: Cool. Cover with a cardboard plate. Pack in a polythene bag. Seal, label and freeze.

To thaw: Unwrap and cover frozen pie with a layer of aluminium foil. Thaw in a medium-hot oven for 15 minutes. Remove the foil and continue to cook for 5 minutes until the top is brown and the pie hot through.

Serve: Warm.

Prune Pie

¼ lb plain flour
Pinch of salt
4 tablespoons cold milk
2 eggs
6 oz butter
20 prunes, soaked and pitted

¼ lb chopped almonds
1 tablespoon butter
1 tablespoon cream
1 teaspoon brandy
2 tablespoons icing sugar

METHOD

1. *To make the pastry:* Sift the flour into a bowl with a pinch of salt. Add the milk and eggs and beat well until smooth. Leave to stand for 2 hours.

2. Roll out the dough on a floured board. Reserve 1 tablespoon butter. Cut the rest into small pieces and dot over the surface of the dough. Sprinkle with flour, fold into three and chill for ½ hour.

3. Divide the pastry in two. Roll out half and line a 9-inch pie plate. Put in the well-drained prunes and chopped almonds. Dot with 1 tablespoon butter cut into pieces.

4. Cover with the remaining pastry.

To serve without freezing: Brush surface of the pastry with the cream mixed with the brandy. Sprinkle with sugar and bake in a hot oven (450°F: Reg. 7) for 20 minutes.

To freeze: Pack pie between two cardboard plates, then in a polythene bag, or wrap in freezer paper or aluminium foil. Seal, label and freeze.

To thaw: Brush frozen pie with cream and brandy. Sprinkle with icing sugar and bake in a hot oven (450°F: Reg. 7) for 40 minutes.

Apple or Peach Meringue Upside-down Cake

1 lb apples or peaches	2 egg yolks
Rind and juice of 1 lemon	1 oz melted butter
1 tablespoon flour	1 tablespoons milk
8 oz granulated sugar	
4 oz plain flour	MERINGUE
Pinch of salt	2 egg whites
1 teaspoon baking powder	4 tablespoons caster sugar

METHOD

1. Well grease an 8-inch pie plate. Cover the bottom with sliced apples or peaches.
2. Sprinkle with ¼ lb sugar, lemon juice and grated lemon rind.
3. Sift the flour into a bowl with the rest of the sugar, the baking powder and salt.
4. Beat the egg yolks with the milk and add to the flour with the melted butter. Beat quickly until well blended.
5. Cover the fruit with the batter mixture and bake in a hot oven (410°F: Reg. 6) for about 30 minutes.

To serve without freezing: Beat the egg whites until stiff. Fold in 4 tablespoons caster sugar. Reverse the cake on to a dish and cover with the meringue. Bake in a slow oven (300°F: Reg. 2) for 15 minutes.

To freeze: Reverse the cake on to a cardboard plate. Cover with another plate and pack in a polythene bag, or wrap in freezer paper or aluminium foil. Seal, label and freeze. Pack egg whites in a suitable container. Seal, label and freeze.

To thaw: Thaw wrapped cake (fruit side up) and egg whites at room temperature for 1½ hours. Unwrap cake. Whip egg whites until stiff, fold in 4 tablespoons caster sugar. Cover fruit with meringue and bake in a slow oven (300°F: Reg. 2) for 15–20 minutes.

Crêpes Suzette

One of the most dramatic and delicious of all puddings. Make plenty at once and freeze in quantities of 4 portions.

PANCAKES
8 oz plain flour
2 eggs
1 pint milk
1 tablespoon brandy
1 teaspoon sugar
Butter

FILLING
2 oz butter
3 oz caster sugar
Grated rind of ½ orange
Juice of 1 orange
Juice of ½ lemon
1 tablespoon orange Curaçao
Icing sugar
3 tablespoons brandy

METHOD

1. *To make pancakes:* Sieve the flour into a mixing bowl. Make a well in the centre.

2. Break the eggs into the well. Add half the milk and gradually mix in the flour until the mixture is smooth.

3. Add the rest of the milk. Beat well and cover and stand for 30 minutes.

4. Add the brandy and sugar and beat again.

5. Melt a little butter in an omelet pan. When it smokes pour in a spoonful of batter. Swirl round the pan until it is evenly coated. Cook pancake over a high heat until brown. Turn and brown other side.

Note: These pancakes should be paper-thin. If necessary add more milk to thin the batter.

6. *To make filling:* Cream butter and sugar until really white and creamy. Slowly beat in orange rind, orange juice, lemon juice and orange Curaçao.

7. Spread each pancake with butter mixture. Fold in half and in half again.

To freeze: Pack pancakes in a suitable container with a layer of freezer paper between each one. Seal, label and freeze.

To thaw: Arrange pancakes in one layer in a shallow buttered dish. Cover with aluminium foil and heat in a moderate oven (350°F: Reg. 4) for 15 minutes or until hot through.

To serve: Sprinkle with icing sugar. Pour over warm brandy and set alight.

Note: For extra effect, after heating pancakes place them in a chafing dish, pour over brandy and heat at the table. When the brandy is nearly hot set it alight.

Raspberry and Redcurrant Ice-Cream

Very refreshing, and easy to make

1 lb raspberries	1 tablespoon water
¼ lb redcurrants	¼ pint double cream
4 oz sugar	

METHOD

1. Combine the raspberries, redcurrants, sugar and water in a saucepan. Bring to the boil and cook over a medium heat for 5 minutes.

2. Press the fruit through a fine sieve or through a food mill. Leave to cool.

3. Whip the cream and fold into the fruit pulp.

4. Spoon into a freezing tray

To freeze: Pack in a polythene bag, or wrap in freezer paper or aluminium foil. Seal, label and freeze.

To thaw: Remove from the deep freeze 10 minutes before required.

To serve: Spoon ice-cream into a glass serving bowl.
Do not keep frozen for longer than 3 months.

Vanilla Ice-Cream

2½ oz sugar   ¾ pint double cream
6 tablespoons water   1 teaspoon vanilla essence
3 egg yolks

METHOD

1. Put sugar and water in a saucepan and cook over a low heat until sugar is dissolved.
2. Bring the syrup to the boil and boil rapidly for 15 minutes – or until a little will form a thread between finger and thumb. Remove from heat.
3. Beat the egg yolks until creamy.
4. Pour the syrup slowly on the egg yolks, beating all the time until the mixture thickens and becomes mousse-like. Stir in the vanilla essence. Cool.
5. Whip the cream and fold into the egg mixture. Pour into a freezer tray and freeze for 2 hours, beating it every ½ hour to prevent crystallization.

To freeze: Pack in cardboard tubs or cartons. Seal, label and freeze.
Do not keep longer than 1 month.

Chocolate Ice-Cream

Follow recipe for vanilla ice-cream.

Mix 1 oz sweetened cocoa with 1 oz unsweetened cocoa and 2 tablespoons water and heat until cocoa is melted. Cool and add to egg mixture before stirring in cream.

Rum and Raisin Ice-Cream

Follow recipe for vanilla ice-cream.

Soak ¼ lb seedless raisins in 3 tablespoons rum for 4 hours until soft. Add to egg mixture before stirring in cream.

Grapenut Ice-Cream

Follow recipe for vanilla ice-cream.

Add 3 tablespoons toasted grapenuts to egg mixture before stirring in cream.

Strawberry Ice-Cream

8 servings

1 lb fresh strawberries, crushed	6 oz caster sugar
1 oz gelatine	1 teaspoon vanilla essence
4 tablespoons cold water	1 pint double cream
2 eggs	2 oz sugar

1. Soften gelatine in cold water. Dissolve over hot water and leave to cool.

2. Beat egg yolks with sugar until creamy. Add the cream, vanilla essence and crushed strawberries.

3. Pour into a refrigerator tray and freeze for 2 hours.

4. Beat egg whites until soft peaks form. Gradually add 2 oz sugar and continue beating until the sugar dissolves and the egg whites are stiff.

5. Break up the partially frozen ice-cream and beat until fluffy. Fold in the egg whites and return quickly to the cold tray.

Note: It is important that the ice-cream should not be allowed to melt.

To freeze: Pack tray in tin foil or freezer paper. Seal in a polythene bag. Label and freeze.

To thaw: Remove from the deep freeze 10 minutes before serving.

Strawberry Ice-Bombe

9 servings

2 oz butter	½ lb ginger nuts
2 oz sugar	3 pints strawberry ice-cream

METHOD

1. Cream the butter with the sugar until almost white, and fluffy.

2. Crush the biscuits with a rolling pin until they become coarse crumbs. Mix with the butter mixture.

3. Line a quart mixing bowl with the crumb mixture. Press in the ice-cream.

To freeze: Cover the surface with a layer of aluminium foil. Pack in a polythene bag. Seal, label and freeze.

To thaw: Remove from the deep freeze 10 minutes before serving. Run a spatula round the sides of the bowl and turn out the bombe.

To serve: Decorate with whipped cream.

Chocolate Roll

¼ lb caster sugar	2 tablespoons unsweetened
3 eggs	cocoa
1 teaspoon vanilla essence	2 tablespoons plain flour
Chocolate or vanilla ice-cream	½ teaspoon cream of tartar

METHOD

1. Separate eggs. Beat yolks with sugar until light and creamy. Add vanilla essence and mix well.

2. Sift flour and cocoa powder together and mix into creamed mixture.

3. Whip egg whites with cream of tartar until stiff and dry. Fold into cake mixture.

4. Line a shallow 8-inch by 12-inch baking tin with greased waxproof paper. Spread evenly with the cake mixture.

5. Bake in a moderate oven (325°F: Reg. 3) for 25 minutes. The cake is cooked if it springs back when pressed. Cool in the tin for 5 minutes.

6. Turn on to a cloth and cut off any crusty edges. Cover with a piece of waxed paper and roll up tightly. Chill in refrigerator.

7. Unroll cake and spread with chocolate or vanilla ice-cream. Re-roll and wrap firmly in moisture- and vapour-proof paper.

To freeze: Wrap roll in freezer paper. Seal, label and freeze.

To thaw: Unwrap chocolate roll 10 minutes before serving.

To serve: Cut into slices.

Blackberry Water Ice

2 lb blackberries
Juice of 1 lemon
½ lb sugar

½ pint water
4 sweet geranium leaves or
    4 blackcurrant leaves

METHOD

1. Place sugar and water, geranium or blackcurrant leaves in a saucepan. Bring slowly to the boil. Cook over a fast flame for 6 minutes.
2. Cool and strain syrup
3. Sieve blackberries or put through a Mouli strainer.
4. Add the syrup to the blackberry purée.
5. Stir in the lemon juice.
6. Pour into a freezer tray and freeze.

To freeze: Pack in a polythene bag or in aluminium foil. Seal, label and freeze.

To serve: Remove from deep freeze 10 minutes before serving. Cut into cubes and serve with sweetened whipped cream.

Frozen Lemons

CASES
4 large ripe lemons

LEMON ICE-CREAM
Lemon juice
Rind of 2 lemons
6 oz icing sugar
½ pint double cream
⅓ pint water

METHOD

1. Cut a slice off the top of each lemon with a sharp fruit-knife. Scrape out all the flesh, being careful to reserve all the juice. Cut a thin sliver from the bottom of each lemon so that it stands squarely.

2. Mash the pulp and strain through a sieve. Reserve the juice.

3. Using a potato peeler or sharp knife, pare off the rind of 2 lemons.

4. Put lemon rind, icing sugar and water into a saucepan. Bring to the boil and cook over a fast flame for 6 minutes. Strain and cool.

5. Whip the cream until stiff.

6. Add the lemon juice to the cooled syrup and pour slowly into the whipped cream, stirring gently.

7. Pour into a freezer tray and freeze for $\frac{1}{2}$ hour. Turn into a bowl and stir well. Return to the freezer for another $\frac{1}{2}$ hour. Stir again and freeze until solid.

8. Spoon ice into lemon cases and replace tops.

To freeze: Wrap each lemon in moisture- and vapour-proof paper. Pack in a polythene bag. Seal, label and freeze.

To serve: Remove lemons from the freezer 10 minutes before serving.

Frozen Oranges

CASES
4 large oranges

ORANGE WATER ICE
$\frac{1}{2}$ pint orange juice
6 oz sugar
$\frac{1}{2}$ pint water
juice and rind of 1 lemon
Rind of 1 orange
2 egg whites

METHOD

1. Cut a slice off the top of each orange. Using a sharp fruit-knife cut the flesh from the inside of the oranges without piercing the skin. Cut a thin sliver from the bottom of the oranges so that they stand squarely.

2. Mash the pulp and put through a sieve to get the juice. There should be $\frac{1}{2}$ pint.

293

3. Using a sharp knife or potato peeler, pare the skin from the lemon and orange.

4. Put the sugar, water, lemon and orange rind in a saucepan. Heat slowly until the sugar dissolves. Bring to the boil and cook over a fast flame for 6 minutes. Strain syrup and cool.

5. Mix syrup with orange and lemon juice. Pour into a freezer tray and freeze for 1 hour.

6. Whip ice with a fork or rotary beater. Fold in stiffly whipped egg whites. Return to freezer until solid.

7. Spoon ice into orange cases. Replace tops.

To freeze: Wrap each orange in moisture- and vapour-proof paper. Pack in a polythene bag. Seal, label and freeze.

To serve: Remove from the freezer 10 minutes before serving.

Apple Mousse

2 lb firm tasty eating apples (eg Cox's)	½ oz gelatine
1 oz butter	½ pint cream
6 tablespoons water	½ teaspoon vanilla essence
3 oz honey	Caster sugar
	Toasted almonds

METHOD

1. Soak the gelatine in 3 tablespoons water.

2. Peel, core and chop the apples. Melt the butter, add the apples and 3 tablespoons water. Simmer until tender.

3. Remove the lid and beat with a wooden spoon over a fast flame until the purée is firm and smooth.

4. Add the honey and the gelatine. Stir well and leave to cool.

5. Whip the cream. Add the vanilla essence and fold into the apple mixture.

6. Turn the mixture into a soufflé dish.

To serve without freezing: Chill for 2 hours. Sprinkle the surface with caster sugar and chopped toasted almonds.

To freeze: Seal the soufflé dish in a polythene bag. Label and freeze.

To thaw: Still sealed, in a refrigerator for about 4 hours or until just thawed.

To serve: Sprinkle the surface with caster sugar and chopped toasted almonds.

Caramel Mousse

6 oz granulated sugar	2 oz sugar
4 tablespoons water	$\frac{1}{4}$ pint double cream
2 egg yolks	$\frac{1}{2}$ oz gelatine
3 whole eggs	Juice of 1 lemon

METHOD

1. Place the granulated sugar in a heavy saucepan and cook over a fierce heat until dissolved and a rich brown. *Do not stir.*
2. Add the water. (The water added to the hot sugar often causes violent spluttering. Cover your hand whilst pouring.) Stir until the sugar has melted. Remove from the heat and leave to cool.
3. Put the egg yolks, eggs and sugar in a basin over hot but not boiling water. Whisk over a low heat until the mixture thickens. Remove from the heat and continue whisking until cold.
4. Whip the cream and fold into the egg mixture with the caramel.
5. Melt the gelatine in the lemon juice and pour into the mousse. Stir gently and pour into a lightly-oiled ring mould. Leave to set.

To serve without freezing: Turn the mousse on to a large plate. Fill the centre with fresh fruit and decorate with whipped cream.

To freeze: Pack the mould in a polythene bag. Seal, label and freeze.

To thaw: Leave for 3 hours at room temperature. Turn out, fill with fresh fruit and decorate with whipped cream. Place in refrigerator until ready to serve.

Note: This pudding can be decorated with caramel strips which can be stored in an airtight tin for up to 1 month.

CARAMEL STRIPS

12 oz granulated sugar	¼ lb chopped blanched almonds

METHOD

1. Melt the sugar in a heavy saucepan over a low heat. When it has completely melted add the almonds. Stir until the mixture bubbles and turns an amber gold.
2. Pour on to a really well-greased baking sheet. Mark into strips with a knife dipped in oil. Using oiled scissors, cut the strips and shape over a glass bottle. This has to be done before the caramel hardens.

Rich Chocolate and Orange Mousse

6 oz plain black chocolate	½ pint cream
4 tablespoons water	Juice and grated rind
2 oz sugar	of 1 orange
4–6 eggs yolks	4 egg whites

METHOD

1. Melt the chocolate with the water in a saucepan over a low heat.
2. Mix the egg yolks and sugar and whisk over hot (but not boiling) water, until thick and frothing. Remove from heat and whisk until cold.
3. Half whip the cream and fold in.
4. Stir in the grated orange rind and juice.
5. Whisk the egg whites and fold into the mixture.
6. Turn into soufflé case or serving bowl.

To freeze: Wrap the bowl in a polythene bag. Seal, label and freeze.

To thaw: Leave the frozen mousse for 3 hours at room temperature.

To serve: Decorate with whipped cream and chopped nuts. Keep in refrigerator until ready to serve.

Chestnut Mousse

1 pint milk	1 lb chestnuts
½ teaspoon vanilla essence	1 oz gelatine
4 egg yolks	½ pint double cream
2 oz sugar	Grated chocolate

METHOD

1. Put the egg yolks with the milk in a double-saucepan over hot but not boiling water. Cook, stirring continually over a moderate heat, until the mixture is smooth and thick. Add the vanilla and leave to cool.

2. Score the chestnuts and put them in a hot oven for 15 minutes. Remove the shells and the inner skin. Put the chestnuts through a sieve or a food mill.

3. Add the sieved chestnuts and sugar to the custard and mix well.

4. Dissolve the gelatine in a little water and stir into the custard.

5. Whip the cream and fold into the mixture. Spoon into a serving dish.

To freeze: Pack the dish in a polythene bag or wrap in freezer paper or aluminium foil. Seal, label and freeze.

To thaw: Leave the packed dish in a refrigerator for at least 5 hours, or at room temperature for 1½ hours.

Serve: Cold with the top sprinkled with grated chocolate.

Pineapple Mousse

3 eggs
½ lb caster sugar
Rind and juice of 2 lemons

½ pint cream
1 oz gelatine
1 tin pineapple pieces

METHOD

1. Separate the eggs. Place yolks, sugar, lemon juice and rind in a basin over simmering water. Whip until thick. Remove from heat and whisk until the basin is cold.

2. Drain the tin of pineapple and using the juice melt the gelatine over a low heat. Fold into the mixture. Add the pineapple pieces crushed with a fork. Reserve a few for decoration. Leave until almost set.

3. Whip cream and fold into the mixture.

4. Whip the egg whites until stiff but not dry and fold into the mousse. Pour at once into a soufflé dish. Decorate with pineapple pieces.

To freeze: Pack the dish in a polythene bag. Seal, label and freeze.

To thaw: Thaw in refrigerator until almost defrosted – about 4 hours.

Serve: Chilled.

Uncooked Chocolate Mousse

4 oz unsweetened
chocolate
4 eggs

2 oz caster sugar

METHOD

1. Melt the chocolate in a double-boiler over hot water.

2. Separate the eggs and beat the yolks with the sugar until light and fluffy.

3. Add the melted chocolate to the egg yolks and beat again.

4. Beat the egg whites until stiff and fold into the chocolate mixture.

5. Pour into a serving bowl.

To serve without freezing: Chill in a refrigerator for at least 3 hours.

To freeze: Pack the bowl in a polythene bag, or wrap in freezer paper. Seal, label and freeze.

To thaw: Leave the mousse in its wrapping in a refrigerator over-night or for at least 4 hours.

Serve: With sweetened whipped cream.

Bavarian Cream

½ pint hot milk
2 eggs
2 oz sugar
2 oz icing sugar
1 oz gelatine

¼ pint water
½ pint double cream
12 sponge fingers or
   macaroons
¼ teaspoon vanilla essence

METHOD

1. Melt the gelatine in the water.

2. Separate the eggs and place egg yolks and sugar in the top of a double-saucepan over hot but not boiling water.

3. Gradually add hot milk, stirring briskly all the time. Stir until the mixture thickens; this takes about 10 minutes but it will happen eventually.

4. Add the gelatine and vanilla essence and cool.

5. Beat egg whites until stiff but not dry. Mix into the egg mixture.

6. Whip the cream and fold gently into the egg mixture.

7. Lightly butter a mould and line with sponge fingers or macaroons. Pour in the cream and leave to set.

To freeze: Pack in a polythene bag or in freezer paper. Seal, label and freeze.

To thaw: Leave in a refrigerator for 5 hours or until thawed.

To serve: Turn out and serve with fresh or stewed fruit.
Do not keep frozen for longer than 3 months.

Chocolate Macaroon Pudding

12 macaroons
1 oz gelatine
1¼ oz unsweetened cocoa
¾ pint milk

4 oz sugar
¼ pint cream
½ teaspoon vanilla essence, or
1 teaspoon rum

METHOD

1. Mix the cocoa and milk together until blended. Add the gelatine and heat until the gelatine is dissolved.

2. Add the sugar and stir well. Leave to cool until the mixture begins to set.

3. Beat the cream until stiff. Add the vanilla essence and the crushed macaroons. Fold into the chocolate mixture.

4. Pour into a damp mould.

To freeze: Pack the mould in a polythene bag. Seal, label and freeze.

To thaw: Leave packed mould in refrigerator for 4 hours or until thawed. Unmould and decorate with crushed macaroon crumbs or whipped cream.

Orange and Pear Jelly

1 pint frozen or tinned
   orange juice

1½ oz gelatine
4 dessert pears, peeled and
   cored

METHOD

1. Melt gelatine in 2 tablespoons orange juice.
2. Mix with the remaining juice and leave until it begins to set.
3. Pour one-third jelly into a mould and cover with half of the pears sliced. Cover with jelly and the rest of the pears. Finish with a layer of jelly. Leave to set.

To freeze: Pack mould in a polythene bag or in freezer paper. Seal, label and freeze.

To thaw: Leave in refrigerator for at least 4 hours or until thawed.

To serve: Turn out and serve with whipped cream or custard.
Do not keep frozen for longer than 3 months.

Variations:
1. Substitute ¼ pint dry white wine for ¼ pint orange juice.
2. Substitute 1 tin fruit cocktail for pears.

Red Fruit Salad

A fruit with a difference. Made from red fruit only, it is attractive and unusual to look at. For special occasions add a tablespoon brandy before serving.

SYRUP
8 oz sugar
1 pint water

FRUIT
½ lb raspberries
½ lb red cherries
½ lb redcurrants
¼ lb strawberries
¼ lb firm red plums

301

1. Make the syrup by boiling the sugar and water together for 10 minutes. Leave to cool.

2. Halve and pit the cherries. Slice the plums and strawberries. Combine the fruit in a bowl and pour over the cold syrup. Mix well.

To freeze: Pour into a suitable container. Seal, label and freeze.

To thaw: Leave in the refrigerator in the container for 4–5 hours until almost thawed through.

Serve: Well chilled, with sweetened whipped cream.

Pear Dessert

9 oz prunes, soaked overnight
4 oz caster sugar
2 teaspoons vanilla essence

1 lemon, sliced
1½ lb small pears, peeled, halved and cored

METHOD

1. Blend together prune syrup, caster sugar and vanilla essence and boil for 8 minutes. Add prunes, lemon slices and pears.

2. Cover and simmer for 20 minutes or until pears are tender.

To freeze: Chill and put into suitable containers. Seal, label and freeze.

To thaw: Leave in refrigerator for at least 5 hours, or overnight.

To serve: Serve chilled with vanilla ice-cream or sweetened whipped cream.

Sunshine Orange Dessert

An orange salad transformed by its golden marmalade topping

4 large oranges	Juice of one orange
6 oz sugar	1 tablespoon Kirsch
1 pint water	(optional)

METHOD

1. Pare off the rind of two oranges as thinly as possible – no white pith should be left on the inside of the skin.
2. Cut the peel into matchstick strips. Blanch in boiling water for 10 minutes and drain well.
3. Put the sugar and the water in a saucepan. Slowly bring to the boil and cook for 15 minutes over a fast flame. Add the rind to the syrup and simmer for 15 minutes over a low flame.
4. Remove the peel and the pith from the 4 oranges. Cut into thin slices and arrange in a dish. Pour over them the juice of 1 orange, the syrup and orange rind.

To serve without freezing: Mix in 1 tablespoon Kirsch. Leave in refrigerator for 2 hours.

To freeze: Pack in a suitable container. Seal, label and freeze.

To thaw: Leave in refrigerator in the container for about 4 hours or until almost thawed through.

To serve: Add 1 tablespoon Kirsch and serve well chilled.

Fruit Fool

2 lb gooseberries, raspberries, blackcurrants or apples	8 oz sugar
¼ pint thick cream	¼ pint water

1. Prepare the fruit for cooking, ie, peel, hull, etc.
2. Stew the fruit with the water and sugar until soft. Leave to cool.
3. Press the fruit through a fine sieve or through a food mill.
4. Add the cream to the fruit and beat well. Pour into a serving dish.

To freeze: Pack in a polythene bag, or wrap in freezer paper or aluminium foil. Seal, label and freeze.

To thaw: Leave fool in refrigerator for 2–3 hours or thaw at room temperature.

Serve: Cold.

Apricot Fool

¼ lb dried apricots
Water
1 tablespoon vanilla sugar
2 tablespoons Kirsch

¼ pint cream
1 egg white
Whipped cream and chopped
  macaroons to decorate

METHOD

1. Place apricots in a baking dish. Cover with water and leave to soak for 6 hours.
2. Bake in a moderate oven (350°F: Reg. 4) for ¾ hour.
3. Drain. Put fruit through a fine sieve or purée in an electric blender.
4. Sweeten with vanilla sugar and flavour with Kirsch.
5. Whip cream and egg white separately. Mix together and fold into apricot purée.

To serve immediately: Top with whipped cream and chopped macaroons.

To freeze: Pour into an unbreakable bowl or dish. Pack in a polythene bag. Seal, label and freeze.

To thaw: Thaw unwrapped at room temperature for 2 hours. Unwrap and keep in refrigerator until required.

To serve: Decorate with whipped cream and chopped macaroons.

Caramelized Oranges

This sweet is to be seen on every sweet trolley in every Italian restaurant in London. Its success depends on the quality of the oranges, which should be firm but very juicy.

4 Jaffa oranges   ½ pint water
8 oz sugar

METHOD

1. Peel the oranges thinly and cut the peel into thin matchstick strips.
2. With a sharp knife, remove all the white pith from the oranges.
3. Put the sugar into a heavy pan and leave it to melt until it turns a deep amber colour. Add the water with care. It is as well to cover the hand you use with a cloth as the syrup will sometimes spit. Stir well.
4. Put the oranges into the hot syrup and poach them over a medium heat for 3 minutes. Remove and leave to cool.
5. Blanch the orange peel in boiling water for 15 minutes to rid it of its bitter taste. Drain and transfer to the syrup. Cook the peel in the syrup over a medium heat for 5 minutes.
6. Pour the syrup and rind over the oranges.

To freeze: Cool quickly. Pack in a suitable container. Seal, label and freeze.

To thaw: Leave oranges overnight in refrigerator in their containers.

Serve: Ice cold.

Note: A tablespoon of Kirsch may be added to the syrup before serving.

Porto Melon

1 large ripe honeydew melon   ¾ pint port
2 oz sugar

METHOD

1. Cut the melon in half and remove the seeds. Scoop the flesh into balls with a spoon or vegetable scoop.
2. Sprinkle the melon with sugar and pour over the port.

To serve without freezing: Chill in refrigerator for at least 1 hour.

To freeze: Pack in a suitable container. Seal, label and freeze.

To thaw: Leave melon in refrigerator or at room temperature until just thawed. About 2 hours at room temperature.

Serve: Well chilled.

Peaches with Raspberry Sauce

8 small ripe peaches (white if   1 tablespoon lemon juice
  possible)   1 lb raspberries
¾ pint water   2 teaspoons Kirsch
¾ lb granulated sugar   2 oz blanched almonds,
½ teaspoon vanilla essence   chopped and browned

METHOD

1. Remove skin from peaches by dropping them in boiling water for 1 minute.

2. Place ¾ pint water with sugar, lemon juice and vanilla essence in a saucepan. Simmer for 4 minutes.

3. Add the peaches to the syrup and poach over a low heat for 5 minutes. Remove peaches and leave to cool.

4. Purée raspberries through a fine sieve. Thin with 4 tablespoons of syrup and stir in the Kirsch.

To serve without freezing: Pour sauce over peaches. Chill and sprinkle with chopped almonds.

To freeze: Pack peaches in waxed container. Pour sauce over. Seal, label and freeze.

To thaw: Leave uncovered in refrigerator for about 4 hours or until thawed through.

To serve: Place peaches on a serving dish, pour the sauce over and sprinkle with chopped almonds.

Peasant Girl with a Tipsy Veil

This is my own variation of a traditional Danish pudding

½ lb ginger biscuits	½ gill water
2 lb cooking apples, peeled and cored	1 wineglass brandy
	6 oz grated chocolate
2 oz sugar	Whipped cream to decorate

METHOD

1. Crush the ginger biscuits into crumbs with a rolling pin.

2. Simmer the apples with the water and sugar until tender. Rub through a sieve.

3. Soak the ginger crumbs in brandy.

4. Fill a dish with alternate layers of biscuit and apple purée. Sprinkle the top with grated chocolate.

To serve without freezing: Chill the pudding and decorate with whipped cream.

To freeze: Pack the dish in a polythene bag. Seal, label and freeze.

To thaw: Leave for 4 hours, or overnight, in the refrigerator.

To serve: Decorate with whipped cream and serve chilled.

Fruit Freezel

8 servings

24 chocolate wafers or thin ginger crisps	1 large tin fruit cocktail
½ pint double cream	1 ripe banana
1 tablespoon sugar	24 tiny marshmallows
2 teaspoons rum	2 oz chopped walnuts

METHOD

1. Line an 8-inch square cake tin or dish with biscuits, reserving 6 for decoration.
2. Whip cream until stiff. Fold in sugar and rum.
3. Drain fruit cocktail and add to cream with chopped banana, marshmallows and chopped walnuts. Mix gently.
4. Spoon into dish and decorate surface with biscuits.

To freeze: Cover surface with moisture- and vapour-proof paper. Pack in a polythene bag or wrap in freezer paper or aluminium foil. Seal, label and freeze.

To serve: Remove from deep freeze ½ hour before serving. Unwrap and serve from dish, cut into squares.

Frozen Lemon Cake

¼ lb butter
6 oz caster sugar
4 eggs
Rind and juice of 1 lemon

1½ dozen sponge fingers
Whipped cream
Toasted almonds

1. Cream the butter and sugar until almost white, and fluffy.
2. Beat in the egg yolks, one by one. Add the lemon juice and rind.
3. Beat the egg whites until stiff. Fold into the cream mixture.
4. Cut the sponge fingers into three lengthways and line an oblong cake tin. Fill with alternate layers of sponge and cream mixture. Finish with a layer of sponge fingers.
5. Press down gently.

To serve without freezing: Cover and chill in refrigerator for 2 hours. Turn out and cover the cake with whipped cream and a sprinkling of toasted almonds.

To freeze: Pack cake in tin in a polythene bag. Seal, label and freeze.

To thaw: Remove cake from deep freeze ½ hour before serving. Turn out.

To serve: Cover with whipped cream and a sprinkling of toasted almonds.

Summer Pudding

This is one of my favourite puddings, and it freezes marvellously. Despite its name it can be made at any time of the year, and you can experiment with your own combinations of fruit, either fresh or from the deep freeze. Below is my favourite combination.

½ lb raspberries
1 lb blackcurrants
½ lb strawberries
4–6 oz sugar

8 or more slices of white
  bread with the crusts
  removed
Whipped cream, sweetened
  with caster sugar

METHOD

1. Heat the fruit with the sugar in a saucepan over a medium heat and cook until the sugar has melted. Do not boil.
2. Allow fruit to cool.
3. Soak the bread with the juice of the stewed fruit and line a greased 1-quart pudding basin with the bread.
4. Pour the stewed fruit over the bread.
5. Cover the top with more bread.
6. Place a plate over the top and a heavy weight on that, so that the fruit is firmly pressed down.
7. Leave in the refrigerator or in a cool place for 4 hours.

To serve without freezing: Dip the basin quickly into very hot water and unmould the pudding. Cover the top and sides with the whipped cream.

To freeze: Seal the basin in a polythene bag. Freeze.

To thaw: Leave in the refrigerator for at least 5 hours or overnight. Turn out.

Serve: With a decoration of whipped cream.

Apple Cake

1½ lb apples
4 oz sugar
1 oz butter

4 oz fresh white breadcrumbs
Grated chocolate

METHOD

1. Peel, core and slice apples.
2. Stew until tender with 2 oz sugar.
3. Melt butter and fry breadcrumbs until crisp.
4. Butter a 7-inch cake tin. Put alternate layers of crumbs and apple, starting and finishing with crumbs.
5. Bake in a medium oven (375°F: Reg. 5) for 1 hour. Leave to cool.

To serve without freezing: Turn out and cover surface with grated chocolate.

To freeze: Freeze in cake tin. Pack in polythene bag. Seal, label and freeze.

To thaw: Thaw still packed, in refrigerator, about 4 hours, or 1½ hours at room temperature. Turn out and cover the surface with grated chocolate.

Serve: Chilled, cut into wedges with a custard or cream sauce.

Bombe Favourite

This pudding, a combination of meringues and a flavoured cream, is served whilst still frozen, and is therefore a useful standby to keep in your deep freeze. It is simple to make.

3 egg whites	¾ pint double cream
3 oz caster sugar	3 tablespoons Kirsch
Grated rind of 1 orange	Caster sugar to taste

METHOD

1. *To make meringues:* Whisk the egg whites until stiff. Add half the sugar and continue beating for 1 minute. Fold in the rest of the sugar with a fork.

311

2. Well oil a baking sheet with olive oil. Drop meringue mixture on to the sheet, a tablespoon at a time.

3. Bake in a slow oven for 2 hours. Turn off heat, and dry meringues for 10 minutes. Remove meringues from baking sheet with a spatula, and when cool break into small pieces.

4. *To make pudding:* Whisk cream until stiff. Flavour cream with sugar, grated orange rind and Kirsch. Fold in broken meringues.

5. Well oil a cake tin or bombe mould. Pour in cream mixture and cover with tin foil.

To freeze: Pack pudding in a polythene bag. Seal, label and freeze.

To serve: Ten minutes before serving dip the mould into hot water and turn out pudding. Accompany with a Melba sauce, or fresh raspberries or strawberries.

Note: Store left-over egg yolks in deep freeze and use for mayonnaise.

Orange Flan

PASTRY
4 oz plain flour
2 oz butter
2 oz vanilla sugar
2 egg yolks

FILLING
3 oz sugar
3½ oz butter
4 egg yolks
2 eating apples
1 oz sugar
Grated rind of 2 oranges

METHOD

1. *To make the pastry:* Sift the flour on to a board. Make a well in the centre.

2. Mix egg yolks, butter and sugar together in a bowl.

3. Pour into the well in the flour. Mix the flour in gradually with the fingertips. When it is blended knead for 1 minute and form into a ball.

4. Wrap in a floured cloth and leave in refrigerator for at least 2 hours.

5. *To make the filling:* Cream the sugar and butter together until white and fluffy. Add the egg yolks one by one, beating until smooth.

6. Add the grated rind of 2 oranges and mix well.

7. Roll out the pastry as thin as possible and line a 7-inch flan case.

8. Turn filling into flan case and cover with the flesh of 2 peeled apples. Sprinkle sugar over the surface.

9. Bake in a moderate oven (350°F: Reg. 4) for 25 minutes.

To serve without freezing: Serve warm or cold.

To freeze: Cool on a cake rack. Wrap, seal, label and freeze.

To thaw: Unwrap pie and thaw at room temperature for 2 hours.

Serve: Cold, or reheat for 20 minutes in a moderate oven.

Fresh Strawberry and Redcurrant Flan

FLAN CASE
8 oz plain flour
5 oz butter
Pinch of salt
1 teaspoon lemon juice
2–3 tablespoons cold water
1 egg yolk

FILLING
½ lb redcurrant jelly
1½ lb strawberries
  (Fraises du bois are best of
  all)

METHOD

1. *To make the flan case:* Sift the flour and salt. Add the butter cut in small pieces and rub into the flour with the fingertips until the mixture resembles coarse breadcrumbs.

2. Mix in the egg yolk beaten with the water and lemon juice.

313

Mix with the hands into a firm dough. Chill in refrigerator for 1 hour.

3. Roll out, and line a flan ring. Press a piece of waxed paper into the flan and fill with rice or dried beans. Bake in a hot oven (425°F: Reg. 6) for 15 minutes. Remove paper and beans and bake for a further 5 minutes. Leave to cool.

4. *To make the filling:* Melt the redcurrant jelly over a low flame. Leave aside to cool, but do not let it jell.

5. Using a pastry brush, brush the bottom of the flan case with a layer of redcurrant jelly. Leave until set.

6. Place one layer of strawberries in the case. Crush lightly with a fork so that the strawberries are evenly spread out. Sprinkle with sugar. Cover with a layer of whole strawberries.

7. Pour over the remaining redcurrant jelly and leave to set.

To freeze: Pack the flan between two cardboard plates. Secure with waterproof tape. Pack in a polythene bag, or in freezer paper. Seal, label and freeze.

To thaw: Leave in refrigerator for at least 4 hours or until thawed.

Serve: Chilled, with a decoration of sweetened, whipped cream.

Note: Any fresh fruit can be used to fill a flan in the same way. The bottom glaze of redcurrant jelly is important as it prevents the pastry getting soggy whilst in the deep freeeze.

Coffee and Rum Chiffon Pie

PASTRY
4 oz flour
⅛ teaspoon salt
2–3 oz butter
1½ oz caster sugar
1 egg yolk

FILLING
¼ pint strong coffee
2 egg yolks
2 oz sugar
⅛ teaspoon salt
1½ teaspoons gelatine
1½ tablespoons water
2 egg whites
1 tablespoon rum

1. *To make the pastry:* Sift flour and salt on to a board.
2. Make a well in the centre and add the butter, sugar and egg yolk. Blend together.
3. Mix to form a dough. Chill in refrigerator for 1 hour.
4. Roll out and line a 6-inch flan ring. Press a piece of waxed paper or muslin into the flan and fill with rice or dried beans. Bake in a hot oven, over 425°F, for 15 minutes. Remove the paper and bake for a further 3 minutes. Leave to cool.
5. *To make the filling:* Make a custard with the egg yolks and the strong coffee. Add the sugar and salt.
6. Dissolve the gelatine in the water and add to the custard mixture.
7. Add the rum and allow to cool.
8. Beat the egg whites. When the custard is nearly set fold in egg whites and pour into pastry case. Chill until set.

To freeze: Place the pie on a cardboard plate and cover with another plate. Secure with waterproof tape. Pack in a polythene bag or aluminium foil. Seal, label and freeze.

To thaw: Leave covered in a refrigerator for about 4 hours or until thawed.

Serve: Cold, with a decoration of whipped cream.

Strawberry Cake

4 eggs
8 oz butter
8 oz sugar
12 oz flour
3 teaspoons baking powder
½ pint milk
1 teaspoon vanilla essence
½ teaspoon grated lemon peel

FILLING
1 lb frozen strawberries
½ pint double cream
2 tablespoons caster sugar

1. Cream the butter and sugar together until light and fluffy.
2. Beat the eggs until thick and add slowly to the butter mixture, beating all the time.
3. Sift the flour with the baking powder and fold into the mixture with the milk, vanilla essence and lemon peel. Mix until well blended.
4. Pour the mixture into two well-greased and floured cake tins. Bake in a moderate oven (350°F: Reg. 4) for 30–40 minutes.
5. Remove from the pans and leave to cool on a cake rack. Cut each cake into two layers.

To freeze: Pack each layer between cardboard plates in a polythene bag, or wrap in freezer paper or aluminium foil. Seal, label and freeze.

To thaw: Leave cake wrapped on a cake rack, at room temperature for 1½ hours.

To fill: Thaw the strawberries. Whip the cream. Mix in the sugar and the strawberries. Spread three layers with the cream and sandwich together. Sift icing sugar over the top of the cake.

Rhubarb Cake

2 eggs	Pinch of cinnamon
6 oz butter	Pinch of nutmeg
6 oz sugar	1 lb rhubarb
6 oz self-raising flour	¼ lb sugar
½ tablespoon lemon juice	

METHOD

1. Sift the flour into a bowl. Add the eggs, the softened butter, sugar and lemon juice. Beat well until a smooth dough is formed.
2. Roll out and line a cake tin with the dough. Fill the centre

with the rhubarb cut into small pieces. Cover with ¼ lb sugar, the cinnamon and nutmeg.

3. Bake in a medium-hot oven (400°F: Reg. 5) for 1 hour or until the cake is cooked. Cool in the tin and turn out carefully.

To freeze: Freeze unpacked cake. When solid pack in a polythene bag or wrap in freezer paper or aluminium foil. Seal, label and freeze.

To thaw: Leave unwrapped cake to stand for 1½ hours on a cake rack. Unwrap and serve.

Cream Puff Ring

This is an easy pudding to make. It looks professional and lends itself to countless variations. I usually sandwich the ring with sweetened whipped cream and fill the centre with raspberries.

CHOUX PASTRY (see page 275)

METHOD

1. Oil a baking sheet and dust with flour. Trace around an 8-inch pie dish to make a circle in the flour. Spoon the mixture on the inside of this circle to make a ring. Smooth into shape with the back of a spoon and score a pattern lightly on the top with a fork.

2. Bake in a hot oven (420°F: Reg. 6) for about 20 minutes until firm and golden. Cool.

To serve without freezing: Cut the top off the ring. Fill the bottom layer with sweetened whipped cream. Replace the top and fill the centre of the ring with raspberries.

To freeze: Place the puff ring carefully in a polythene bag. Seal, label and freeze.

To thaw: Unwrap frozen ring and place in a slow oven (300°F: Reg. 2) for 15 minutes. Cool. Cut the top off the ring and fill.

Other fillings:
1. Fill the ring with ice-cream just before serving. Pour over a hot chocolate sauce.
2. Fill the ring with 1 small tin of chestnut purée mixed with $\frac{1}{2}$ pint of whipped cream, 2 tablespoons caster sugar and 1 tablespoon Kirsch.
3. Fill the ring with Swiss black cherry jam. Serve with cream.

Profiteroles

(Small Eclairs)

CHOUX PASTRY (see page 275).

METHOD

1. Drop dough in dessertspoonfuls on to a greased baking sheet, or use a forcing bag.
2. Bake in a moderate oven (375°F: Reg. 5) for 20–25 minutes until well risen and a pale gold. Make an incision halfway through and return to a slow oven (240°F: Reg. $\frac{1}{4}$) for 10 minutes to dry the insides.
3. Cool on a cake rack.

To freeze: Fill with ice-cream and pack in a suitable container with a sheet of moisture- and vapour-proof paper between each layer, or pack unfilled in the same way. Seal, label and freeze.

To thaw: Remove filled puffs from the deep freeze 15 minutes before serving. Put frozen unfilled puffs in a moderate oven (325°F: Reg. 3) for 10 minutes. Cool and fill.

Suggested fillings:
1. Sweetened whipped cream served with a hot chocolate sauce.

2. Fill frozen puffs with Swiss cherry jam and heat as above. Serve hot.

Rum Baba

SYRUP

6 oz flour
½ oz yeast
2 eggs
6 tablespoons warm milk
1 teaspoon sugar
¼ teaspoon salt
2 oz butter
3 oz sugar
2 oz raisins
2 oz chopped peel
2 oz currants
Small pinch saffron

4 oz sugar
4 tablespoons water
2 tablespoons rum

METHOD

1. Dissolve the yeast in the warm milk.

2. Sift the flour into a large bowl. Make a well in the centre and add the yeast and milk. Add the eggs. Mix to a stiff dough and knead for 3 minutes.

3. Cover with a cloth and leave in a warm place until doubled in bulk – about 20 minutes.

4. Add the softened butter, sugar and salt. Beat until well blended. Mix in the raisins, chopped peel, currants and saffron.

5. Cover with a cloth and leave to rise in a warm place until doubled in bulk.

6. Pour into a rounded cake tin or savarin mould and bake in a medium hot oven (375°F: Reg. 5) for 1 hour. Turn out and cool on a cake rack.

To freeze: Cool. Freeze uncovered. Pack in a polythene bag. Seal, label and freeze.

To thaw: Let the baba stand unwrapped on a cake rack for 3 hours at room temperature until thawed. Unwrap and puncture the surface with a knitting needle or skewer. Pour over the warm syrup made by boiling the sugar and water together for 10 minutes, then add the rum. Baste the cake well with the syrup so that it is really moist.

Bread, Cakes and Biscuits

Bread Rolls

1 lb plain flour	1 teaspoon sugar
1 teaspoon salt	$\frac{1}{4}$ pint milk
1 oz butter	$\frac{1}{4}$ pint water
$\frac{3}{4}$ oz yeast	1 beaten egg

METHOD

1. Heat the milk, water and butter together in a saucepan until the butter is melted.

2. Cream the yeast and sugar together. Add the warm liquid and leave for 5 minutes.

3. Sift the flour and salt together. Add half the flour to the yeast and liquid, and beat until a smooth batter is formed. Add the rest of the flour and beat in.

4. Turn the dough on to a floured board and knead for 10 minutes until smooth and elastic.

5. Put the dough in an oiled bowl. Turn to make sure the surface of the dough is well oiled. Cover with a cloth and leave in a warm place for 40 minutes or until double in bulk.

6. Punch down the dough. Knead lightly and form into twenty small rolls. Place on a greased baking sheet. Cover and leave in a warm place for a further 20 minutes or again doubled in size. Brush with beaten egg and bake in a hot oven (425°F: Reg. 6) for 15 minutes.

To freeze: Cool. Pack in polythene bags. Seal, label and freeze.

To thaw: Place frozen rolls on a baking sheet. Bake in a hot oven (425°F: Reg. 6) for 10 minutes or until golden brown and piping hot.

Note: Poppy or caraway seeds can be sprinkled over the rolls after they have been brushed with beaten egg.

Croissants

1 lb plain flour	¼ pint warm water
½ oz yeast	¼ pint warm milk
1 teaspoon caster sugar	1 teaspoon salt
4 oz butter	

METHOD

1. Sieve the flour and salt into a large bowl. Warm in a slow oven for 5 minutes.

2. Cream the yeast and sugar. Add to the warm flour.

3. Pour over the milk and water and mix to a fairly stiff dough. Knead lightly. Cover with a cloth and leave for about 1 hour to rise, in a warm place, until doubled in bulk.

4. Divide the butter into three portions. Roll out the dough into a long strip and dot one portion of the butter over two-thirds of the dough. Fold into three and seal the edges together.

5. Roll out the dough twice more, repeating the process with the remaining butter and sealing the edges each time.

6. Leave the dough in a warm place to rise for 30 minutes.

7. Roll out the dough to ¼ inch thick. Cut into 4-inch squares and then into triangles. Brush the edges with a little milk and roll, starting with the wide edge. Bend into crescent shapes and leave to prove on a greased baking dish for 20 minutes.

8. Bake in a hot oven (410°F: Reg. 6) for 15 minutes.

To serve without freezing: Brush with beaten egg and bake for a further 5 minutes until golden brown.

To freeze: Cool. Pack carefully with a sheet of freezer paper between each layer. Seal, label and freeze.

To thaw: Brush frozen croissants with beaten egg. Bake in a hot oven (410°F: Reg. 6) for 10 minutes or until golden brown.

Serve: Hot.

Note: The croissants can be frozen uncooked but should not be kept in the deep freeze for longer than 2 weeks.

French Bread

1 lb plain flour
1 oz yeast
2 beaten eggs
1 oz butter
1 teaspoon salt

1 teaspoon sugar
½ pint warm milk
A little melted butter
Beaten egg

METHOD

1. Sift the flour and salt into a large bowl. Rub in the butter with the fingertips and place in a slow oven for 3 minutes to warm.

2. Cream the yeast and sugar. Stir in the warm milk and 1 beaten egg.

3. Add the liquid to the flour and beat well. Turn on to a board and knead thoroughly.

4. Grease the bowl with melted butter. Put in the dough. Brush the top with melted butter. Cover and leave to rise in a warm place for about 1 hour until doubled in bulk.

5. Shape into plaits or long rolls. Prove on a greased baking sheet for 10 minutes. Brush with beaten egg and bake in a hot oven (410°F: Reg. 6) for 20 minutes until golden brown and crisp.

To freeze: Cool. Pack in polythene bags. Seal, label and freeze.

To thaw: Leave in wrapping to thaw at room temperature for 1 hour, or thaw frozen bread in a moderate oven for 10–15 minutes.

Sally Lunn

4 oz butter
4 oz sugar
3 eggs
½ lb plain flour

3 teaspoons baking powder
¾ teaspoon salt
½ pint milk

METHOD

1. Beat the butter and sugar until light and creamy.
2. Add the eggs one at a time, beating well each time.
3. Add the sifted flour, salt and baking powder in three parts, alternately adding the milk. Beat the butter lightly until just blended.
4. Pour into a well-greased 9-inch × 12-inch pan and bake in a hot oven (425°F: Reg. 6).

To serve without freezing: Break the bread into squares and serve hot.

To freeze: Cool in the tin. Pack in the tin in a polythene bag, or wrap in freezer paper or aluminium foil. Seal, label and freeze.

To thaw: Thaw bread still wrapped for 1 hour. Unpack, cover with aluminium foil and heat in a hot oven for 5 minutes.

To serve: Break into squares and serve hot.

Fruit Bread

1 medium tin fruit cocktail
7 oz plain flour
2½ oz soft brown sugar
1½ teaspoons baking powder
Pinch of nutmeg

1 beaten egg
1 oz melted butter
½ tablespoon grated lemon
 rind
1 oz toasted chopped almonds

1. Drain the fruit cocktail and add enough water to the syrup to make 4 liquid oz.

2. Sift together the flour and baking powder. Add the sugar and nutmeg and stir well.

3. Add the syrup and butter to the egg and mix well. Pour the liquid into the flour and beat until well blended.

4. Mix in the lemon rind, fruit cocktail and almonds.

5. Pour into a greased loaf pan and bake in a moderate oven (350°F: Reg. 4) for 1 hour or until done. Leave to cool in the pan for 10 minutes. Turn out and cool on a cake rack. Refrigerate before cutting.

To freeze: Wrap in a polythene bag, freezer paper or aluminium foil. Seal, label and freeze.

To thaw: Leave wrapped to thaw for 1½ hours at room temperature.

Note: A tin of chopped apricots can be substituted for the fruit cocktail.

Coffee Gâteau

CAKE
10 oz plain flour
1 tablespoon baking powder
10 oz soft brown sugar
3 tablespoons instant coffee
½ pint milk
6 fl oz corn oil
1 teaspoon vanilla essence
4 eggs

ICING
6 oz unsalted butter
12 oz icing sugar
2 tablespoons coffee essence
¼ teaspoon vanilla essence
4 oz shelled walnuts

METHOD

1. *To make the cake:* Sieve the flour and baking powder into a large bowl. Add the brown sugar.

2. Dissolve the coffee in the milk and add to the corn oil, vanilla essence and egg yolks. Mix well and add to the dry ingredients. Beat until smooth.

3. Whisk the egg whites stiffly and fold into the cake batter.

4. Divide the mixture between two well-greased round cake tins.

5. Bake in a medium-hot oven (370°F: Reg. 5) for 40 minutes. Turn out and leave to cool. Split each cake into two layers with a sharp knife.

6. *To make the icing:* Cream the butter and icing sugar together until soft and fluffy. Add the coffee and vanilla essence. Beat well.

7. Chop the walnuts, reserving a few for decoration.

8. Spread each layer with butter icing and sprinkle with chopped walnuts. Sandwich the layers together and decorate the top with the whole walnuts.

To freeze: Freeze the cake unwrapped. When frozen, pack between two cardboard plates and in a polythene bag. Seal, label and freeze.

To thaw: Unwrap cake and leave to thaw at room temperature for 2 hours on a cake rack.

Note: The cake can be frozen un-iced in which case it should be thawed whilst still wrapped before icing.

French Chocolate Cake

¼ lb butter
½ lb unsweetened block
   chocolate
4 eggs, separated
¼ lb sugar

1 tablespoon flour
1 teaspoon vanilla essence
1 teaspoon grated almonds

METHOD

1. Soften the butter with a wooden spoon. Melt the chocolate in a basin over hot water.

2. Combine the butter and chocolate. Stir in the egg yolks one by one, beating until smooth.

3. Add the sugar and beat well. Stir in the flour, almonds and vanilla essence and mix well.

4. Beat the egg whites until really stiff. Fold carefully into cake mixture.

5. Pour into a buttered cake tin and bake in a medium-hot oven (375°F: Reg. 5) for 40 minutes. Test with a knife blade to see if the cake is properly cooked. The blade should come out clean. Turn out on to a cake rack.

To freeze: Cool. Freeze without packing. When solid, pack in a polythene bag. Seal, label and freeze.

To thaw: Stand wrapped cake on a rack and leave to thaw at room temperature for 1½ hours.

Note: The cake can be glazed with apricot jam and filled with sweetened whipped cream.

Spice Cake

¼ lb butter	½ teaspoon mixed spice
6 oz sugar	½ teaspoon ground ginger
2 eggs	6 oz flour
¼ pint milk	2 teaspoons baking powder
½ teaspoon ground cinnamon	

METHOD

1. Beat the butter with the sugar until light and creamy.

2. Beat in the eggs one by one.

3. Sift the flour with the baking powder and spices. Fold into the butter mixture in three parts alternately with the milk. Beat thoroughly until the mixture is smooth and well blended.

4. Pour into two well-greased 9-inch baking tins. Bake in a moderate oven (350°F: Reg. 4) for 25–35 minutes. The cake is cooked when an inserted knitting needle comes out clean.

5. Turn on to a cake rack and leave to cool.

Note: The cake can be filled and iced with a butter icing before freezing.

To freeze: Pack cake between two cardboard plates. Seal in a polythene bag, or wrap in freezer paper or aluminium foil. Seal, label and freeze.

To thaw: Thaw cake on a cake rack at room temperature for 1½–2 hours. Leave wrapped if un-iced, or unwrap if the cake was frozen in icing.

Fruit Cake

This is my standby at harvest time. I make four at a time, freeze them and then use one every three days.

12 oz flour	4 oz treacle
4 oz brown sugar	8 oz raisins
6 oz butter	6 oz currants
4 eggs	4 oz mixed peel, chopped
2 teaspoons baking powder	

METHOD

1. Cream the butter and sugar together until soft and fluffy. Add the treacle and beat in the eggs one by one. Beat the mixture well.

2. Sieve the flour with the baking powder and add to the cake mixture with the fruit. Mix well.

3. Bake in a well-greased tin (I use a loaf tin) in a moderate oven (270°F: Reg. 4) for 1½ hours. Leave to cool in the tin.

To freeze: Cool. Pack cakes in polythene bags or wrap in freezer paper or aluminium foil. Seal, label and freeze.

To thaw: Leave cake wrapped and thaw on a cake rack at room temperature for 1½–2 hours.

Chocolate Fudge Cake

5 oz butter	8 oz flour
14 oz sugar	1¼ teaspoons baking powder
2 eggs	½ teaspoon salt
1 teaspoon vanilla essence	½ pint cold water
3 oz unsweetened block chocolate	

METHOD

1. Cream butter with sugar, eggs and vanilla essence until mixture is pale and fluffy – about 5 minutes by hand.

2. Melt chocolate over hot water. Cool and blend into butter mixture.

3. Sift flour, baking powder and salt. Mix into creamed mixture, alternating with the cold water. Beat well after each addition of flour.

4. Bake in two well-greased 9-inch sponge tins in a moderate oven (350°F: Reg. 4) for 30 minutes. The cake is done when it springs back when pressed with a finger.

Cool and fill with chocolate butter icing.

To freeze: Freeze cake unpacked. When solid, pack in a polythene bag or wrap in freezer paper or aluminium foil. Seal, label and freeze.

To thaw: Stand wrapped cake on a cake rack and leave for 1½ hours at room temperature.

Queen Cakes

4 oz butter	4 oz self-raising flour
4 oz caster sugar	2 oz sultanas, chopped
½ teaspoon vanilla essence	1 tablespoon hot water
2 eggs	

METHOD

1. Beat the butter and sugar until light and creamy. Add the vanilla essence and beat well.

2. Beat the eggs into the butter mixture one at a time.

3. Fold in the flour, chopped sultanas and hot water. Mix until just blended.

4. Fill greased patty tins two-thirds full and bake in a moderate-hot oven (350°F: Reg. 4) for 15 minutes. Turn out and cool on a cake rack.

To freeze: Pack cooled cakes in a polythene bag. Seal, label and freeze.

To thaw: Place cakes, still wrapped, on a cake rack and thaw at room temperature for about 1 hour.

Genoese Cake

6 oz butter 6 oz plain flour
4 eggs 1 teaspoon vanilla essence
8 oz sugar

METHOD

1. Melt the butter over hot water. Cool.

2. Combine the eggs and sugar in a bowl over hot but not boiling water. Beat for 5 minutes or until the mixture has doubled in bulk.

3. Fold in the flour and butter with a spatula, lifting the mixture to get as much air as possible into it. Gently stir in the vanilla essence.

4. Pour into a buttered 9-inch cake tin. Bake in a moderate oven (350°F: Reg. 4) for 35 minutes or until a needle inserted into the cake comes out dry.

5. Run a knife round the edge and turn on to a cake rack to cool.

To freeze: Freeze cake without wrapping. When frozen pack in a polythene bag, or wrap in aluminium foil or freezer paper. Seal, label and freeze.

To thaw: Leave wrapped cake on a cake rack at room temperature for 1½ hours. Unwrap, split and fill.

Note: The cake can be filled and iced with a chocolate butter icing made from ¼ lb unsalted butter creamed with ¼ lb sugar and 1 tablespoon unsweetened cocoa. Thaw iced cakes wrapped for 2 hours on a cake rack. It is also delicious split and well buttered with unsalted butter. Heat in a moderate oven for 5 minutes or until the cake is warm and the butter melted. Serve cut into slices with jam.

Quick-mix Cake

This cake is so quick and easy to make it is almost a surprise to find it tasting delicious too.

7 oz self-raising flour	¼ pint milk
4 oz sugar	2 teaspoons baking powder
4 oz softened butter	1 teaspoon vanilla essence
2 eggs	

METHOD

1. Sift the flour into a large bowl. Add the remaining ingredients and beat with a wire whisk or electric beater until well blended, about 3–5 minutes.

2. Pour into two well-greased 8-inch cake tins. Cook in a moderate oven (350°F: Reg. 4) for ½ hour. The cake is done if it springs back when lightly pressed with the fingertips.

To freeze: Freeze the cake without packing. When solid pack in a polythene bag or wrap in freezer paper or aluminium foil. Seal, label and freeze.

To thaw: Leave the cake, still wrapped, to stand on a cake rack. Thaw for 1½ hours at room temperature. Unwrap and ice.

Notes:

1. The cake can be filled and iced with a butter icing before freezing, in which case it will need about 2 hours, wrapped, to thaw at room temperature.

331

2. The cake can be varied by flavouring with grated orange or lemon rind, or by using 4 tablespoons cocoa instead of 4 tablespoons of the flour.

Gingerbread

4 oz butter	$\frac{1}{4}$ pint milk
$\frac{1}{2}$ lb golden syrup	$\frac{1}{2}$ lb self-raising flour
3 oz granulated sugar	1 teaspoon ground ginger
1 tablespoon orange	1 teaspoon cinnamon
marmalade	1 teaspoon bicarbonate of
1 large egg	soda

METHOD

1. Put the butter, syrup, sugar and marmalade into a saucepan and heat gently until the sugar has dissolved. Leave to cool.
2. Beat the egg with the milk and add to the syrup mixture
3. Sift the flour with the ginger and cinnamon and soda. Pour in the liquid and beat to a smooth batter.
4. Butter an 8-inch square cake tin and pour in the batter. Bake in a moderate oven (350°F: Reg. 5) for 1 hour. Test with a skewer or knitting needle. If it comes out clean the cake is cooked.
5. Turn out on to a cake rack.

To freeze: Cool. Freeze before packing. When frozen pack in a polythene bag, or wrap in freezer paper or aluminium foil. Seal, label and freeze.

To thaw: Leave at room temperature, unwrapped, for $1\frac{1}{2}$ hours on a cake rack.

To serve: Cut into slices as a cake. Or heat gently in a moderate oven and serve with a marmalade or apple sauce as a pudding.

Chocolate Eclairs

½ pint cream
2 tablespoons caster sugar
Vanilla essence
Choux pastry (see page 275)

4 oz unsweetened chocolate
4 tablespoons water
1 lb icing sugar

METHOD

1. Pipe dough through a large pastry tube into 3-inch lengths. Bake in a medium-hot oven (375°F: Reg. 5) for 20–25 minutes until well risen and golden. Cool and slit along the sides. Remove any soft dough from the centre.

2. Whip the cream and flavour with caster sugar and a few drops of vanilla essence.

3. Melt the chocolate in the water in a double-boiler. Add the icing sugar slowly, stirring constantly.

4. Fill the éclairs with the whipped cream and spread each one with a thin layer of chocolate icing.

To freeze: Freeze éclairs unpacked. When solid, pack in a rigid container with a sheet of moisture- and vapour-proof paper between each layer. Seal, label and freeze.

To thaw: Unwrap frozen éclairs and thaw at room temperature for 30–45 minutes.

Muffins

½ lb flour
3 teaspoons baking powder
½ teaspoon salt
2 oz sugar

2 oz melted butter
½ pint milk
2 eggs, well beaten

METHOD

1. Sift the flour, sugar, baking powder and salt into a large bowl.

2. Beat the egg with the melted butter and milk.

3. Stir the liquid quickly into flour. Don't worry about lumps – over-mixing will result in tough muffins.

4. Pour the butter into greased muffin pans. Fill half full.

5. Bake in a hot oven (425°F: Reg. 6) for 25 minutes. Remove immediately from the tins and cool on a cake rack.

To freeze: Pack cooled muffins in polythene bags. Seal, label and freeze.

To thaw: Leave muffins to thaw in unopened bags on a cake rack for about 1 hour at room temperature. Reheat in a paper bag in a hot oven for 5 minutes.

BLUEBERRY MUFFINS

Use an extra ounce of sugar and fold into the batter ¼ lb blueberries lightly dusted with flour.

PINEAPPLE MUFFINS

Add ¼ pint well-drained crushed pineapple to the batter.

BACON MUFFINS

Use only 1 tablespoon sugar, and 1 tablespoon bacon fat instead of butter. Chop and fry 4 rashers bacon until crisp. Add to the flour before mixing in the combined eggs, milk and bacon fat.

Bran Muffins

¼ lb flour	½ pint milk
1 teaspoon baking powder	4 tablespoons golden syrup
1 teaspoon salt	1 egg
½ lb bran	

1. Sift the flour, baking powder and salt into a mixing bowl. Add the bran and mix well.
2. Beat the egg with the milk. Add the syrup and mix well.
3. Add the liquid to the dry ingredients. Mix quickly. Pour into greased muffin tins, filling half full. Bake in a medium-hot oven (375°F: Reg. 5) for 30–40 minutes. Turn out immediately and cool on a cake rack.

To freeze: Pack cooled muffins in polythene bags. Seal, label and freeze.

To thaw: Leave muffins in unopened bag to thaw for 1 hour at room temperature. Reheat in a paper bag in a hot oven for 5 minutes.

RAISIN BRAN MUFFINS

Add 6 oz raisins to the bran mixture.

Rock Cakes

½ lb flour	1 beaten egg
6 oz butter	Pinch of salt
2 oz sugar	1 teaspoon baking powder
2 oz currants	Milk
1½ oz candied peel, chopped	

METHOD

1. Sift the flour, salt and baking powder. Rub in the butter with the fingertips.
2. Add the sugar, currants and peel and mix to a stiff dough with the beaten egg and a little milk.
3. Place in spoonfuls on a greased baking sheet. Bake in a hot oven (410°F: Reg. 6) for 10–15 minutes until browned.

To freeze: Cool. Pack in a polythene bag. Seal, label and freeze.

To thaw: Leave cakes wrapped to stand on a cake rack for 1 hour at room temperature.

Cheese Scones

6 oz plain flour
2 teaspoons baking powder
1 oz margarine
1 teaspoon dry mustard

4 oz grated cheese
Salt and pepper
Milk

METHOD

1. Sieve flour and baking powder with salt, pepper and mustard.
2. Rub in margarine with fingertips until the mixture resembles coarse breadcrumbs.
3. Add the cheese and mix well.
4. Mix with enough milk to form a stiff dough.
5. Roll out on a floured board to $\frac{1}{2}$-inch thickness. Cut into rounds with a floured cutter.
6. Brush scones with milk and bake on a greased tin in a very hot oven (475°F: Reg. 8) for 10 minutes until well risen and golden brown.

To freeze: Cool, pack in a polythene bag. Seal, label and freeze.

To thaw: Leave uncovered at room temperature for $1\frac{1}{2}$ hours until thawed, or heat through in a medium-hot oven for 8 minutes until hot through.

Note: The scones can be frozen before baking. Pack with a sheet of moisture- and vapour-proof paper between each layer. Brush frozen scones with milk. Leave for 10 minutes and then bake in a very hot oven (475°F: Reg. 8) for 10 minutes until well risen and golden brown.
Do not store unbaked scones in the deep freeze for longer than 6 weeks.

Chocolate Chip Cookies

The glory of these cookies is that you can keep the roll of dough in your deep freeze, cutting off slices as you require the cookies, and returning the rest to your freezer.

½ lb sugar
4 oz soft butter
1 egg
1 teaspoon vanilla essence
9 oz plain flour

2 teaspoons baking powder
Pinch of salt
2 oz chopped nuts
2 oz chopped bar chocolate

METHOD

1. Beat the sugar and butter together until light and creamy.
2. Beat in the egg.
3. Add the vanilla essence.
4. Sift the flour, baking powder and salt, and stir into the creamed mixture.
5. Mix in nuts and chocolate pieces.
6. Using floured hands, shape the dough into a long sausage shape 2 inches across. Wrap in waxed paper.

To freeze: Wrap in freezer paper or aluminium foil. Seal, label and freeze.

To thaw: Cut the thinnest possible slices from the frozen dough. Place on a greased baking sheet and bake in a hot oven (410°F: Reg. 6) for 10 minutes. Be careful not to burn. Leave to cool on a cake rack.

This recipe may be used for:
Lemon Cookies: Substitute 1 tablespoon lemon rind for chocolate and nuts.
Orange Cookies: Substitute 1 tablespoon orange peel for chocolate and nuts.
Plain Sugar Cookies: Leave out chocolate and nuts and sprinkle cookies with icing sugar when cold.

Almond Cookies

½ lb butter
1 lb flour
1 lb sugar
1 lb coarsely ground almonds
¼ lb candied orange peel

1½ tablespoons lemon juice
1 egg
Pinch of cinnamon
1 egg yolk, beaten

METHOD

1. Rub the butter and flour together until the mixture resembles fine breadcrumbs.
2. Add the sugar, almonds, candied orange peel, cinnamon and lemon juice. Bind with the egg and knead on a floured board until smooth.
3. Shape in a long roll 2 inches in diameter.

To freeze: Wrap in moisture- and vapour-proof paper. Pack in a polythene bag. Seal, label and freeze.

To thaw: Cut thin slices from frozen dough. Re-seal dough not required and return immediately to the deep freeze.

Brush biscuits with beaten egg yolk and bake on a greased baking sheet in a hot oven (450°F: Reg. 7) for 8 minutes until golden brown. Be careful not to burn.

Cake Icings that Freeze Well

LEMON OR ORANGE ICING

1 lb icing sugar
2 oz butter

Grated rind and juice of 1 lemon or grated rind and juice of 1 small orange
2 teaspoons double cream

METHOD

1. Soften the butter without melting. Add the sugar and beat well until the mixture is light and creamy.

2. Beat in the lemon or orange rind and juice. Add the cream and mix well.

CHOCOLATE COFFEE ICING

2 oz unsweetened block chocolate	4 tablespoons hot coffee
2 oz butter	1 teaspoon vanilla essence
	1 lb icing sugar

METHOD

1. Melt the chocolate in a saucepan over a very low flame. Add the butter and stir until melted.
2. Add the coffee and remove from the heat. Stir until cool.
3. Add the vanilla essence, and gradually beat in the softened icing sugar until a suitable spreading consistency is reached.

COFFEE RUM ICING

1 lb icing sugar	3 tablespoons strong hot coffee
¼ lb butter	1 teaspoon rum

METHOD

1. Beat the butter until soft. Gradually add the softened sugar and beat the mixture until creamy.
2. Add the hot coffee and continue beating for 2 minutes or until the mixture is cool. Add the rum and mix well.

PINEAPPLE ICING

1 lb icing sugar	½ teaspoon vanilla essence
2 oz butter	4 tablespoons well-drained crushed pineapple
1 teaspoon lemon juice	

METHOD

1. Beat the butter until soft. Add the softened icing sugar and beat until light and creamy.
2. Beat in the lemon juice, vanilla and pineapple. Leave to stand for 5 minutes. Beat again until the icing is creamy.

Savoury Butters

Green Butter

To serve with poached fish

¾ lb butter   3 oz parsley
3 anchovy fillets   Freshly ground black pepper

METHOD

1. Boil the parsley in a little water for 5 minutes. Drain and press through a fine sieve.
2. Pound the anchovies and add with the parsley to the softened butter. Season with freshly ground black pepper.

To freeze: Shape the butter into a long roll. Wrap in freezer paper and pack in a polythene bag. Seal, label and freeze.

To serve: Unwrap frozen butter and cut into slices.

Mustard Butter

To serve with baked fish; mackerel, herring, etc, and with grilled or boiled gammon or bacon

4 oz butter   Pepper
1½ tablespoons Dijon mustard

1. Cream the butter. Work in the mustard a little at a time.
2. Season with pepper.

To freeze: Shape into a long roll. Wrap in freezer paper and pack in a polythene bag. Seal, label and freeze.

To serve: Unwrap frozen butter and cut into slices.

Chive Butter

To serve with fish and baked potatoes

¼ lb butter
2 teaspoons chopped chives

½ teaspoon lemon juice
Salt and pepper

METHOD

1. Cream the butter. Work in the chives and lemon juice.
2. Season with salt and pepper.

To freeze: Shape into a long roll. Wrap in freezer paper, pack in a polythene bag. Seal, label and freeze.

To serve: Unwrap frozen butter and cut into slices.

Mint Butter

To serve with lamb cutlets and boiled vegetables

¼ lb butter
4 tablespoons finely chopped mint

Salt and black pepper
1 teaspoon lemon juice

1. Cream butter.
2. Add the lemon juice and mint and mix well.
3. Season with salt and pepper.

To freeze: Shape into a long roll. Wrap in freezer paper and pack in a polythene bag. Seal, label and freeze.

To serve: Unwrap frozen butter and cut into slices.

Miscellaneous Accompaniments

Apple and Mint Ice

4 large cooking apples
¼ pint water
Grated rind of 1 lemon
Juice of 1 lemon

8 sprigs of fresh mint
¼ pint water
6 oz sugar

METHOD

1. Core apples and chop roughly. Do not peel.
2. Put in a saucepan with ¼ pint of water and simmer until tender. Rub through a fine sieve. Add lemon juice and rind.
3. Boil the sugar with ¼ pint water for 3 minutes.
4. Chop the mint very finely. Add to the syrup.
5. Cool syrup and add slowly to the apple purée stirring well.
6. Pour into an ice-cube tray.

To freeze: Freeze unpacked. When frozen, pack, seal, label and return to deep freeze.

To serve: Unmould and serve frozen cubes with roast lamb.

Yorkshire Puddings

Keep a supply of these light crisp puddings in the deep freeze. Traditionally served with roast beef they are delicious with any roast meat and a useful standby to serve instead of potatoes.

| 4 oz flour | ½ pint milk and water mixed |
| 1 egg | A pinch of salt |

METHOD

1. Sieve the flour and salt into a bowl. Make a well in the centre and add the egg and a little liquid. Beat until smooth.
2. Gradually add the rest of the liquid, beating continually until the mixture is like thin cream.
3. Cover and leave to stand for 30 minutes.
4. Put a small knob of dripping in twelve patty tins. Place the tins in a hot oven (425°F: Reg. 7) until the fat is smoking. Half fill the tins with the batter and cook in a hot oven (425°F: Reg. 7) for 20 minutes until crisp and brown.

To freeze: Cool puddings on a cake rack. Pack in a rigid container with a sheet of moisture- and vapour-proof paper between each layer. Seal, label and freeze.

To thaw: Place frozen puddings on a greased baking sheet in a medium-hot oven (380°F: Reg. 5) and heat for 10 minutes until crisp and hot through.

Hot Garlic Bread

| 1 long French loaf | 2 large cloves garlic |
| 6 oz butter | |

METHOD

1. Squeeze garlic in a garlic press or chop very finely.
2. Mix garlic with softened butter.
3. Slice loaf diagonally ¾-way through in ½-inch slices.
4. Spread garlic butter evenly on both sides of each slice.

To freeze: Wrap the loaf in a good covering of tin foil. Seal in a polythene bag. Label and freeze.

To thaw: Remove polythene bag but leave loaf in its tin-foil covering. Place on a baking sheet in a medium oven for 15 minutes. Remove tin foil and replace loaf in a hot oven for 5 minutes or until the butter is melted and the bread crisp.

Serve: Hot.

Note: Garlic loses its flavour in the deep freeze. Take extra care with wrapping and sealing to avoid the garlic odour tainting other produce.
Do not keep frozen for longer than 1 month.

Hot Cheese Bread

1 long French loaf	1 teaspoon French mustard
6 oz butter	½ teaspoon cayenne pepper
6 oz grated Cheddar cheese	

METHOD

Combine butter, cheese, mustard and cayenne pepper and proceed exactly as for garlic bread above.

Cheese Sticks

12 oz flour	1 oz grated Gruyère
½ lb grated dry Cheddar cheese	1 egg yolk
6 oz butter	1 tablespoon water
¼ pint cold water	Paprika pepper
1 teaspoon salt	

METHOD

1. Sift the flour and salt into a large bowl. Add 2 oz of the cheese and rub in the butter with the fingertips.

2. Add the cold water and mix to a firm dough. Chill for 15 minutes.

3. Roll out into an oblong. Fold in three and roll in the opposite direction. Sprinkle with 2 oz cheese and fold in three again. Chill for 15 minutes.

4. Repeat the rolling and folding, etc, twice more, chilling for 15 minutes each time.

5. Roll out to $\frac{1}{8}$-inch thickness. Cut into thin strips.

To serve without freezing: Brush with the egg yolk beaten with 1 tablespoon water. Sprinkle with grated cheese and a dusting of paprika pepper. Bake in a very hot oven (450°F: Reg. 8) for 6–8 minutes.

To freeze: Freeze unpacked sticks. Pack in suitable containers with a sheet of moisture- and vapour-proof paper between each layer. Seal, label and freeze.

To thaw: Place frozen sticks on a baking sheet. Brush with egg yolk and sprinkle with grated cheese and a little paprika. Bake in a very hot oven (480°F: Reg. 8) for 10 minutes or until golden brown.

PART THREE

Seasonal Menus

Seasonal Menus for Special Dinner Parties

These menus are for the occasions when you really want to provide your guests with superb and well-balanced meals. Menus for the time when you aim to impress and to make a name for yourself as a hostess. Most of the dishes can be cooked and frozen days or even weeks before the party itself so that, by careful planning, your cooking time before the arrival of your guests will be cut to a minimum, leaving you free to arrange your house and yourself to perfection.

Remember to check carefully how much time is needed for the thawing, heating or cooking of your dishes. Nothing is more demoralizing than presenting some wonderful creation that looks perfect but is frozen solid in the centre.

If you do a lot of entertaining, it is well worth while cooking two sets of the same meal to serve at two separate dinner parties but do be careful that your guests are not the same on each occasion.

Spring Menus

Jellied Tomato Ring with Prawns and Watercress	Allow time for thawing
Hot Cheese Bread	Allow time for heating
Steak au Poivre	
Pommes Duchesse	Allow time for heating
Spinach with Mushrooms	
Frozen Oranges	Needs no thawing
Assorted Cheeses	

Smoked Salmon and Crab Rolls with thinly cut Brown Bread and Butter	Allow time for thawing
Escalopes a l'Estragon	
Potatoes Laurette	Allow time for cooking
Green Peas	
Green Salad	
Pineapple Mousse	Allow time for thawing
Iced Camembert	Needs no thawing

Bortsch Soup	Allow time for heating
Cheese straws	
Ham Rolls with Creamed Spinach	
Straw Potatoes	Allow time for cooking
Mixed Salad	

| Orange Flan | Allow time for thawing |

Assorted Cheeses

| Fruits de Mare Alexa with
    Brown Bread and Butter | Allow time for heating |

| Chicken Caesar
Buttered Rice
Harvard Beets
Spring Cabbage | Allow time for heating |

| Porto Melon | Allow time for thawing |

Assorted Cheeses

Summer Menus

| Lobster Newburg
Thin slices Brown Bread and
    Butter | Allow time for heating |

| Spécialité Lamb Cutlets
New Carrots aux Fines Herbes
Mashed Potatoes | Allow time for cooking |

| Summer Pudding | Allow time for thawing |

Assorted Cheeses

| Lobster Mousse with thin slices
    Brown Bread and Butter | Allow time for thawing |

Beef Rolls
Shoestring Potatoes   Allow time for heating
Peas
Green Salad

Raspberry and Redcurrant   Needs no thawing
  Ice-cream
Filled Cream Puff Ring   Allow time for thawing

———————

Chilled Chicken Curry Soup   Allow time for thawing
Hot Rolls

Fillet of Pork with Prunes
Crisp Fried Onion Rings   Allow time for heating
New Potatoes
Green Salad

Frozen Lemon Cake   Allow $\frac{1}{2}$ hour for thawing

Fresh Fruit and Assorted Cheeses

———————

Moules Marinières   Allow time for reheating
Garlic Bread

Stuffed Escalopes   Allow time for reheating
Pommes Duchesses
Braised Lettuce

Cold Curried Fruit Salad   Allow time for thawing

Assorted Cheeses

Scampi Provençale   Allow time for heating
Hot Rolls

Wild Duck with Olive Sauce
Buttered Rice   Allow time for heating
Cauliflower
Peas

Bombe Surprise   Allow time for thawing
Fresh Fruit Salad

Potted Partridge   Allow time for heating
Hot Toast and Butter

Beef Rosettes
French Fried Potatoes   Allow time for heating
Aubergines with Tomatoes

Apple Mousse   Allow time for thawing
Bavarian Cream

Quiche Lorraine   Allow time for heating
Hot Rolls
Casserole of Venison
   or
Partridge with Red Cabbage
Brussels Sprouts with   Allow time for heating
   Chestnuts
Mashed Potatoes

Orange Dessert with Kirsch
Profiteroles with Ice-cream Allow time for thawing

Assorted Cheeses

Game and Liver Pâté   Allow time for thawing
Hot Toast and Butter

Boeuf Stroganoff
Buttered Rice
French Beans with Almonds   Allow time for heating
Green Salad

Chestnut Mousse   Allow time for thawing

Assorted Cheeses

————————

Crêpes Bolognaises   Allow time for heating

Louella's Lamb Kidneys
Buttered Rice
Creamed Spinach   Allow time for heating
Julienne Carrots

Caramelized Oranges   Allow time for thawing

Assorted Cheeses

————————

Coquilles St Jacques   Allow time for heating
Garlic Bread

Duck in Red Wine Sauce   Allow time for heating
Mashed Potatoes
Broccoli
Green Salad

Caramel Mousse   Allow time for thawing

Assorted Cheeses

Winter Menus

Soupe Chasseur   Allow time for heating
Bread Rolls

Chicken à la King
Pommes Duchesse   Allow time for heating
Green Salad

Chocolate and Orange Mousse   Allow time for thawing

Sole Walewska   Allow time for heating
French Bread

Tongue Véronique
Buttered Noodles
Creamed Cucumber   Allow time for heating
Brussels Sprouts

Crêpes Suzette   Allow time for heating

Assorted Fruits and Cheeses

Recipes Index

General Index

Mackerel, 66, 250
Mangoes, 50
Margarine, 69
Marjoram, 107, 109, 144, 152
Marmalade, 231, 243, 332
Marrow, 30, 121
Marshmallow, 308
Mayonnaise, 253–4, 264
Meals, preventing time-expired, 20
Meat, 8, 10, 19–22, 56–9, 165–218; chopped, 57; cooked, 184, 186; glaze, 178; in cream sauce, 75; minced, 13, 57, 177–85; mousse, 73; preparing for freezers, 56–9; 20% saving, 9
Mediterranean prawns, 66
Melons, 50, 132, 306
Milk, 86, 88–9
Mincemeat, 277, 282
Mint, 132, 341, 343
Mixed vegetables, storing, 11
Monosodium glutamate, 193
Mullet, 249
Mushrooms, 11, 30, 100; ketchup, 139, 171; storing, 11
Mussels, 67, 94–5, 135
Mustard (as powder), 172, 205, 255, 265, 336; (as vegetable), 28; French, 162, 174, 241, 345
Mutton, 19, 58, 90, 182, 185

Nectarines, 50
Nutmeg, 112
Nutrition, correct freezing preserves, 3
Nuts, chopped, 297, 337

Offal, 10, 210–18; maximum storage time, 57
Okra pods, 30, 119

Olive oil, 94, 102
Olives, 1 45, 160
Onions, 81–7, 89–95
Orange, 50, 106; Curaçao, 286; juice, concentrated, 115, 301; peel, 243; peel, candied, 338
Oregano, 223
Oxtail, 91
Ox tongue, 216–17
Oyster plant, 32
Oysters, 67, 173–4, 199

Packaging, 12–17; containers, 12; materials, types of, 13
Parsley, 83, 89
Parsnips, 30
Partridge, 62–3, 91–2, 150, 153, 235, 240
Pastry, -ies, 8, 11, 69–71, 219, 272–6; care in handling, 70; choux, 275, 317–18, 333; puff, 138, 165, 186, 187–8, 200, 228; storing, 11
Pâté, 73, 151–6, 160–61
Patties, 13–14, 76
Peaches, 52, 279, 306
Pearl barley, 90
Pears, 52, 301, 302
Peas, 23–4, 30, 84; mangetout, 30
Peel, chopped, 319, 328, 335
Peel (sea trout), 65
Pepper, black, 81, 84; cayenne, 136; paprika, 99, 345
Peppercorns, 82, 97, 144, 168, 216, 217, 248
Peppers, green, 11, 30, 89; red, 102, 133, 145, 221
Persimmons, 50
Pheasant, 63, 91, 153, 235–6, 239–40
Pickles, 159, 161, 202

Marika Hanbury Tenison
Deep-Freeze Sense 75p

The definitive guide to the sensible and economical use of your deep
freeze. Marika Hanbury Tenison, herself a deep freeze user for over
sixteen years, tells you everything about the practicalities, advantages
and pitfalls involved.

There is much useful advice on such aspects as preparation and
packaging, costs and economy, buying in bulk, and length of freezer
life of various foodstuffs. In addition to the delicious recipes in the
book there is a seasonal guide to fresh products.

Eat Well and Be Slim 40p

Published in association with the *Sunday Telegraph*

Here is a cookery book that offers you no temptations yet gives you
and your family delicious and filling recipes and a balanced diet. Whether
you have been on a diet and want to keep your new-found shape, or
whether you just want to stay the same weight – or even lose a few
pounds – this is the book for you.

You can buy these and other Pan books from booksellers and
newsagents; or direct from the following address:
Pan Books, Cavaye Place, London SW10 9PG
Send purchase price plus 15p for the first book and 5p for
each additional book, to allow for postage and packing
Prices quoted are applicable in UK

While every effort is made to keep prices low, it is sometimes
necessary to increase prices at short notice. Pan Books reserve the
right to show on covers new retail prices which may differ
from those advertised in the text or elsewhere